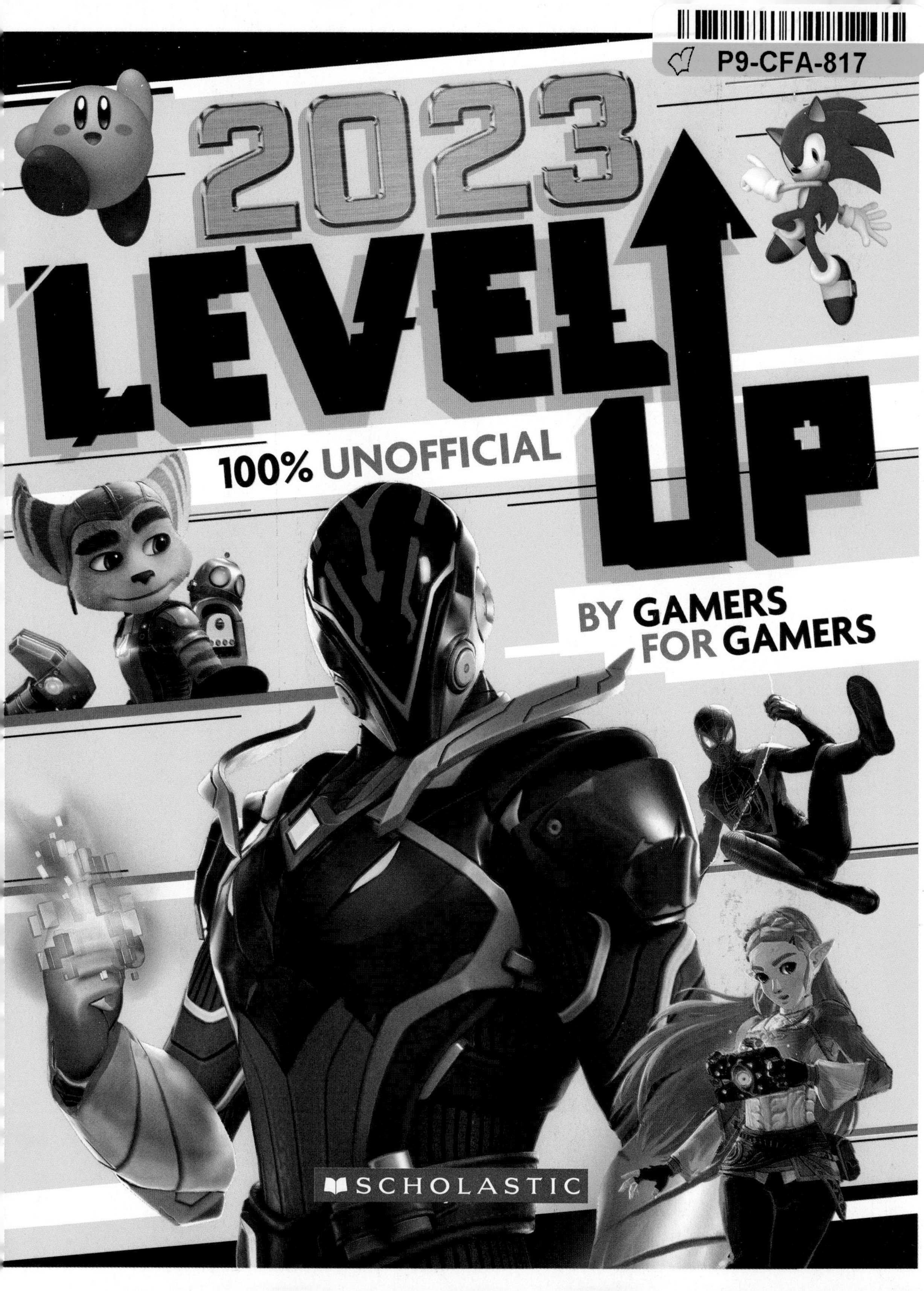
P9-CFA-817
2023
LEVEL UP
100% UNOFFICIAL
BY GAMERS
FOR GAMERS
SCHOLASTIC

LEVEL UP 2023

Editor:
Stuart Andrews

Design:
Andrew Sumner

Contributors:
Phoebe Andrews

ISBN 978-1-338-76731-5
10 9 8 7 6 5 4
22 23 24 25 26
Printed in the U.S.A. 40
First printing, September 2022

STAY SAFE AND HAVE FUN!

■ Games are awesome, but you need to know how to stay safe while you're playing, especially when you're playing online. Follow these simple rules to have a great time!

1 Talk to your parents and fix up rules on which games you can play, when you can play them, and whether you can play them online.

IT'S TIME TO LEVEL UP!

This is an exciting time for video games. We're still seeing awesome games on the Xbox One, PlayStation 4, and Switch, while the new superconsoles are getting games that look so good you could mistake them for a movie. New mobile games, handheld consoles, and cloud gaming services are changing where and how we play, while brilliant indie game developers are creating new and different styles of game.

Level Up is your guide to this incredible world of games—and we want to help you get even better at playing them. We hope you find new games to love inside, and the tricks and tips you need to beat them!

2 Never give out any personal information while you're gaming, including your real name, where you live, your parents' names, where you go to school, any passwords, or your phone number. Don't agree to meet someone you've met online or through a game in person.

3 Tell your parents or a teacher if you find something online that makes you feel uncomfortable.

4 Be nice to other players, even when you're competing against them. Don't say anything that might hurt someone's feelings or leave them feeling bad.

5 Take regular breaks when you're gaming. Give your eyes, hands, and brain a rest, and get your body moving.

6 Don't download, install, or stream any games or software without first checking with your parents. Pay attention to the age ratings on games. They exist to protect you from content that might upset or disturb you, or that your parents won't be comfortable with you experiencing.

7 If you play mobile games outside, keep aware of your surroundings. Don't play them alone and wander around the neighborhood.

CONTENTS

34

92

100

78

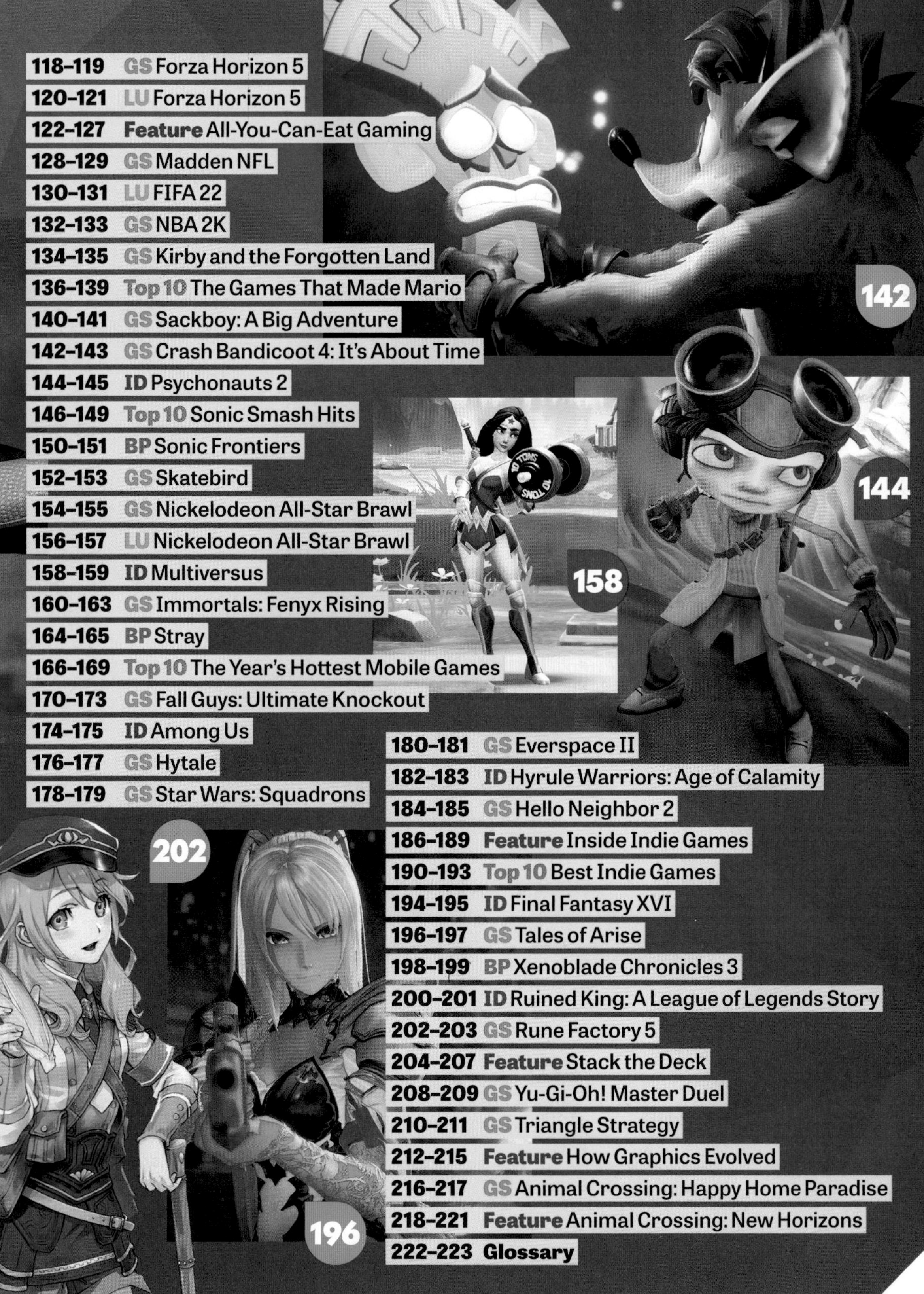
142
144
158
202
196

THE
BIG
GAMES
28 Monster Hunter Rise
82 Genshin Impact
118 Forza Horizon 5
194 Final Fantasy XVI
150 Sonic Frontiers
50 Ratchet and Clank: Rift Apart

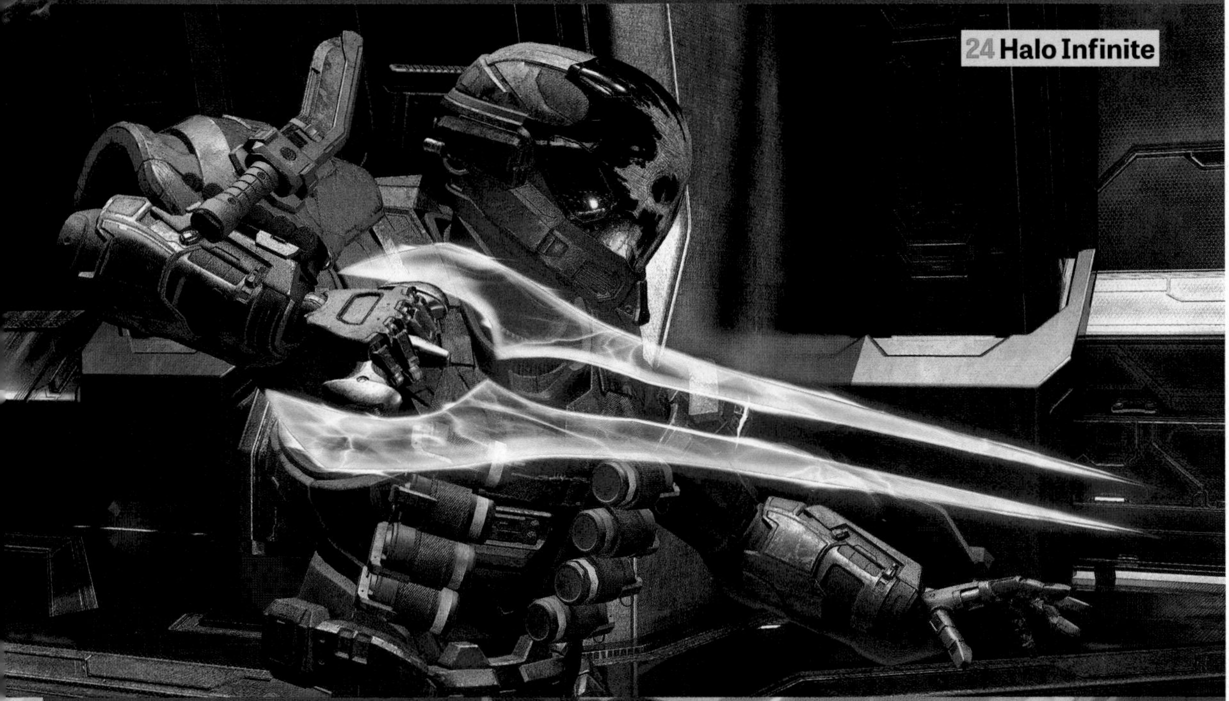

24 Halo Infinite

Whatever games or styles of game you love, we want to help you level up! Read on and get the inside info on the best and biggest games we've played and the games we're most excited about playing, along with hints and tips that are going to help you boost your skills, beat the toughest bosses, or win if you're playing online.

Along the way, we hope to introduce you to some games you haven't played, tell you about the hottest gaming machines, and give you some ideas on where gaming might be headed. Strap in. It's going to be a ride!

44 Pokémon Legends: Arceus

62 Fortnite

184 Hello Neighbor 2

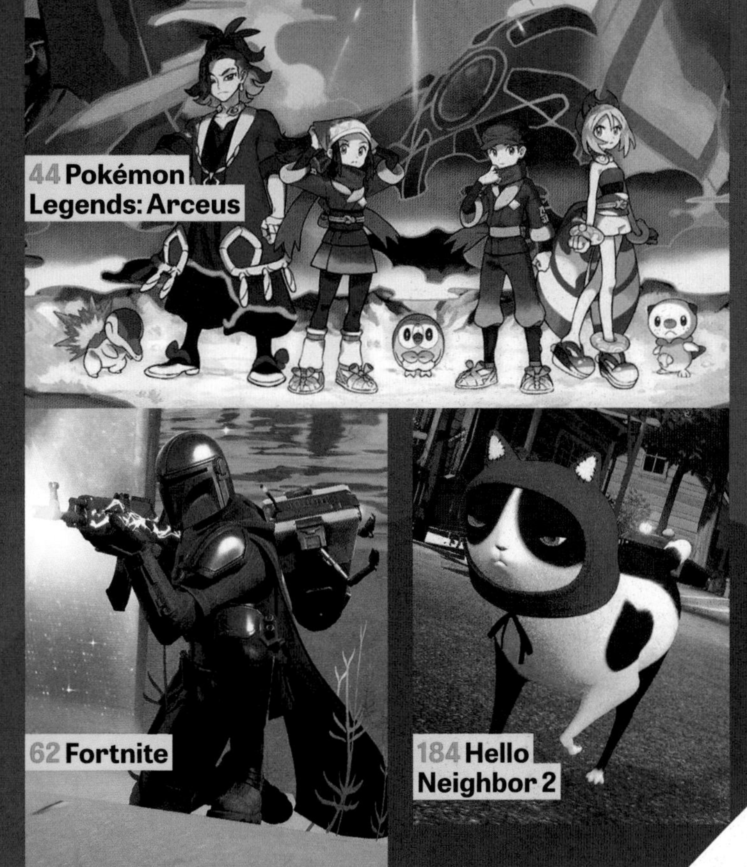

50 GREATEST GAMING MOMENTS

Our gaming highlights from the last two years

50 BATTLE ROYALE RUMBLE
Rumbleverse

■ After *Fortnite* and its Impostors mode, Epic Games is used to getting grief for basing great games on other people's best ideas. Now with *Rumbleverse*, it has its own new concept: a massive battle royale game that's all about the melee action, going big on mighty fighters and overpowered wrestling moves. Think wrestling in a city-size ring, where your favorite stars defy the laws of physics and can deal out colossal blows. This game deserves to be huuuuge!

49 MAKING EVERY SHOT COUNT
Cursed to Golf

■ Couldn't play golf if your life depended on it? Well, how about if it could save your soul? In *Cursed to Golf*, there's only one way out of purgatory, and that's to drive, chip, and putt your way to freedom. It's a clever mix of platform, puzzle, and golf game, crammed with impossible holes and tricky traps, and it makes each shot matter as you navigate each dungeon course on a mission to escape your curse. And if you have to cheat with the odd power-up? All's fair when your soul is on the line.

48 SHAGGY VS. SUPERMAN
Multiversus

■ Does the world need another clone of *Smash Bros*, even with a cast of cartoon favorites and DC superheroes? Having played *Multiversus*, we think it does. There aren't many games where Batman can take on *Scooby Doo*'s Shaggy, or Steven Universe can battle Arya Stark. Plus, with more characters on their way and everyone's favorite price (zilch), we suspect this one could run and run.

47 SUCKING UP THE SLIMES
Slime Rancher 2

■ Who knew slimy critters could be this lovable? Beatrix LeBeau is back on another slime-ranching adventure. She's on a new island crawling with the cuddly little blobs of goo, and she's sucking them up in her vacpack and taking them to her all-new slime conservatory. There's a nice mix of action, exploration, and slime breeding going on, and even when you're tackling the evil tarr slimes, it's a heap of fun. Get out there and corral some slimes!

46 HEROES IN A HALF SHELL

Teenage Mutant Ninja Turtles: The Cowabunga Collection

■ It's time for turtle power! *Teenage Mutant Ninja Turtles: The Cowabunga Collection* brings back thirteen arcade and console classics, ranging from the much-loved *Turtles in Time* to the fabulous *Tournament Fighters*. Leonardo, Donatello, Michelangelo, and Raphael feel like nineties throwbacks, but we love the way the game leans into it with its game guides and arcade cabinets. Together, there is nothing that four minds cannot accomplish!

45 THE CONQUEST OF SPACE

Kerbal Space Program 2

■ Kerbal Space Program was such a big left-field hit that we knew there had to be a sequel. The big surprise, though, is how ambitious this one is. Those cute li'l Kerbonauts are back in a game that still goes heavy on the rocket science. However, this one's easier to learn while still making you think hard about your spacecraft design. What's more, you can now build colonies on other planets and use them as a springboard to explore whole new star systems. To the stars, little Kerbal dudes!

44 DUELING LIKE A MASTER

Yu-Gi-Oh! Master Duel

■ For too long *Yu-Gi-Oh!* hasn't had the respect that it deserves. One of the first and best collectible card games has been sitting on the sidelines while its rivals soak up all the glory. Well, with *Master Duel*, it's back, and it's never been as exciting to play, as great to watch, or as easy to learn. You'll be surprised how far you can get into it without needing to spend any real-world cash. Could you become the next Yugi or Seto?

43 THAT PERFECT RUN!

OlliOlli World

■ *OlliOlli World* isn't what you'd call a realistic skateboarding game. In fact, it owes as much to Sonic and Mario as it does to *Tony Hawks Pro Skater*. All the same, it's an awesome game for split-second timing, tricks, and daring stunts, and nothing else in years has given us this kind of satisfaction with a perfect run. You need to put in the practice and the dedication, but when it all pays off, you want to pump your fist and yell in triumph.

42 IT'S YOUR CALL
Triangle Strategy

■ *Triangle Strategy* isn't for everyone. It's a bit slow to start and talky, never hitting you with one long dialogue scene when three in a row will do. Yet it manages something few strategy RPGs ever do: make you feel like your choices matter. Suddenly you're the hot-headed young lord trying to work out when to go to war and when to push for peace. You're the one whose decisions could save a country or destroy its peoples' lives. It's a great RPG for any gamer with a brain for tactics.

41 DESIGN A DREAM HOME
Animal Crossing: Happy Home Paradise

■ If you're looking for a feel-good moment, you can't beat Animal Crossing. And its feel-good moments don't get any better than when you let an excited client find their way around their new pad once you've created it in the *Happy Home Paradise* expansion. We could watch them walk around grinning from ear to ear for ages, all backed by an infectious, happy tune. If this doesn't put a smile on your face, nothing will.

40 BIGGER AND BRIGHTER
Nintendo Switch OLED

■ A lot of people were disappointed that the new Switch was just a Switch with a better screen. But just look at that lovely OLED display, based on the same technology as today's top TVs and smartphones. Doesn't it make *Mario 3D World* and *Monster Hunter Rise* look amazing, or bring out all the colors in *Splatoon 3*? Don't you want to see how good *Legend of Zelda: Breath of the Wild 2* can look on this big, bright, beautifully crisp screen? Of course you do.

39 FABLE RETURNS
Fable

■ Lionhead's series of oddball British fantasy adventures delivered some of the biggest highlights of the Xbox 360 era, so it's a shame that we haven't seen a Fable for so long. Well, now that's changing, and with the Forza Horizon team at Playground Games behind it, we can't wait! Expect a very different take on the sword-and-sorcery RPG, with great characters, a silly sense of humor, and a world you can make your own.

38

APEX PREDATOR
Apex Legends Mobile

■ Even after Fortnite and Call of Duty came to phones and tablets, Apex Legends looked like a stretch. Yet it's here and it looks amazing. You can play as most of your favorite Legends, grab the same weapons, and use the same skills as in the console versions. It even plays well with touch controls. Gaming on the go keeps getting better, and *Apex Legends Mobile* is amazing!

37

MARIO GETS SPORTY
Mario Golf: Super Rush and Mario Strikers: Battle League

■ We love that Mario has taken some time off from battling Bowser and rediscovered his inner jock. He's still kart racing on the weekends, but now you'll find him on the golf course in *Mario Golf: Super Rush*, or hitting the soccer field in *Mario Strikers: Battle League*. Maybe one day he'll take on football or ice hockey, though we can't see Toad and Luigi holding on to the puck with Bowser and the Goombas charging at 'em!

36

THE LEAGUE EXPANDS
League of Legends: Ruined King

■ *League of Legends* has had an incredible few years. Being one of the biggest online games around was never going to be enough, but now we have an amazing cartoon spin-off, *Arcane*, and the superb RPG *Ruined King*. Sure, it's short by Final Fantasy or Dragon Quest standards, but it packs in a brilliant story and some of the main games' most exciting heroes and villains. The turn-by-turn combat is as good as it gets. Let's have more!

35

NOW NOWHERE'S SAFE!
Hello Neighbor 2

■ *Hello Neighbor* was a game built on a handful of great ideas, but how could you keep a sequel scary? By expanding the action to fill out the whole town, and making sure that players can't relax even when they're well outside the Neighbor's house. In *Hello Neighbor 2*, you can be chased or followed almost no matter where you are or what you're doing by some of the creepiest characters you'll find outside of a full-on horror game. Get ready for the jump scares or get caught screaming like a baby!

34 HYRULE HISTORY LESSON
Hyrule Warriors: Age of Calamity

■ We knew that *Hyrule Warriors: Age of Calamity* would give us a different perspective on the story of *Legend of Zelda: Breath of the Wild*. What we didn't know is that it would give us a fresh take on Hyrule's past. This was a chance to see Hyrule's heroes in their prime, taking on the might of Ganon's armies with courage, sorcery, and skill. Where the first *Hyrule Warriors* felt like an interesting side-story, *Age of Calamity* became a must-have for any serious Zelda fans.

33 COMPLETING THE PHOTODEX
New Pokémon Snap

■ What a difference twenty-two years makes. The original *Pokémon Snap* was cool, but the new one puts the *wild* in wildlife photography. Simply snapping your favorite Pokémon is brilliant, but *Snap* kept on adding new layers and tools to coax even more weird and wonderful responses out of them. You could even go on night shoots and make these fantastic creatures glow. Who knew that filling out a photo album could be this much fun?

32 PLAY FOR FREE
Genshin Impact

■ Along with *Fortnite*, *Genshin Impact* has rewritten the rulebook on free games. Sure, we all know that you can spend real money unlocking new characters and weapons, but the amazing thing is that you don't have to. You can explore a huge and incredible world, painted with the most fantastic cartoon graphics, and there are hours and hours of stories and adventures to enjoy for nothing!

31 GOING DOWNHILL FAST
Riders Republic

■ *Riders Republic* is one crazy game. Where else can you mountain bike, ski, and snowboard through America's great national parks? Or strap on a wingsuit and fly through Bryce Canyon? But just when you think things can't get more wacky than hurtling down a mountain at eight zillion miles per hour, you enter a mass race event and join sixty-three other idiots doing the same thing. It's all kinds of chaos and like nothing else in games. Just finishing feels like a triumph!

30

GET A MOUTHFUL OF THIS!
Kirby and the Forgotten Land

■ Kirby has never quite made it into Nintendo's top rank of heroes, but the shape-changing pink blob has earned his place with his first fully 3D adventure. This is one of the best 3D platformers since *Super Mario Odyssey*, with imaginative levels, great boss battles, and incredible shape-changing puzzles. And with Mouthful Mode, *Kirby*'s creative team came up with some fantastic new forms. From cars to traffic cones, vending machines, big rigs, and even roller coasters, Kirby proves he can make any shape look super.

29

CARTOON KERFUFFLE
Nickelodeon All-Star Brawl

■ It's not hard to see how much *Nickelodeon All-Star Brawl* owes to a certain Smash Bros. series, but—give credit where it's due—it works hard to capture the same magic. The stages are impressive and packed with clever tricks, while the characters have been cleverly built to show attacks and abilities that fit in with their cartoon antics. There are hidden depths here that you'll never find in your average cartoon fighter, and it all works brilliantly to bring the Nickelodeon universe to life.

28

HANDHELD DREAM MACHINE
Valve Steam Deck

■ Valve has made some old dreams come true with this incredible handheld games machine. This is a proper gaming PC you can hold in both hands, and it'll play the latest games without collapsing in a pool of melted plastic. The screen looks great, the controls feel great, and, while it's not cheap, there's a chance you could save up and own one. We're saving our dimes and dollars for a Steam dream machine.

27

DISNEY DOES ZELDA
Kena: Bridge of Spirits

■ If you want to see how far game graphics and animation have come along, you only have to look at the award-winning *Kena: Bridge of Spirits*. It's not just that graphics have caught up with CGI cartoons, but the team at Ember Labs made *Kena* with the same kind of skill and love that the likes of Disney and DreamWorks Animation put into blockbuster movies like *Encanto*. It's a superb adventure set in one jaw-dropping fantasy world.

26 THE RISE OF THE SKYWALKERS
LEGO Star Wars: The Skywalker Saga

■ Whether you prefer the prequels, the sequels, or the classic original movies, *LEGO Star Wars: The Skywalker Saga* is on a mission to win your heart. It has everything you could want in a *Star Wars* game—space battles, stormtroopers, Sith Lords, and lightsaber duels. It also has the best shooting, platforming, and puzzle gameplay in the whole LEGO series, and assembles one impossible-to-beat cast of *Star Wars* stars. And if you want Baby Yoda, you just have to grab the *Mandalorian* expansion!

25 SERIOUSLY SPEEDY
Gran Turismo 7

■ How much do you love cars? Not as much as the makers of *Gran Turismo 7*. It's a fan letter to the world's favorite four-wheeled vehicles, in all their shiny glory, with stunning tracks that reimagine courses your mom or dad might have been driving on twenty-five years ago. What's more, these cars have never been so good to drive, with the game making full use of the PS5's Dual Sense controller to put you right in the driver's seat. Whether you'd rather race a Ford or a Ferrari, no driving game gets it better than this.

24 SOMETHING TO CROW ABOUT
Death's Door

■ Here's another Zelda-like game that dares to do something different, combining the magic of Nintendo's classic series with the hard-hitting combat of a challenging action game. The amazing thing is that *Death's Door* can be tricky, but it never feels unfair, and there's so much to love about its weird fantasy world and warped monsters that you can't resist another run. Who knew a crow hero could be this cool?

23 BACK IN ACTION
Overwatch 2

■ It's been delayed so many times we thought we'd never see it, but we've actually played *Overwatch 2*. Blizzard has refined its awesome formula, cutting back the player count to 5v5, adding new maps, modes, and heroes, plus a cool new progression system. But at heart, it's still the same awesome hero shooter, with the best and most exciting roster of champions in town. Whether you're dealing out the damage as Hanzo or wielding a railgun as new star Sojourn, you're in for a ride!

22 RETRO WARGAMES

Advance Wars 1+2: Re-Boot Camp

■ Here's a real blast from the past! In the days when people said you couldn't make a strategy game work on a handheld console, *Advance Wars* on the plucky Game Boy Advance showed them that it could. Now the first two games are back in a brilliant retro war game that'll see you fighting battles both on land and sea and in the air. It looks simple, but there's a lot going on beneath the surface, and the revamped graphics and cool Commanding Officers give this old soldier buckets of charm.

21 THE CHRONICLES CONTINUE

Xenoblade Chronicles 3

■ *Xenoblade Chronicles 2* and *Xenoblade Chronicles: Definitive Edition* brought one of the all-time great RPG series to the Switch. Now we have a third chapter in the saga, and it answers some of the outstanding questions left by both. It's hard to believe that so much imagination can fit into one game, let alone a game you can pick up and play on a handheld. With more action and drama than your average anime show, it's as epic as RPGs get.

20 MORE MARIO KART

Mario Kart 8 Deluxe Booster Course packs

■ Much as we'd like to see a proper sequel, we love the way Nintendo has expanded *Mario Kart 8 Deluxe* with forty-eight extra tracks. That means favorites from *Mario Kart 64*, *Mario Kart 7*, *Mario Kart Wii*, and even the mobile *Mario Kart Tour*, and they've all been given a new lick of paint to look their best on Switch. Sure, you had to pay for all this DLC goodness, but it's given us another excuse to restart old rivalries and tell Toad and Waluigi to eat our dust!

19 STOPPING A CAT-ASTROPHE

Stray

■ *Stray* would have had our attention for its beautifully animated cat, but what's captured hearts and minds is its stunning sci-fi world, with its sad robots, rain-soaked streets, and brash neon lighting. From its first moments, it's a game that makes you want to explore—to climb up to the rooftops and search every alley—but underneath the spectacular graphics, there's a game with a lot to say. The outlook might be gloomy, but there's a light of puss purr-fection creeping through.

18 AN ALL-NEW FINAL FANTASY
Final Fantasy XVI

■ We've waited years for an all-new Final Fantasy—and, no, the *FFVII remake* and *Stranger of Paradise* don't count! Well, we're finally getting one, and it's looking great! *Final Fantasy XVI* has cool characters and an interesting story, not to mention a brilliant approach to summoning that reinvents one of the sage's finest features. Who knows if we'll ever see a final Final Fantasy, but this one looks like a stormer!

17 SAMUS STRIKES BACK!
Metroid Dread

■ It's been years since she has had a decent outing, but *Metroid Dread* puts Samus back in the spotlight. It's a dazzling and imaginative 2D action-adventure, with a rich alien planet to explore along with a story full of mystery. The indestructible E.M.M.I. robots also make for some of the most tense and terrifying moments of any Metroid game. We're still desperate for *Metroid Prime 4* to come out, but we'd happily take a Metroid Dread 2.

16 WE ARE GROOT!
Marvel's Guardians of the Galaxy

■ Here's another nice surprise: *Marvel's Guardians of the Galaxy* is a brilliant game. Yes, the characters don't look much like they do in the movies and their back stories aren't quite the same, but the game sticks closer to the original comics, and all the action, humor, and adventure is right there. We could spend hours exploring alien worlds with Star-Lord, Drax, Rocket, Gamora, and Groot just listening to their yapping, but the brilliant, team-based combat and ingenious puzzles mean there's so much more to this Guardians game than that!

15 SUDDENLY, IT ALL MAKES SENSE
Tunic

■ You can play *Tunic* for hours and still see it as a clever clone of *Legend of Zelda*. Then, all of a sudden, something clicks, and you realize that it goes much deeper! This isn't a rip-off, but a game made with memories of the early days of gaming, brought bang up to date with gorgeous graphics and a wicked sense of fun. Give it a try and let its magic work on you!

14

CALL OF THE WILD
Legend of Zelda: Breath of the Wild 2

■ How do you follow a game many call the best game of all time? The sequel to *Legend of Zelda: Breath of the Wild* looks set to do it in style. It takes all the exploration and free-roaming adventure of the Switch classic, then adds some daring new twists, much as *Legend of Zelda: Majora's Mask* did when it followed *Ocarina of Time* all those years ago. It's a shame that the game's been bumped until next year, but if it helps Nintendo make it perfect, we can wait!

13

QUEEN OF LIES
Destiny 2: The Witch Queen

■ The latest *Destiny 2* expansion is everything you'd want from the legendary team at Bungie. It's massive, has a great main story line, and has one of the most incredible worlds we've seen in any game. It's also scary, thanks to a new breed of Hive monsters with the same superpowers as your guardian heroes, and Destiny's most sneaky, treacherous, and fiendish villain yet: the Witch Queen herself! Destiny 2 has always been best played with friends, but it's easier to take the scares if you've got your buds around you.

12

RACING THROUGH MEXICO
Forza Horizon 5

■ We could fill up half of this list with moments from *Forza Horizon 5*. How about chasing storms in the desert or speeding off-road along muddy jungle tracks? Or would you rather hit the rain-slicked streets of the city, taking on its top racers, or take Baja buggies for a spin along the beach? Either way, the game's real stars are its cars and its take on Mexico, making it your destination for one awesome racing vacation, where the supercars keep coming and you're never low on gas.

11

GETTING SCHOOLED
Hogwarts Legacy

■ For years kids have wanted to jump on the train and enroll for a year at Hogwarts. Now, with *Hogwarts Legacy*, they can do exactly that. Of course, things aren't quite like they are in the books or movies—the new game is set roughly 100 years before—but you can still take classes in potions, herbology, and defense against the dark arts, then explore the world around Hogsmeade and the legendary school, foiling a dark plot. Which house are you going to join?

10 THE NEXT CHAPTER
Fortnite

■ *Fortnite* should be running out of road by now, yet it keeps on trucking! Maybe it's because each season brings in new areas, new weapons, new gadgets, and new game modes to try out. Maybe it's because the Creative community keeps coming up with fantastic new ideas for maps or games. Or maybe it's because each chapter takes the chance to reinvent the game without throwing out what makes players love it, or all the cool stuff they've collected over the years. Taking risks and kicking battle royale butt, *Chapter Three* shows why *Fortnite* is the ultimate survivor.

9 INTO THE SPIDER-VERSE
Marvel's Spider-Man: Miles Morales

■ After the movie magic of *Into the Spider-verse* and *No Way Home*, Spider-Man has never been stronger. Everyone's favorite neighborhood web-crawler is having just as good a time in games. *Marvel's Spider-Man* looks even better remastered on PS5, while *Marvel's Spider-Man: Miles Morales* transformed from a side story into one of Spidey's best video game adventures. Now we're looking at a new game featuring both Peter Parker and Miles Morales, and our spider-senses won't stop tingling!

8 OFF THE HOOK!
Splatoon 3

■ Only Nintendo could have made a hit out of such a weird ink-splattering shooter, and only Nintendo would have had the imagination to roll out two sequels full of fresh ideas. *Splatoon 3* isn't just more Splatoon with a bunch of new maps and weapons, but a deep dive into the world of the Squidlings and Octolings, featuring a new furry foe and a better-than-ever co-op Salmon Run mode. Don't just sit there and stink, get out there and ink!

COMEBACK KING
Sonic Frontiers

■ First the movies, then *Sonic Frontiers*. Now we can all remember what made Sonic one of the world's biggest video game stars! The movies get the speed and spiky style of SEGA's hedgehog mascot, while *Sonic Frontiers* gives him an open-world platform adventure that takes our hero somewhere new and gives the gameplay a much-needed update. The result? Sonic's looking fresher than he has in years!

RISE AND SHINE!
Monster Hunter Rise

■ Were you expecting *Monster Hunter Rise* to be a cut-down *Monster Hunter World*? Us too! Luckily, we were wrong. For one thing, *Monster Hunter Rise* added even more features, giving us new ways to get around the landscape, track terrifying targets, and slay them. For another, it made all this stuff even easier to get into, so that just about anyone could pick up a Switch and get into the role of a Hunter's Guild hero in just an hour or two of play. Once you've started crafting new armor and weapons from monster bones and hide, it's impossible to stop!

HEADING TO THE COAST
Horizon: Forbidden West

■ The *Horizon: Zero Dawn* sequel is one seriously beautiful game, but it holds back some of its most spectacular sights for when you make it to the coast. Battling monster robot dinosaurs on the beach is pretty cool, but then you dive down into underwater ruins, hiding from speedy, shark-toothed Tiderippers and Snapmaws. Come in for a swim—the water's deadly!

HOT-TEMPERED!
Bowser's Fury

■ Mario and Bowser have clashed before, but never at the scale they clash in *Bowser's Fury*. Every few minutes, Bowser wakes from his black sludge sleep and turns into the huge Fury Bowser, raining fire and brimstone down on Lake Lapcat. But if Mario can ring the Giga Bell, he can transform into Giga Cat Mario and defeat him. Watching these two titans slug it out has to be one of the best moments of any Mario game so far.

3 CATCH 'EM ALL
Pokémon Legends: Arceus

■ Just when Pokémon seemed stuck in its ways, along came *Pokémon Legends: Arceus*. Not only did it take us back to the Sinnoh region in the days when all Pokémon were wild, but it opened up the action to a true open-world style of play, where you could go almost anywhere you wanted and discover that there is more than one way to catch 'em all. Throw in a great time-traveling story and some seriously lovable critters, and we had Pokémon's finest hour in years.

2 RIVET MEETS CLANK
Ratchet and Clank: Rift Apart

■ *Ratchet and Clank: Rift Apart*—what a showcase for the PS5! A game that blitzed through worlds and dimensions at a crazy rate, yet never felt like it was running out of ideas. Yet beneath those awesome graphics and overpowered weaponry, it still found time to introduce great characters, like Ratchet's cross-dimensional equivalent, Rivet, and her new bot bestie, Kit. These were heroes you could root for on an adventure that broke the laws of physics when it came to thrills.

1 FINISHING THE FIGHT
Halo: Infinite

■ After all the delays and disappointing reveals, *Halo Infinite* turned out to be a triumph. The multiplayer has never been so exciting or so much fun, but it's the single-player story that we're going to remember. With a massive Halo ring, packed with UNSC marines to rescue and Banished bases to capture or destroy, *Infinite* made Halo work as an open-world game, while the Master Chief's new gadgets made exploring it amazing. From its ferociously evil villains to its epic sci-fi moments and action scenes, *Infinite* is Halo at its very best.

LEGEND OF ZELDA: BREATH OF THE WILD 2

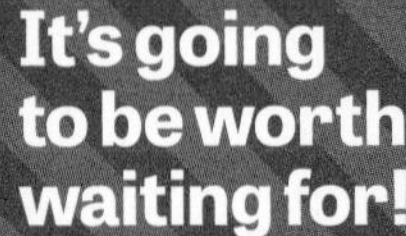

It's going to be worth waiting for!

We've been waiting a long time for the *Breath of the Wild* sequel, but it's finally coming out in 2023. For most of that, Nintendo has kept it tightly under wraps, telling us little about the story, Link's adversary, or what's going on with our hero's arm. With Calamity Ganon defeated, what ancient evil has spread out to corrupt it—and the land of Hyrule? We want answers, and the only way to get them is to play it!

■ Link isn't quite the same hero he was in *Breath of the Wild*. Forces of evil have infected his arm and wreaked havoc on the Master Sword! Luckily, he also has new powers. Can he save himself and rescue Hyrule?

FAST FACT

Only one enemy has appeared in every single Legend of Zelda: the skeletal Staflos. He's always got a bone to pick with you . . .

■ Nintendo promised us new ways to explore Hyrule, both on land and in the air! Link can still rely on his trusty glider, but he can also rise up and phase through the chunks of land that now float in the skies above. This is just one way that the *Breath of the Wild* sequel seems to look back to an earlier Zelda, *Skyward Sword*.

■ Calamity Ganon might have gone, but there's a new evil out there, and it's bringing enemies old and ancient out of the woodwork. We're not done with the Moblins and Bokoblins, and what's going on with this big guy? Is he an update of that classic Zelda enemy, the Armos?

HALO INFINITE

THE MASTER CHIEF FACES HIS TOUGHEST CHALLENGE YET!

Humanity is up against it. The UNSC ship *Infinity* has been destroyed, and its forces are scattered across the remains of an incomplete Halo ring. That ring is under the control of a renegade Covenant army, the Banished, and they're working with an ancient and mysterious being to rebuild it and destroy humankind once and for all. With the remaining UNSC troops outnumbered and outgunned, only one Spartan super soldier stands between these evil goons and their goals: John 117, The Master Chief. With a new AI companion, Weapon, he's going to take on the Banished and win!

While it follows on from the events of *Halo 5*, *Halo Infinite* feels like a new start for Halo. On the one hand, it's gone open world, with a whole ring to explore and dozens of side missions beyond the main story line. On the other, it's recaptured the magic of the early Halo games, with the Master Chief right at the center of Halo's best campaign in years. The Banished might be fearsome, but the Master Chief is going to do what he does best: fight!

QUICK TIPS

GET GRAPPLING

Master Chief's new gadgets aren't just for show, but are essential to winning the war. Use the Grappleshot to reach new areas or get out of trouble. Use the Repulsor to repel incoming grenades and shells.

SCAN FOR CLUES

Don't forget to use your Scan ability – press down on the D-Pad. You can see inside locked rooms, find switches that activate doors, track down weapons and objectives, and a whole lot more.

CAPTURE THE FOBS

The Banished have taken over UNSC Forward Operating Bases, but the Master Chief can take them back. You can use them to deploy vehicles or collect unlocked weapons, but also to locate Banished targets, collectibles, and missions in the area around.

BEAT THE BANISHED

■ This isn't going to be an easy battle. The Banished are spread across the surface of the Zeta Halo, and they have their own bases, super troops, and high-powered weapons.

BOSS OF THE BANISHED

■ The Banished are now led by Escharum, and he might be the Master Chief's toughest adversary yet. He's smart, brutal, and obsessed with beating the Master Chief in single combat.

UNDER CONSTRUCTION

■ Zeta Halo isn't like any other Halo you've visited yet. It's vast and rebuilding itself as you watch. Crammed with weird Forerunner installations and Banished fortresses, there's a lot of Halo to explore.

COMBAT EVOLVED

■ The Master Chief is one mighty solder, and he's now got the best lineup of weapons of any Halo game. Why settle for the standard rifles when you can skewer the Banished or melt them with a light beam?

DON'T LEAVE ANYONE BEHIND

■ The Banished have captured many UNSC troops and are doing their best to eliminate the rest. Rescue your old allies, and they'll join you as you take the battle to the bad guys.

FAST FACT

The Banished aren't brand-new to Halo. They put in their first appearance in the Halo strategy spin-off *Halo Wars 2*, where you could command them through one half of the campaign.

LIKE THIS? TRY THIS:

SPLITGATE

■ It doesn't have a campaign like *Halo Infinite's*, but *Splitgate* is the freshest multiplayer FPS in years. Think classic Halo team deathmatch with added portals you can use to take your foes by surprise.

FINISH THE FIGHT IN HALO INFINITE

Want to make your mark in the new Halo multiplayer? Here's how:

Tired of getting kicked around in *Halo Infinite* and want to score more eliminations? There are several tricks that Halo veterans will know, plus some fresh ones specific to the new game. Put in the practice, build your map knowledge, and develop a few strategies, and you might start coming out on top!

1 Battle the bots

■ *Halo Infinite* gives you the option of a Bot Bootcamp playlist, where you fight with other players against a team of bots. It's a great way to learn the maps and get used to the different weapons, modes, and mechanics without getting blasted by players with superior skills.

2 Get in close

■ Don't be afraid to use melee attacks, especially if you can get your hands on a Gravity Hammer or Energy Sword. Many players will panic as you charge them, and your shields can soak up a lot of firepower. Rush in, take your swing, and you could rack up some kills.

3 Play the objectives

■ Unless you're playing Slayer matches, you need to do more than just rack up a high kill count. If you're playing Strongholds, capture and hold the three zones, and keep an eye on which zones are under attack from the enemy team. Playing Oddball? Grab and hold that skull!

4 Plasma destroys shields

■ It takes a while to wear down a Spartan's shields, but plasma weapons will do it much faster than a gun that fires bullets. Use Plasma Pistols, Ravagers, Needlers, and Pulse Carbines to take your enemy's shields down, then switch to a kinetic or shock weapon for an easier kill.

5 Team Up

■ You can do a lot of damage as a lone-wolf hero, but you'll do more if you fight in a pack. When two Spartans are up against one, they're usually more likely to win. And if you are outnumbered? Use grenades or other explosive weapons to hit more than one opponent at a time.

FAST FACT

You can customize almost every part of your Spartan's armor, even your AI.

Target practice

■ Whether you're playing against human players or practicing against bots, try to switch between the different weapons and get a feel for how they aim and fire. Some maps give you space to snipe targets at a distance, while others are all about close-quarters combat. You need to get your head around both!

MONSTER HUNTER RISE

DID ANYONE CALL PEST CONTROL?

Kamura village has a serious problem. It's not bad enough that monsters are causing panic in the local area and blocking all the trade routes—now they're threatening to mass together and overrun the streets. Luckily, Kamura can rely on the good folks of the Hunter's Guild, dedicated to dealing with unruly monsters and slaying the biggest and baddest of the bunch. And guess who's just moved to Kamura and joined up with the local Guild?

Monster Hunter Rise might be the greatest Monster Hunter yet—and it's definitely the easiest to get into! What's more, it's spread its monstrous dragon wings to expand out from the Kamura region into new territories, thanks to the spectacular *Sunbreak* expansion. So grab your gear, call your buddies, and get ready to slay some mighty beasts. How else are you going to get the stuff for this year's hottest weapons and armor?

QUICK TIPS

GET WIRED

■ It's easy to forget the new line-spinning critters, but don't. They can work as a grappling hook for reaching high spots or a quick way to get into and out of battle. Or use the new Silkbind attacks!

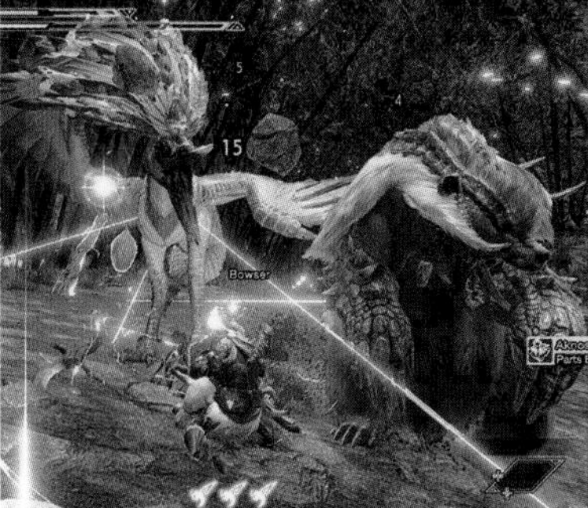

RIDE 'EM

■ Your Palamute can help you in combat or become a mount to help you get around the landscape faster. Need to chase a fleeing monster? Hop on board!

FOCUS ON THE VILLAGE QUESTS

■ While you can tackle Hub quests early on, focus on the village quests instead. You'll learn the ropes of monster hunting, get some better gear, and push through the first stages of the story line faster.

GET READY TO HUNT!

Hunter's Guild members are sure of a warm welcome in Kamura, so make the most of the village before you head out on the next hunt.

USE THE STORES

Kamura is bustling with stores and merchants, where you can buy health potions, antidotes, and other essentials, or grab a tasty snack for your next adventure.

FORGE NEW GEAR

Head to the Smithy in Kamura—or upstairs in the Hub—to get new weapons and armor forged or upgraded. You'll need the necessary metals or monster parts first, though, so get out there, slay, and scavenge.

HIT THE HUB

The Gathering Hub is where you can pick up new Hub quests. You can play these solo or with other players online. You can also craft and upgrade new gear and sign up for challenging man vs. monster arena fights.

FAST FACT

It turns out that monster hunting is big business! In fact, 2018's *Monster Hunter World* is Capcom's bestselling game ever, selling over 20 million copies—more than any of its Resident Evil or Street Fighter games.

BUDDY UP!

The Buddy Plaza is the area to go to when you need some extra muscle. Why not hire in new Buddies to battle alongside you or get tips and training for your existing Palicoes and Palamutes?

SLAY IT YOUR WAY!

■ Hunting monsters is a dangerous business. Fight badly or fail to watch your health and energy levels, and you'll wake up back at camp after a knockout—if you're lucky! Yet there's more than one way to bring a monster down...

FIGHT SMART

■ Monster Hunter combat is all about the timing. Learn how the monsters move and when it's safe to whack them. Watch for their tells—the moves or animations that mean they're going to unleash a big attack. Dodge out of the way, then rush back in and give it all you've got!

MONSTER RODEO!

■ Do enough damage to a monster or hit it with wirebug attacks and you can jump on its back and ride it—and even make it take on other monsters. It's a great way to do a lot of damage fast, and you can sometimes take advantage of two monsters fighting to wear both of them down.

GIVE CHASE

■ When monsters take enough damage, they get weak and tired—they might even make a run for it. If a beast looks out of breath or poorly, this is your chance to rush in and finish it off. Show no mercy! And if it makes a dash for freedom? Pursue it on your Palamute and deal the final blow.

BEST BUDS

■ Palicoes and Palamutes are every monster hunter's best friends. The feline Palicoes will help you take on the mightiest varmints, and can also heal you if things get rough. The canine Palamutes will speed you around the game's locations on their backs, or rush in and fight your monstrous targets, tooth and claw.

Both Palicoes and Palamutes level up as you hunt, and don't forget to get new weapons and armor crafted for them at the Buddy Smith next to Hamon the Blacksmith. The better their gear, the harder they can fight!

SUNBREAK

You wanted more *Monster Hunter Rise*? You got it, in the shape of the *Sunbreak* expansion. You're leaving Kamura behind to explore the realms around the outpost of Elgado. Make sure you're ready for a new challenge, as this place has the most terrifying monsters you've faced yet.

The outpost has everything a hunter needs, including new allies, a friendly tea shop, and a smithy crafting all-new arms and armor. It's also a leading hub for monster research, so go out and slay them in the name of science!

The area is threatened by three massive monsters known as the Three Lords. The Elder Dragon, Malzeno, drains the life energy from living creatures. Meanwhile, Garangoim is a huge, brutish beast that can turn the plants growing on it into weapons of destruction.

Finally, Lunagaron is a fierce wolflike critter with a nasty line in freezing breath. You're also going to meet new species of monsters, so get ready for electrifying wyverns, pinecone-throwing flyers, and razor-clawed giant bugs!

LIKE THIS? TRY THIS:

DAUNTLESS

Dauntless feels a bit like Monster Hunter lite, but it's a fun, furious, and approachable online monster hunting game with a great line-up of big bads in serious need of slaying. Best of all, it's free to play!

Hogwarts Legacy

Something sinister's afoot at the legendary school

You'll see sides of Hogwarts that you've never seen before in this all new Potterverse prequel. It's a spellcasting action RPG that takes us back to the late 1800s, where a new student at the school of witchcraft and wizardry gets caught up in a goblin rebellion and a conspiracy of dark witches and wizards. As well as attending your classes in the school, you'll need to explore the wider world outside and underneath it, using the magical skills you're busy learning to battle the forces of evil.

Enroll at Hogwarts

Who wants to play as the same ordinary student when you can design your own witch or wizard using the game's cool customization tools? Get them sorted into one of the four Hogwarts houses, then enhance their skills and talents through a brilliant system of upgrade cards. You can even craft new gear to boost their magical abilities and make them perfect for the way you want to play.

FAST FACT

As *Hogwarts Legacy* is set so long before the books, Hogwarts won't have the same teaching staff. You will see some familiar faces, though: Nearly Headless Nick and the other Hogwarts ghosts.

Don't cut classes

You're a late starter, so you'll need to spend some of your time catching up. Classes in charms, defense against the dark arts, potions, and herbology will give you the skills you need to survive in the lands outside the school. You'll learn more powerful offensive and defensive spells for dueling, and also how to brew skills-boosting potions and use magical beasts and plants in battle.

Fantastic beasts

It's not hard to find weird critters around Hogwarts, and you can learn how to take care of them and get them on your side. You'll also meet beasts in need of rescue and corrupted beasts thirsty for a young witch or wizard's blood. Save the threatened beasts and deal with the corrupted!

Explore the world

In between classes, you can explore the secret realms inside and underneath the castle, as well as the countryside beyond the walls. Head to Hogsmeade to buy supplies or search for mysterious vaults and dungeons. Just take care that you don't find more adventure than you bargained for!

Challenges and companions

Changing seasons and smart weather systems mean that the land around Hogwarts never stays the same for long. Keep an eye out for some sneaky puzzles, too. These will test your magical skills and your brainpower as you probe further into the sinister goblin plot. Luckily, you'll make new friends who can help in your investigations.

MARVEL'S SPIDER-MAN: MILES MORALES

EVEN BETTER THAN OG SPIDEY?

If you're looking for a game to show off your PS5, you can't do better than *Marvel's Spider-Man: Miles Morales* – and it still looks great on PS4. It's both a sequel to and an expansion of the amazing *Marvel's Spider-Man*, giving you all the same awesome web-slinging, wall-crawling action, but with a new hero who has his own special spider skills.

What's more, he's got a brand-new story, with the junior Spider-Man on his own in New York City and up against a mysterious new enemy, the Tinkerer, and an army of thugs armed with futuristic weapons. They're at war with a powerful high-tech corporation, with consequences for Miles and his family, as well as the Big Apple itself. Miles has sworn to protect his city, but can he also protect the people that he loves?

SPIDER-MOVES

BASIC COMBAT

■ Miles has the same basic moves as Peter Parker. He can leap into an enemy and teach them a lesson in a flurry of blows, and he can also blast them with his web-shooters. Or why not use webbing to whack them with a nearby trash can?

FEEL THE STING

■ Miles can also build up stores of energy and unleash it in furious Venom attacks. These can smash straight through high-tech shields or armor, or send whole crowds of enemies flying. With an upgrade, he can even heal automatically as he fights.

NOW YOU SEE ME . . .

■ Miles also has the power of camouflage, making him almost invisible to evildoers. It won't last long, but you can use it to escape a battle and heal yourself, or to sneak up on enemies and catch them by surprise!

FAST FACT

Universes are so 2019—it's all about the multiverse these days! The Spider-Man games take place in a separate world from the movies, the *Into the Spider-Verse* film, or even the Marvel comics, so don't expect everything to turn out the same.

QUICK TIPS

FIGHT LIKE SPIDEY

■ This isn't some straight-up brawler, so don't rely on your fists to win fights. Keep moving, use your web-shooters, and dodge attacks when your spider-sense tingles.

FRIENDLY NEIGHBORHOOD

■ The story missions are important, but don't forget you're a friendly neighborhood spidey. Use the app and help out with folks' smaller problems, and you'll earn extra gear and upgrades.

START SNEAKY

■ Miles has some brilliant stealth attacks, so use them before you head into combat to get rid of enemies who might overwhelm you later.

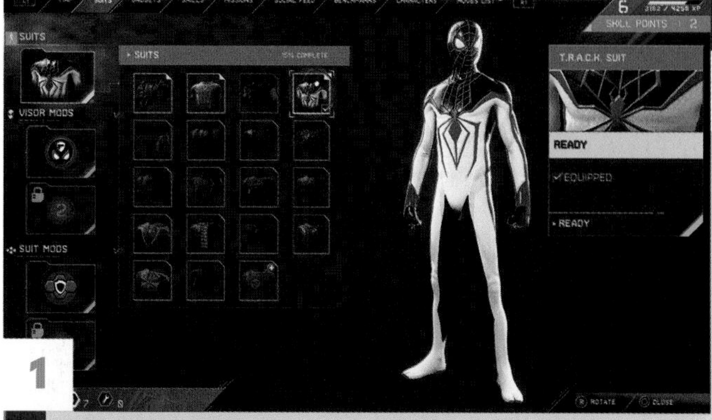

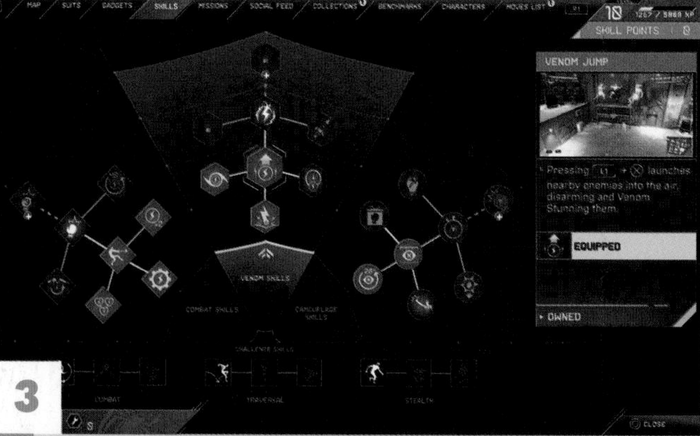

GET AN UPGRADE

1 SPIDEY STYLE

One thing that makes Miles Morales so enjoyable is that you can try so many different outfits on for size. There are nineteen different suits to unlock, ranging from his home-made sportswear suit, to this sporty number, to the suit he wears in *Into the Spider-Verse*.

2 COLLECT THE MODS

Each suit also comes with its own unique mod, giving you new perks, combat moves, and finishers. You'll also get new Visor Mods that make it easier to track your enemies or generate Venom Power. Mods aren't locked to the suit they come with, so feel free to mix things up!

3 WITH GREAT POWER...

As you level up, you'll also get skill points you can use to enhance your powers. These might give you new Venom attacks and fighting moves, or they might improve the ones you already have. Keep using those skill points to make the ultimate Spider-Man.

4 ... COMES AWESOME GADGETS

Collect resources while you're completing missions, and you can splash out on new gadgets and upgrades. Don't you want new web-slinging moves, drones, and shock mines? Show off what a little science can do!

LIKE THIS? TRY THIS:

MARVEL'S AVENGERS

While it's never quite taken off as a superhero version of *Destiny*, *Marvel's Avengers* packs in a great single-player campaign starring Ms. Marvel, Iron Man, the Hulk, and many other classic Marvel stars. It puts the fun in the god of thunder.

PUBLIC ENEMIES?

THE UNDERGROUND

■ The Tinkerer leads a growing gang of thugs and criminals who seem intent on disrupting life in NYC and stealing the latest technology from Roxxon Energy. Can you find out what they're up to and why they're doing it?

ROXXON

■ Led by its charismatic CEO, Simon Krieger, Roxxon is a massive corporation with plans to transform how New York gets its energy through revolutionary new technology. But is Roxxon hiding secrets, and why all the gun-toting, armored goons?

THUGS, THIEVES, AND HIJACKERS

■ Of course, NYC hasn't lost all its ordinary criminals. Keep an eye on your Friendly Neighborhood Spider-Man app, and it'll send you up against robbers, violent gangs, and even thieves on a mission to spoil Christmas! Take them down in classic Spidey style!

CLASSIC VILLAINS

■ It wouldn't be a Spidey game without some of your favorite villains. One big, bad bruiser makes an unforgettable appearance right at the start of the game, but there's still time for some classic Marvel bad guys, including the Prowler and a certain toothy symbiote.

MASTERS OF MAYHEM

■ Did you know that *Marvel's Spider-Man* and *Miles Morales* come from the same studio that brought us Ratchet and Clank? Insomniac Games first became famous for developing the Spyro the Dragon games, but after Ratchet and Clank, they're best known for fast-paced games combining awesome action with crazy weapons, as they did in *Resistance: Fall of Man* and *Sunset Overdrive*. Next up? A Spidey sequel starring both Peter Parker and Miles Morales.

SUPERCONSOLES COMPARED

A new generation of consoles is here to rock the gaming world. How do they match up?

THE POWERHOUSE: XBOX SERIES X

PROCESSOR (CPU)

■ The Xbox Series X has an eight-core custom AMD Zen 2 processor running at 3.8GHz, which is much, much faster than the processor in the old Xbox One X. This means the new console can run more complex games at higher speeds—and it's slightly faster than the similar Zen 2 processor in the PlayStation 5. With 16 GB of RAM, the Xbox Series X also has more working memory for data and graphics, which is crucial when you're making games to run on 4K TV sets.

CONTROLLER

■ The Xbox Series X controller is very similar to the existing Xbox One controller, but Microsoft has made the grips more grippy and added a Share button for taking and sharing screenshots and videos in games.

GRAPHICS PROCESSOR

■ The Series X's AMD graphics processor is built into the same chip as the CPU and can run through 12 trillion (trillion!) floating-point operations a second. That's over twice as many as the Xbox One X could handle, and it makes the Series X's graphics processor slightly more powerful than the one in the PlayStation 5.

■ Running 4K games at a smooth sixty frames per second isn't a problem for the Xbox Series X, and it also supports ray tracing. This technology is new to consoles and creates much more realistic reflections, shadows, and lighting effects.

STORAGE

Old-fashioned hard drives are out! In come super-speedy solid-state drives, or SSDs. The Xbox Series X has a 1TB SSD, which means games load faster and you spend less time reloading when you die. It also helps game developers create bigger and better game worlds.

You can also run old Xbox One games on a USB hard drive and save that SSD for Xbox Series X games and games enhanced for the new console. If you're running out of space, you can also buy a special expansion drive that slots in at the back.

SOUND

The Xbox Series X doesn't have a dedicated sound chip, but its processor can process Dolby Atmos audio, which can create sounds all around you in your favorite games through a pair of headphones or a home theater speaker system.

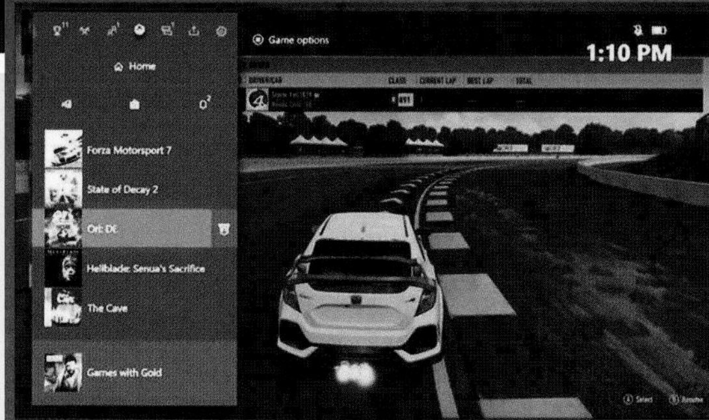

TOP FEATURES

Smart Delivery:

The Xbox Series X can run nearly all the games designed for the old Xbox One, and many will come with enhancements that make them look and play even better. You don't even have to download a special version. Smart Delivery will download the Xbox Series X version automatically.

Quick Resume:

Thanks to that fast SSD, you can switch from one game to another almost instantly, with the action starting just where you left off. You can even switch between several games at once, hopping from one to another and back again without any boring waits while the game loads up.

120fps:

If you've got a really fancy new 4K TV, you might be able to play games at 120fps, which makes the action incredibly smooth. Not many TV sets support this yet, though, although some gaming monitors will do it.

THE INVENTOR:

PLAYSTATION 5

PROCESSOR

■ The PlayStation 5 runs on a different version of the AMD Zen 2 processor also used in the new Xbox consoles. It runs at a slower 3.5GHz, but you wouldn't know it from the leading games, which play just as well on PS5 as they do on the Xbox Series X. That's also more than twice the speed of the processor in the original PS4, so the PS5 won't have any problems running bigger and more complex games.

GRAPHICS PROCESSOR

■ On paper, the PS5's AMD graphics processor is less powerful than the one in the Xbox Series X. Whereas the Series X can work through 12 trillion clever floating point operations per second, the PS5 is stuck at just over 10 trillion.

■ That doesn't make it much less powerful, though. Sony customized the AMD processor to make it really quick at switching between different jobs, and while it doesn't have as many compute units to do all those complex calculations, the ones it does have run at higher speeds. The PS5 can still pump out incredible 4K graphics, complete with slick ray tracing effects.

STORAGE

■ Storage might sound boring, but it's actually where the PS5 gets really exciting. It combines a super-fast 825-GB SSD with a whole new storage system that's even faster than the storage systems on today's incredibly powerful gaming PCs.

■ This means faster loading times, but it also allows game developers to load all the data needed for a new area of a game—or even a new world—in a tiny fraction of a second. This should really help them build games with even bigger and more interesting worlds to explore, where you're never stuck waiting while the next area loads.

■ The PS5 comes in two editions: one with a Blu-ray drive for games and 4K Blu-ray discs, and one without. This costs less, but it will only play games downloaded from Sony's PSN store.

SOUND

Sony has come up with some brand-new sound technology for PlayStation 5, which it calls Tempest 3D Audio. This works a bit like the surround sound you get in the cinema when watching the latest Marvel movie, only the PS5 can track dozens of different noise sources, all at the same time, with incredible precision so that you can track the footsteps of an enemy as they move around you, or the sound of a dragon's wings beating as it flies over your head.

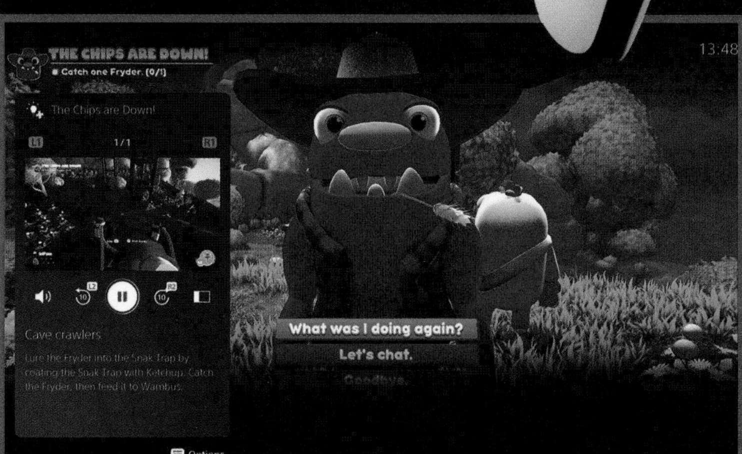

CONTROLLER

The new Dual Sense controller is Sony's most ingenious controller yet, with two absolutely brilliant new features. The first is a new high-definition rumble, where different motors in different parts of the pad can make it vibrate in different ways so that when you land heavily in a platform game or blast an enemy in a game like Fortnite, you feel more like you're inside the game.

The Dual Sense also has motorized triggers that give you different levels of resistance depending on what you're trying to do in a game. You'll feel the effects when you press down on the gas pedal in a racing game, grab hold of a ledge in a platform game, or fire your weapon in an action game. Gaming isn't just about what you hear and see anymore, but also about what you can feel!

TOP FEATURES

Activity Cards:

PS5 doesn't have a Quick Resume feature, but it does have special Activity Cards that can take you straight from the dashboard to the level you're playing through in a platform game, your favorite mode in *Fortnite*, or a particular track or event in a racing game. Less waiting, more playing. Win!

Astro's Playroom:

The PS5 has a free game pre-installed onto every console, which shows off all the clever features of the new Dual Sense controller. You'll want to play it, as it's a brilliant 3D platform game that's just packed out with cool ideas.

Built-in tips:

The PS5 has its own built-in tips system, where you can pause the game and bring up the new Control Center and check out Game Help cards that show you how to find a secret item or get past a difficult section of the game.

THE PEOPLE'S CHAMP:

XBOX SERIES S

PROCESSOR

■ The Xbox Series S is designed to run all the same games as the Xbox Series X, but on a full HD TV or PC gaming monitor rather than a fancy 4K screen. That means it has the exact same AMD Zen 2 processor as the Series X, but it runs at a slightly slower speed (3.6GHz rather than 3.8GHz).

■ As it doesn't need as much RAM for gorgeous 4K graphics, it can also get away with having less. Where both the PS5 and Xbox Series X have 16 GB, the Xbox Series S has just 10 GB.

GRAPHICS PROCESSOR

■ The Series S also has a less powerful graphics processor. It has fewer than half the number of compute units to generate its 3D graphics, and those units run at a lower speed. With enough power to crunch through 4 trillion floating point operations, it's still a bit smarter than you or me at math, but it's a long way behind the Series X and PS5.

■ Amazingly, this doesn't matter all that much. The Series S GPU still has the same ray tracing features as its Series X bigger brother, and games still have most of the same graphical features. It runs at HD not 4K resolutions, but the games still look great!

Does S stand for small? This thing is tiny!

CONTROLLER

■ The Xbox Series S controller is just like the Xbox Series X controller, only it comes in white. As there's only one new button, you can still use any old Xbox One controllers you have lying around. Score!

STORAGE

The Series S has a much smaller SSD than the Series X. It can store up to 512 GB of data, but some of that is already taken up by the Xbox software and Quick Resume features.

This means you can only store a few big games at the same time, but—thanks to Smart Delivery—each one takes up less space than it does on the Series X, and you can store any games you aren't playing right now on a USB hard disk drive.

SOUND

As with the Series X, there's no new sound technology, but you can still have awesome digital surround sound through the built-in audio or the Dolby Atmos app.

TOP FEATURES

Digital only:

The Xbox Series S has no Blu-ray drive, so you can only download games rather than buy them in the shops. That's not a problem if you subscribe to Microsoft's Xbox Games Pass subscription service, where you can download any game from a massive games library as long as you keep paying the monthly charge. Series S and Games Pass go together like biscuits and gravy!

Cloud Gaming:

The Series S has all the same software features as the Series X so you don't miss out on any of its Instant Resume or Smart Delivery goodness. You can also play your Xbox games on your smartphone while you're away from your console, thanks to the magic of cloud gaming.

Price:

The Xbox Series X and PS5 are seriously expensive consoles; if you get one for Christmas, you must have hit the top of Santa's nice list. The Series S is a whole lot cheaper, so you've got a decent shot at persuading your mom and dad to buy it!

POKÉMON

SO MANY WAYS TO CATCH 'EM ALL

Pokémon reached its 25th anniversary last year, and the series has never been stronger. We've had remakes of *Pokémon Diamond* and *Pearl* and a cool new take on *Pokémon Snap*. *Pokémon Unite* has given us a brand-new way to battle, while *Pokémon Legends: Arceus* took us on a trip back in time that opened up the classic gameplay. And now we're looking at a new Pokémon generation, with *Pokémon Scarlet* and *Pokémon Violet* taking that open-world style even further and into an all-new region!

SCARLET AND VIOLET

■ The ninth generation Pokémon games build on the open-world style of play we saw introduced in *Pokémon Sword* and *Shield* and expanded in *Pokémon Legends: Arceus*. After the British style of the Galar region and Arceus's exploration of the history of Sinnoh, Scarlet and Violet bring us up to date in the present day and a setting with the feel of Spain and Portugal. We hope you like the heat, because this one's going to be a scorcher!

■ We're also getting three new starter Pokémon. Sprigatito is a grass-type cat Pokémon, while Fuecoco is a chilled-out crocodile fire Pokémon who loves to set his opponents ablaze. The coolest, though, has to be Quaxly, the duckling water Pokémon with an awesome pompadour hairdo. He's got a torrent attack ready for anyone who mocks that ice-cold coiffure!

BRILLIANT DIAMOND AND SHINING PEARL

■ *Pokémon Diamond* and *Pokémon Pearl* are Pokémon fan favorites, so it's great to see them reproduced on Switch as *Pokémon Brilliant Diamond* and *Shining Pearl*. The originals came out on the Nintendo DS, so they've had a big graphical upgrade, but the story and the classic gameplay are mostly unchanged, with just a few adjustments that make them easier to play.

For instance, your current Pokémon now all get XP when you battle, just like they have in the last few games. This means you don't need to keep rotating the little critters in and out of the fight just to make sure they all level up!

■ If you want to see what the Hsui region in *Pokémon Legends: Arceus* looks like 200 years later, give the remakes a shot...

FAST FACT

***Pokémon Scarlet* and *Violet* are the first pair of Pokémon games where your character's initial look will be different depending on your version, and the first where both the boy and girl characters wear the same outfit!**

FIND THE GRAND UNDERGROUND

■ One of the biggest areas—and one of the best for catching Pokémon—is hidden under Eterna City. Find the legendary Underground Man and he'll give you an Explorer Kit, which opens up the Grand Underground. This massive dungeon area is packed with free-roaming monsters to collect, including some you won't find anywhere else in Sinnoh!

POKÉMON LEGENDS: ARCEUS

■ It might be a weird, time-traveling, historical side story, but *Pokémon Legends: Arceus* is the most revolutionary and exciting Pokémon in years!

It takes you back to the Sinnoh region of *Pokémon Diamond* and *Pokémon Pearl*, only 200 years in the past. This is when it was called Hsui and was a whole lot wilder—and that goes double for its Pokémon!

As a young Pokémon enthusiast who's dropped in from the future, you're soon enlisted to help Professor Laventon and the Galaxy Team's Survey Corps fill in the region's first Pokédex. The locals are only just beginning to bond and battle with the crazy critters, so get ready for a very different style of Pokémon game.

SIGN UP FOR THE SURVEY CORPS

■ *Pokémon Sword* and *Shield* dabbled with free-roaming gameplay in its special Wild Areas and its two expansions, but *Pokémon Legends: Arceus* doubles down on it, with five huge areas where you can wander around at will. You pick up missions at the base camps or the central HQ in Jubilife Village, and once you have them you'll need to explore that region, looking for the Pokémon you need to catch or battle or the opponents you need to conquer.

■ There are no gym leaders to defeat or tournaments to win—it's all about making your way up the Survey Corps ranks and finding out what's really going on behind the scenes in Hsui.

■ These areas are big, but you don't have to walk them all on foot. As you play, you'll catch and unlock new Pokémon who'll let you ride them. Wyrdeer and Ursalunar will get you around faster on the land, while Bascalegion can speed you across the water in style.

■ Sneasler's backpack is a great way to tackle walls, trees, and cliffs, or catch a lift with Braviary and glide across the landscape!

CATCH 'EM ALL!

It won't take you long in *Pokémon Legends: Arceus* before you realize that different Pokémon take a different approach if you want to catch them.

QUICK CAPTURES

With the easiest Pokémon, all you need to do is throw the right Poké Ball. Get 'em in your sights and throw that sucker! You might need a Great Ball or Heavy Ball to catch some tricky Pokémon, or a Jet Ball or Feather Ball if they're flying in the air.

CATCH 'EM BY SURPRISE

Timid Pokémon need to be snuck up on. Just crouch and sneak your way through the long grass, then throw the ball while they're unawares. Move slowly, throw a back strike from behind, and don't let them spot you, or they'll run away!

DODGE 'EM!

Aggressive Pokémon will sometimes rush you, so make sure that you master the Dodge move. Tap it when they charge, or you might get whacked!

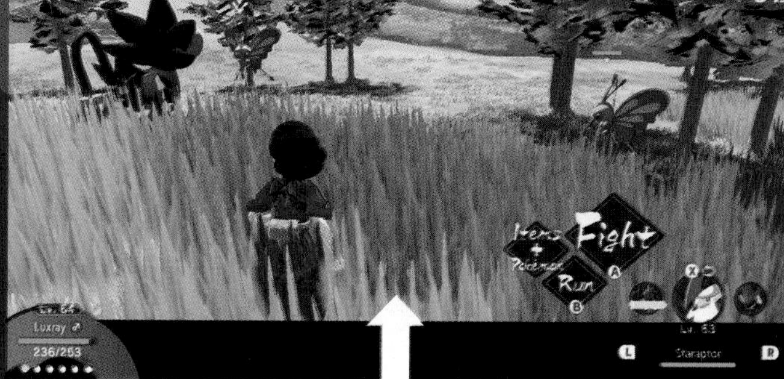

BATTLE 'EM

With aggressive Pokémon, you need to go old-school. Ready a Poké Ball packed with your strongest little monster and throw it their way to start a battle. Don't worry—you can still switch Pokémon in and out of the fight if they're getting weak and you need to heal them.

POKÉMON UNITE

■ *Pokémon Unite* takes Pokémon into a whole new world of action that's closer to multiplayer online battle arena games like *League of Legends* or *DOTA 2*.

FIVE VERSUS FIVE

■ Two teams of five Pokémon battle over a series of control points using their moves to fight and catch wild Pokémon—or battle members of the other team.

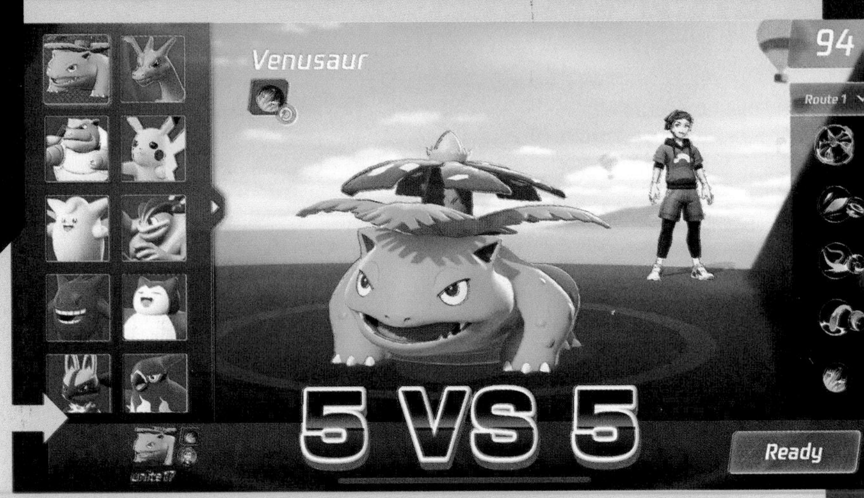

MIGHTY MOVES

■ Keep leveling up and you can unlock unique Unite moves that can hit several opponents hard at the same time. You need to think about when to use your Unite move and when your opponent might use theirs.

TRAINING UP

■ The Pokémon you control begin each battle at level 1, but by defeating the wild Pokémon, they can level up, evolve, and learn new moves. You can choose which moves you learn as you level to match your Pokémon to your favorite style of play.

DON'T GO SOLO

■ Winning in *Unite* is all about teamwork. Work with your teammates to occupy and protect the control points, surround your opponents, and stop them stealing precious points. The team with the most points at the end of the match is the winner.

POKÉMON SNAP

■ *Pokémon Snap* was a weird and wonderful hit on the old Nintendo Gamecube, where instead of training and battling with your Pokémon, you became a kind of Pokémon wildlife photographer.

■ Now it's back on the Switch, giving you a chance to watch—and snap—your favorite Pokémon out in the wild.

■ You'll get to explore different coastal, ocean, plains, and jungle areas, where you can pull out your camera and catch the critters in your frame. Get the right shot from the right angle, and you'll not only fill up your new Photodex but win awards for your artistic shooting style. Get snapping!

LIKE THIS? TRY THIS:

DIGIMON SURVIVE

■ Looking for a Pokémon-style game with a little more edge? The latest title in the Digimon series has the same kind of creature-collecting action, but more tactical battles and a deeper story line. Can you and your Digimon escape a mysterious world and fight your way back home?

RATCHET AND CLANK: RIFT APART

GAMING'S GREATEST DOUBLE ACT SPLITS?

It wasn't meant to go down like this! One minute Ratchet and Clank are celebrating years of heroic adventures, the next they're in an alternative dimension, where the evil Dr. Nefarious is Emperor Nefarious and all hope for the universe seems lost. To make things worse, our dynamic duo has been separated, with no way to save this dimension or get back to their own.

Luckily, this dimension has its own potential saviors: a female Lombax, Rivet, and a lonely warbot, Kit. Can this foursome pull together to stop Emperor Nefarious and make some new friends along the way?

QUICK TIPS

BAG THOSE BOLTS

Every level is crammed with collectibles, so look around, smash the crates, and bag those bolts. Look out for the special golden bolts, and pocket Raritanium for weapon upgrades.

USE YOUR WRENCH

You can't level up Ratchet's wrench through combat, but it's a great way to destroy weak enemies when you're short on ammo, and it's the best tool for smashing crates and boxes.

SPEND, SPEND, SPEND

Look out for Ms. Zurkon, and don't be shy about spending those bolts. The only way to get new weapons is to buy them, and you'll need all the guns and power gloves you can carry.

THROUGH THE RIFT

Switching dimensions is a big deal in *Rift Apart*, and the new universe our heroes find themselves in is full of new friends, new enemies, new challenges, and new gadgets!

BUDDY UP!

Each of our heroes gets paired up with a partner from the new dimension. Ratchet learns to rely on the insecure Kit, while Clank teams up with the Lombax rebel Rivet.

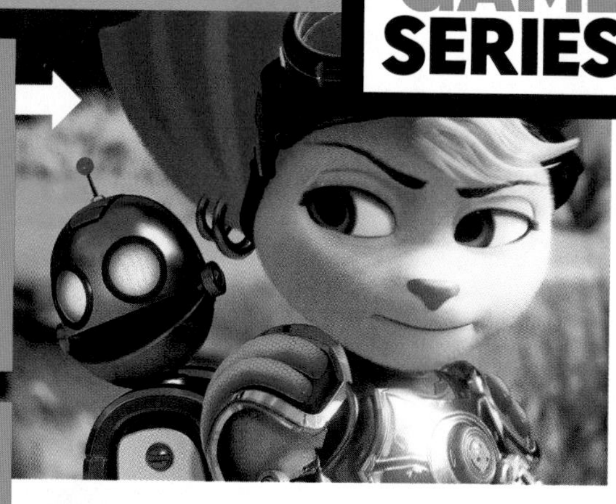

FIND 'EM, GRIND 'EM

Rift Apart is full of the jumping, swinging, and grinding action we expect from a Ratchet and Clank. Think fast and use your new wall-running moves if you want to survive.

JUMP, JET, AND BOOST

Once you've found them, the Hoverboots are a great way to travel – or escape scary, speeding monsters. Use the ramps to reach and explore new areas.

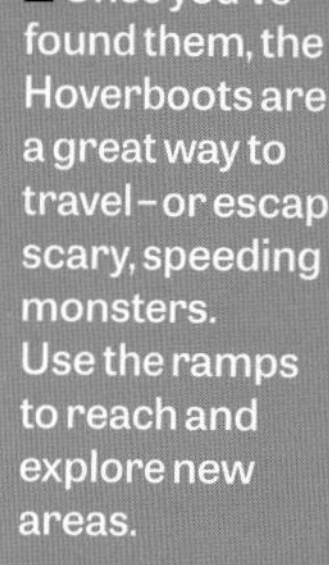

MEET THE CHALLENGE

Rift Apart is also packed with clever challenges, including mind-bending puzzles where you figure out a path for potential Clanks, and sneaky arcade hacking games featuring a new friend, Glitch.

AST ACT

Classic Ratchet and Clank characters reappear in different forms in *Rift Apart. Tools of Destruction*'s Rusty Pete is now Pierre Le Fer, while Captain Qwark becomes the more heroic Captain Quantum.

LIKE THIS? TRY THIS:

SOLAR ASH

If you like *Rift Apart*'s high-speed grinding and platforming sections, you're going to love Solar Ash. It's all about skating and leaping through spectacular cosmic landscapes on a mission to save your world.

FIGHT A BETTER BATTLE IN RATCHET AND CLANK: RIFT APART

Improve your combat skills and make the most of those wacky weapons

It might look like Pixar made a classic 3D platform game, but *Ratchet and Clank: Rift Apart* features some deadly combat. Unless you can master the moves and the weaponry, Ratchet and his new friend Rivet will be toast! You'll need to handle large packs of enemies and switch between weapons on the go. Listen up—we're here to teach you how!

1 Keep moving

■ You won't have any problems picking off three or four enemies at a time, but *Rift Apart* is full of sequences where you'll have to battle armies of robot warriors, alien bruisers, or space pirates. The trick is to keep moving. Run backward while you're blasting to deal with charging enemies before they hit you, and learn to strafe, moving left and right while keeping your foe in your sights.

2 Work around their armor

■ Some enemies are heavily armored or carry a shield that protects their front from your attacks. Work around their defenses using guns like the Ricochet or Buzz Blades that can hit them from the sides or behind. Mr. Fungi or the Glove of Doom are also handy for exposing your foes to a sneaky rear attack.

3 Go for your guns

■ While some guns and gloves work well in most situations, you'll find that many are particularly good in a certain situation or against a particular type of enemy. Being harassed by packs of alien crabs or those nasty little spinning blots with the sharp blades? Hit them hard with the Enforcer. Tackling tough, single enemies? Reach for the Shatterbomb, Drillhound, or Negatron Collider. And remember—the more you use each weapon, the faster it levels up!

4 Crowd control

■ If you're being swamped, escape to a safe spot and try to grab a health recharge along the way. Weapons like the Shatterbomb, Buzz Blades, and Mr. Fungi can be great for tackling multiple enemies at once, while the Lightning Rod can affect a whole bunch of bad guys. Keep firing and the deadly charge will spread to take out a squad of varmints in one go.

FAST FACT

Every Ratchet and Clank game has its share of amazing weapons, and the R.Y.N.O. and the Glove of Doom date back to the 2002 original game. Every new installment features at least one gun that turns enemies to chickens, sheep, or harmless plants. Here it's the Topiary Sprinkler.

5 Use the rifts

■ Ratchet's and Rivet's rift-shifting moves are brilliant for a fast escape or for getting behind an enemy and giving them a shock. Target the rift, press L1 to go through it, then spin around and hit 'em where they least expect it. Also, look out for opportunities to use rifts, wall runs, or grapple points to reach health and ammo. You're going to need all the ammo you can find.

Don't forget to upgrade!

■ With all the new guns to collect and the way that weapons level up, it's easy to forget to upgrade them. Don't. Grab all the raritanium you can find and use it in the Ms. Zurkon shops to increase the capacity, accuracy, range, and damage of your favorite guns. When you do, prioritize the upgrades that surround the orange clusters. You'll unlock the bonus upgrades held inside!

BOWSER'S FURY

ONE GIANT LEAP FOR MARIO-KIND!

CAT SHINE!

Make the Lighthouse Shine

Bowser's Fury isn't your old-school Mario game. Bundled with the *Super Mario 3D World* remake, it's a short but very sweet adventure that shows Nintendo playing around with new ideas. For one thing, this isn't a game with individual levels or words. Instead, it all takes place on one big map, with new areas emerging as you fight back against a giant-size, bad-tempered Bowser!

Meanwhile, Big B isn't just waiting at the end of the level for a boss battle. Instead, he wakes up every few minutes and comes looking for you, bringing a storm of driving rain, fireballs, and flaming Bowser-breath along with him. Don't want to get cooked? You'd better avoid him, or better still, defeat him!

QUICK TIPS

LIGHTHOUSE SECRETS

■ As you play, you'll free the lighthouses from the evil goo that covers them and Bowser. When you do, climb to the top. There could be something useful up there.

GRAB A KITTY

■ Those cats aren't just there to look cute. Pick one up, and you can use its crazy claws to break through crates and teach the local Goombas a lesson.

LISTEN TO JUNIOR

■ Bowser Jr. is on your side this time, and he's full of good advice. He can also investigate mysterious objects for you or fight off enemies with his paintbrush. Nice work, little B!

FIGHT THE FURY!

The action in *Bowser's Fury* follows a definite cycle. When Bowser's sleeping and the world is sunny, Mario gets out there and collects the Cat Shines. But when Bowser wakes and things turn stormy, Mario must fight to survive.

COLLECT THE CAT SHINES

Mario collects the Cat Shines by exploring the map. He needs to make his way up to its highest platforms and complete the weird and wonderful tasks that will reveal another gleaming Shine.

RING THE BELL

Collect enough Cat Shines and Mario unlocks the Giga Bell. Ring it when Bowser's on a rampage, and Mario will power up to take him on. It's giant Cat Mario vs. Bows-zilla!

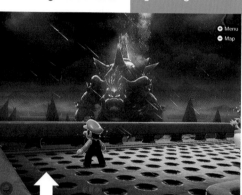

INCOMING!

Every few minutes, the weather will turn dark and stormy, meaning Bowser is waking up again. Watch out for fireballs and Bowser's flaming breath, but also look for new blocks that appear or chunks of scenery that get destroyed. Can you use them?

GET READY TO RUMBLE

Each time these titans clash, it's like an epic-scale boss battle. Watch Bowser's moves and work out how to bring him down in style. Don't think it's over, though. Bowser keeps coming back for more!

FAST FACT

Mario hasn't been the hero of every game he's starred in. In *Donkey Kong Jr.* (1982) he was the bad guy, having locked Donkey Kong Sr. in a cage! Still, you could say the big ape deserved it . . .

LIKE THIS? TRY THIS:

CRASH BANDICOOT 4: IT'S ABOUT TIME

We can't say this enough. Crash's comeback adventure is one of the smartest, most inventive 3D platform games of the last decade, even if it can be tough!

THE BEST GAMES OF THE LAST GENERATION

Which Xbox One and PS4 games should go down as all-time greats?

So, we've come to the end of one amazing console generation. From 2013 through 2020, the Xbox One and PS4 served up great game after great game, from the biggest and best open-world adventures to all-action shooters that changed the way we play online. Then along came the Nintendo Switch and turned our gaming world upside down again! But which of these games deserve a spot in the gaming Hall of Fame? We've picked our favorites. Can you pick yours?

20

NBA 2K18

■ Madden can be magic, and FIFA has its fans, but for the Xbox One and PS4, NBA 2K was the top dog of sports games. *NBA 2K18* was the series at its peak, shooting baskets and pulling off trick shots like a champ, with great online action and a fantastic career mode where you could tell your own basketball tale.

19

FINAL FANTASY XV

■ Final Fantasy hit this generation looking tired and over-the-hill. The *Final Fantasy XIII* games were okay but a bit messy, and *Final Fantasy XIV* looked, at first, like a bad attempt at a Final Fantasy take on *World of Warcraft* (though it's brilliant now). *Final Fantasy XV* turned that around, thanks to a great story, lovable stars, and a brilliant road trip theme.

18

APEX LEGENDS

■ *PUBG* got there first and *Fortnite* was unstoppable, but *Apex Legends* could be the best battle royale of the bunch. Its action and gunplay are as good as you'd expect from the guys that brought us Titanfall, and the different characters, weapons, abilities, and gadgets make each match a thriller where you never know whatis going to happen next.

17

HOLLOW KNIGHT

■ Every console's game library is now stuffed with tough 2D platformers where you explore and battle monsters, but *Hollow Knight* is in a different class. It has its own weird cartoon style, a cast of mysterious and sinister creepy-crawlies, and one of the strangest worlds of any game. If you're looking for a new kind of adventure, these battling beetles have the real deal.

16

NO MAN'S SKY

■ Some gamers will never forgive *No Man's Sky* for turning up unfinished after so much hype, but Hello Games kept working on it until it became the best space exploration epic for a decade. You could spend hours wandering around its millions of planets, finding new life-forms and beautiful alien landscapes, or just trade and battle in your starship in the inky depths of space.

15

SUPER SMASH BROS ULTIMATE

■ Nintendo's fighting game doesn't always get the credit it deserves, but no game tried harder to pack in so many classic stars from Nintendo's greatest hits—and then some from a ton of other classic games. What other game pits Solid Snake against Pikachu or Donkey Kong against Minecraft's Steve? It's packed with fun stuff to do and fiercely competitive. You can't stop coming back for more!

14

ROCKET LEAGUE

■ Who would have seen that a mix of jet-powered cars and soccer would become one of the biggest online games in years? Well, *Rocket League* made it all look easy, thanks to brilliantly simple gameplay, great controls, and a whole lot of style. It's a slice of fast-paced, car-crazy mayhem that never seems to get old, so start your engines and race for the goal.

13

FIRE EMBLEM: THREE HOUSES

■ Nintendo's superb strategy RPG series seemed to take inspiration from Harry Potter for its Switch debut. As the new professor in a military academy in a fantasy kingdom, you had to train your students in battle and help them through their school life in a story full of twists and teenage drama. The best game to ever mix magical warfare with cake and a nice cup of tea.

12

CELESTE

■ Retro games don't get meaner or better than *Celeste*. The blocky pixel graphics and precision platforming gameplay take you straight back to the early days of gaming, but it's the hard-as-nails yet addictive action that keeps you coming back for more. Sure, you might die another twenty times trying to get through the next screen of spikes and death traps, but the challenge is part of the fun.

11

SPLATOON 2

■ Nintendo launched its paint-splattering shooter on the old Wii U, but perfected it for this Switch sequel. *Splatoon 2* has it all—incredible team-based multiplayer mayhem, great single-player and co-op game modes, along with a whole heap of charm. And who can resist a game where you can go online to settle some of life's big questions, like what's best: cats vs. dogs or burgers vs. pizza?

10

MONSTER HUNTER WORLD

■ Japan has loved Monster Hunter for ages. With *Monster Hunter World*, the rest of us finally caught on. The best-ever Monster Hunter didn't mess with the classic formula—hunt and kill the titanic beasts, then use their bones and hides to craft new weapons and armor. But it made it much, much easier to get into and a lot more fun, with some of the best online co-op play around.

OVERWATCH

■ Who would have thought that the makers of Diablo and World of Warcraft could make one of the best competitive shooters ever made? Well, Blizzard did it with *Overwatch*, creating a game full of cool heroes and villains battling it out with their own awesome, superpowered abilities. It still has millions of fans nearly six years later, who love watching it almost as much as they love playing it.

9

8

FORZA HORIZON 4

■ What started out as an offshoot of Forza Motorsports has become this generation's essential racing game. *Forza Horizon 2* took the crazy racing festival to Europe, while *Forza Horizon 3* took it all the way to Australia, and *Forza Horizon 4* went to England and Scotland for the most thrilling on- and off-road racing we've ever had. And the LEGO expansion was genius as well!

7

ORI AND THE WILL O THE WISPS

■ *Ori and the Blind Forest* showed what you could do with a classic 2D platform adventure and today's beautiful HD graphics. The sequel took that even further, with an epic tale full of challenging combat, brilliant boss battles, new abilities, and incredible scenery. It's all the best bits of Mario, Zelda, Castlevania, and a dozen other greats rolled into one game.

6

ANIMAL CROSSING: NEW HORIZONS

■ Some people don't get Animal Crossing. Doesn't all that home building, decorating, fishing, and chatting with your animal friends get pretty old, pretty fast? But these people are missing out on the way your island changes over time and the relationships you build with its eccentric characters. When things get tough, Animal Crossing makes the world feel better.

5

DESTINY 2

■ Having built one of the best shooters ever with Halo, Bungie seemed to mess up big time with *Destiny*. Its online co-op shooter looked amazing and had fantastic gunplay, but the rest of it was too complicated, and the story made no sense at all.

■ In the years since, though, Bungie kept working, refining *Destiny* through expansions and one amazing sequel. If you want sweeping sci-fi adventure on alien worlds and the chance to create your own legend, then *Destiny 2* is impossible to beat. And it's even better if you can pull some friends together in a fireteam!

4

SUPER MARIO ODYSSEY

■ Don't call it a comeback—Mario never went away—but *Odyssey* was his best outing since *Super Mario Galaxy* on the Wii. There's a real sense of going on a journey, as the Mushroom Kingdom's mightiest plumber battles Bowser's minions across different worlds, and his new hat-flicking, monster-controlling moves made for some truly ingenious gameplay.

■ Some gorgeous cartoon graphics and a brilliant soundtrack showed that the Switch could pull off some spectacular stuff. And who can forget fighting Bowser himself, all dressed up in his best wedding gear?

3

MARVEL'S SPIDER-MAN

■ Spidey's starred in some amazing video games in his time, but nothing before has captured his superpowered spirit in the way that Marvel's Spider-Man did. It gets the speed and excitement of swinging through Manhattan's glass-and-concrete canyons, sprinting up the side of a building, and hurling yourself off with a somersault.

■ It also nails the combat by focusing on fast moves, acrobatic dodges, and web-slinging special attacks. And, best of all, it has a brilliant story packed with Spidey's greatest characters and super-villains, along with plenty of callbacks to his classic comics and movies. Some say it's the greatest super-hero game ever made, and with respect to *Batman*, we agree.

2

FORTNITE

■ Did *Fortnite* invent the battle royale? Nope, but it made it a lot more fun. Epic took the colorful cartoon graphics and great gunplay from an unsuccessful co-op shooter and used them to build a brilliant game where 100 players fought to be the last one standing. Then it added its masterstroke—building—where you could craft your own cover or ramp up to get some height.

■ But what really makes *Fortnite* sing is its Battle Pass full of challenges, its cool and crazy costumes, and the way that each new season adds new twists, modes, and gadgets to mix things up. The result has been a money-making monster that's changed the way the world enjoys games. And while it's going to go up and down in popularity, we don't reckon it's running out of steam at all.

1

LEGEND OF ZELDA: BREATH OF THE WILD

■ *Breath of the Wild* isn't just Zelda at its biggest and most beautiful, but also one of the bravest games Nintendo has ever made. Where every Zelda since *Ocarina of Time* has followed the same basic style and blueprint, *Breath of the Wild* threw it out for a much more ambitious open-world adventure. You could go almost anywhere and do almost anything within a few hours of starting a new game, but what you really needed to do was explore, develop your skills, and prepare yourself for the tougher challenges that lay ahead.

■ *Breath of the Wild* has a sense of freedom that you won't find in many other games, and there's so much to see and do that you could spend months just wandering Hyrule. Yet it still had great characters, awesome boss fights, ingenious puzzles, and a whole bunch of weird stuff going on beneath the surface. It's still the best game on Switch—and one of the best games ever made.

FORTNITE

ANOTHER YEAR AS THE BEST BATTLE ROYALE

Is *Fortnite* ever going to run out of steam? Not while each season keeps on throwing in such great ideas, or while the biggest names in entertainment keep lining up for crossover events. In the last year, we've had the stars of Spider-Man and Uncharted, guest spots from NBA ballers, and even The Rock in a central role. And we know there are more guest stars to come.

While the battle royale is still the main course, *Fortnite*'s Creative Mode keeps dishing up delicious sides of team-based modes, party modes, and remakes of other multiplayer hits. Whatever you want to play, there's almost always a way to play it in *Fortnite*. And there's just as much fun to be had playing Hide and Seek as there is blasting away in Zone Wars games and Boxfights.

QUICK TIPS

LEARN TO EDIT

In the early years of *Fortnite*, your building skills were what made you a champ, but these days you need to be an editing expert, too! Learn how to quickly edit corners and windows to surprise your enemies—and blast 'em!

PRACTICE MAKES PERFECT

Creative Mode is full of practice maps where you can hone your skills in sniping, building, editing, close combat, and more. Try these out to develop as a *Fortnite* player, or to warm up before you start playing proper matches.

BE BOLD (BUT NOT STUPID)

Don't rush in against other players when you might be outnumbered or outgunned. Playing it safe will help you reach the final ten. Don't avoid every fight, though. If you never battle, you'll never get better!

THE BEST GETS BETTER

■ *Fortnite*'s battle royale never stops evolving. Every season brings new changes to the map, new gimmicks and gadgets, and new heroes to join the fight.

DRIVE THEM CRAZY

■ Vehicles have made a big difference to *Fortnite*, giving you a chance of making it to the storm circle alive even if you're halfway across the map. The only problem? Other players will hear you coming, and they love to destroy your wheels!

GUEST STARS

■ Strong themes and new outfits make every Fortnite season feel different from the last. We've already had some of Marvel's mightiest heroes and the biggest stars in the Star Wars universe, including Darth Vader, the Mandalorian, and Fennec Shand and Krrsantan from *The Book of Boba Fett*.

CHANGING WORLDS

■ If there's one thing you can be sure about with Fortnite, it's that the map won't stay the same for long. *Chapter 3* has redrawn the map once again, bringing back Tilted Towers and introducing a bunch of brand-new locations to discover.

MEET THE MONSTER

■ Klombos might go down as one of the best Fortnite additions ever! Throw the big galoot some delicious Klomberries and it might just spew out useful items. You can also climb up and use its blowhole to get some air and glide across the map. Just don't start shooting at them. It only makes these gentle giants angry, and then it's trampling time!

AST ACT

Chapter 2's big finale, the Cube live event, showed that Fortnite can still pull in a massive audience. On top of millions of players actually fighting UFOs, over 3.5 million viewers watched the action on YouTube or Twitch!

GET CREATIVE

■ *Fortnite* is now so much more than a battle royale game, thanks to Epic's own ingenuity and the awesome powers of the game's creative community. If you want a break from the fighting, there's always something cool to do!

HIDE AND SEEK

■ Who doesn't love a game of Hide and Seek? Well, it's just as much fun in *Fortnite*, especially when the maps feature secret areas where sneaky players can lie low. The fun doesn't end if you get caught—you'll just join the seeking team.

SUPER FORTNITE KART

■ Love Mario Kart? Love *Fortnite*? Why not combine the two? Creative Mode features some amazing race-course maps where you can speed around in karts, glide through rocky canyons, or even float around a sci-fi track on a hoverboard.

RUNNERS VS. SNIPERS

■ Team games don't get better than Runners vs. Snipers. One team tries to make it from one end of the map to the other, while the other team tries to stop them the painful way—with bullets! In the awesome Kitty Box Run map, blackout shutters and cardboard boxes make things twice as exciting!

IMPOSTORS

■ Fortnite's finest bonus mode might be this brilliant tribute to *Among Us*. Can your team of agents get their work done and spot the Impostor, or will they meet a sticky end?

BORN TO BOXFIGHT

Boxfighting is *Fortnite* at its most intense, making Boxfight maps some of the most popular Creative Mode maps. It's a great way to practice your building, editing, and fighting skills!

BUILD AND BATTLE

Each match takes place in a small arena, and you have a few moments at the start to build some cover. Build walls around you and get ready to ramp up and get moving. You could be under attack in seconds!

TAKE 'EM BY SURPRISE

Boxfights are all about building, editing, and shooting. You need to be able to build quickly and edit out doors, windows, and corners to surprise your enemies and get them in your sights. The faster you can switch between editing and shooting, the longer you'll survive.

DON'T PANIC

Fights can be sudden and deadly, so don't freeze when the bullets start flying. Stay calm, move to avoid incoming fire, take aim at your enemy, and shoot. Assault rifles are good at a distance, but up close you want a shotgun. One hit and it could all be over!

LIKE THIS? TRY THIS:

APEX LEGENDS

If *Fortnite* is the number-one battle royale, then *Apex Legends* is a close number two. It looks great and beats *Fortnite* on moving fast and gunplay, and the lineup of legends and abilities just keeps on getting better.

APEX LEGENDS NEW LEGENDS

Four ace Legends – and how to use them!

MAD MAGGIE

REAL NAME: Margaret Kōhere
AGE: 55
HOME WORLD: Salvo

■ A fearsome mercenary and ex-partner of fellow Legend Fuse, Mad Maggie is a force to be reckoned with on the battlefield. Her Riot Drill ability fires a drill that can touch her enemies even when they're ducking behind a shield or cover. Her Warlord's Ire passive highlights enemies you've damaged and increases her movement speed while she wields a shotgun. Finally, her Wrecking Ball releases speed-boosting pads, then detonates in close contact with the enemy.

HOW TO PLAY Mad Maggie:

■ Play aggressively and pack a shotgun. Tag your enemies, then use Warlord's Ire to hunt them down relentlessly. Use Wrecking Ball's speed pads, and you can move even faster!

ASH

REAL NAME: Dr. Ashleigh Reid
AGE: 121
HOME WORLD: Unknown

■ Working as a scientist double agent in an experimental fuel research facility, Dr. Ashleigh Reid should have died when it self-destructed. She didn't. Her mind was moved into an android shell, and like that other fiendish man-machine, Revenant, she's joined the Apex Games. She can throw a spinning Arc Snare that tethers and damages her enemies or use her Phase Breach ultimate to warp to a targeted location. Her Marked for Death passive reveals where other players have died and marks surviving attackers.

HOW TO PLAY Ash:

■ Use Arc Snare to trap and break down your opponents and Phase Breach to get closer to a hostile team fast. Marked for Death is great for spotting weak targets for the team.

SEER

REAL NAME: Obi Edolasim
AGE: 26
HOME WORLD: Boreas

Born under a bad sign and despised as a cursed child, Obi Edolasim became a hero in the Apex Games arenas. Using psychic abilities and cutting-edge tech, he's a master of the ambush and the ultimate Apex showman. His Heart Seeker passive enables him to visualize the heartbeats of nearby foes while he's aiming down the sights, while his Focus of Attention skill brings out microdrones that can reveal enemies through walls. And if Seer needs more info, his Exhibit ultimate creates a sphere of drones where nobody can hide.

HOW TO PLAY Seer:

Seer is a powerful leader or support character. Use the information his abilities deliver to locate enemies, track their movements, and feed it all back to your squad. Play it smart.

FAST FACT

Apex Legends takes place in the same universe as *Titanfall* and *Titanfall 2*. You'll even see some of the same weapons and technology in both series of games. Now how about *Titanfall 3*?

VALKYRIE

REAL NAME: Kairi Imahara
AGE: 30
HOME WORLD: Angelia

Kairi Imahara has always been trouble, stealing her father's Titan as a child. But when he disappeared on a mission, she started her own quest for revenge. Now she's in the Apex Games, strapped into a sleek new jetpack, and she's going to do her dad proud. She can use her jetpack to fly, with her VTOL Jets passive enabling her to soar into the sky. When she's on the attack, her Missile Swarm ability fires a horde of mini rockets at her foes. Finally, she can launch into the sky with her Skyward Dive ultimate, and take the rest of her squad with her. That's air support!

HOW TO PLAY Valkyrie:

Your jetpack can make you an easy target, but it's great for leading a team into battle or taking them out of danger. Don't overuse it!

DESTINY 2

THE WITCH QUEEN

Destiny 2 keeps dishing out the good stuff to its fans, taking our brave Guardians to new worlds to battle even more terrifying foes. The latest era of Bungie's smash hit started with a bang in 2020's *Beyond Light* expansion, and the latest, *The Witch Queen*, is even better. But don't worry if you haven't yet become a legend. The basic game is free to play, and there's never been a better time to start.

In case you don't know, *Destiny 2* puts you in the awesome space boots of a Guardian, a sort of superpowered sci-fi knight defending the last remnants of humanity from evil. Up until now, Guardians have worked for a mysterious alien sphere, the Traveler, using its powers of light to battle alien creatures that want to wipe out the human race. *Beyond Light* mixed things up with a fight against a renegade Fallen clan, while *The Witch Queen* hits us with Destiny's deadliest enemies yet!

QUICK TIPS

WATCH YOUR SHIELDS

■ When you're fighting, keep an eye on your health bar at the top of the screen. If your health drops and the bar goes red, try to find some cover or jump around until it recovers. This goes double in an area where you can't respawn.

CHECK THE LEVEL

■ In *Destiny 2*, you have a power level, based on the combined levels of all your weapons and armor. If this is lower than the recommended level for a mission, think about trying something else instead. There's always loads to do in Destiny, and you'll have an easier time if you've leveled up.

USE YOUR POWERS

■ Every Guardian has three core abilities that recharge over time, including a melee attack, a grenade attack, and a special class ability. Make sure you use these as they recharge, and watch for your fourth, "super" power charging up. These do a lot of damage and can destroy even tougher bad guys.

NEW WORLDS, NEW ENEMIES

We're now in a new era for Destiny—they could have called it *Destiny 3*! While some old *Destiny 2* locations and story lines have disappeared, there's a lot of new stuff to make up for it.

A NEW DESTINATION

Beyond Light takes us to the frozen wastes of Europa, a moon of Jupiter, where you can help one of your old Fallen enemies fight a dangerous new Kell—a leader of a Fallen clan.

NEW FOES

The new Kell, Eramis, has managed to harness the powers of the Darkness, giving her and her greatest warriors Stasis abilities they can use to freeze and kill you. Praksis the Warrior, Phylaks the Technocrat, Bakris the Adamantine, and Eramis herself must be destroyed!

STOLEN LIGHT

The Witch Queen's big bad, Savathun, has stolen the powers of light for herself. She's created her own Hive Lightbringers—scary alien monsters with a Guardian's superpowers. Can you stop them?

FAST FACT

Bungie is no stranger to epic sci-fi action – it created *Halo* for Microsoft and went on to make *Halo 2*, *Halo 3*, and *Halo: Reach*. Perhaps that's why the combat in Destiny still has a lot of that classic Halo feel!

THRONE WORLD

Defeating the Witch Queen means traveling to her Throne World, an eerie domain of haunted castles and creepy caves, crawling with the fiendish Hive. It's Savathun's place, so watch your step!

1

2

POWER UP!

You can't have a new *Destiny 2* expansion without new weapons and abilities, and today's Guardians are even more like sci-fi superheroes. Between Stasis abilities, the new Glaive weapons, and the beefed-up Void subclasses, your enemies won't know what hit 'em!.

1 The Glaive is *The Witch Queen* expansion's signature weapon: a customizable spear you can tune to the way you play. Not only can you poke and swipe at your monstrous foes, but blast them with a bolt of explosive energy from a distance.

2 If *Beyond Light* was all about its ice-cold Stasis powers, *The Witch Queen* brings in revamped Void subclasses. Pick one of these and you'll have a whole bunch of super-skills, which you can buff with class-specific Aspects and collectible Fragments. Become the ultimate Hive-smasher!

COMING SOON

The *Destiny 2* story is far from over. First, *Beyond Light* had us embracing the Darkness and fighting the Fallen Kell Eramis. Then *The Witch Queen* puts us up against Savathun, who's been hanging around in the background since the days of the original Destiny. Next up comes *Lightfall*, bringing us closer than ever to the mysterious Darkness, before a fourth (and possibly final) expansion, *The Final Shape*, brings the current *Destiny 2* saga to an epic conclusion. We've got some legendary battles ahead!

MULTIPLAYER MAYHEM

Destiny 2 is mostly about fighting with your fellow Guardians to defeat the galaxy's worst nightmares, but sometimes it's about fighting against your fellow Guardians for glory, fame, and cooler weapons.

You can travel to the Crucible and battle it out in awesome team vs. team Guardian battles, or join the Drifter for a Gambit match, where two teams compete to battle enemies for cash rewards, which they can bank to summon up an ancient monster. Now that's a team sport we'd like to watch!

CHOOSE YOUR WEAPON

We all love Destiny for its stunning sci-fi worlds and amazing action, but every Destiny fan has a soft spot for its awesome armor and incredible guns.

GRAB THE GEAR

You can collect a lot of weapons, helmets, breastplates, boots, and bracers just by defeating foes in *Destiny 2*'s missions—they'll drop the engrams when they fall. Most will be everyday blue items, but if you're lucky, you'll get a legendary purple item—or even a gold exotic!

TAKE THE QUEST

Other exotic weapons, like the Parasite grenade launcher, can only be won by completing a series of challenging quests. Want Parasite? You'll need to finish *The Witch Queen*'s main campaign, then tackle some of the most fearsome targets on Savathun's Throne World.

MAKE IT PERSONAL

The great thing about exotic and legendary weapons is that you can upgrade them by feeding them with the Light-containing components of lesser guns or unlocking new Resonant patterns. Do that and you can build some of the most powerful weapons in the game.

LIKE THIS? TRY THIS:

WARFRAME

Warframe is another brilliant sci-fi action game where you shoot the bad guys and grab their loot, all in the name of getting bigger, better guns. It's free to play but seriously complicated. You might want to study how it works before you play!

EXPLORE THE FORBIDDEN WEST

Horizon: Forbidden West is the game your PS5 was made for

H*orizon: Forbidden West* might be the most incredible PS5 game yet, bringing to life a world where fearsome robot dinosaurs prowl a post-apocalyptic North America. Where the first game took us to a grim far future version of Colorado, Arizona, and Utah, the second heads west to California and Nevada, where parts of San Francisco lie sunk beneath the ocean and the remains of Las Vegas are concealed beneath the desert sands. It's tragic stuff, but it sure looks pretty!

■ It's not just the land you'll be exploring this time. Forbidden West takes Aloy on an adventure beneath the waves. Here you'll meet strange new machine creatures and discover more about what happened to the world.

■ Aloy's world is beautiful but full of danger. You'll have to fight against new rebel tribes and a menace from the past. And there are still plenty of mecha-monsters out there, including the dreaded Clawstrider. Some humans are using these as mounts!

BIG
PICTURE
See these flying critters? These are Sunwings, and eventually Aloy will be able to take one for a ride. Flying beats walking when you've got huge distances to cross!
Aloy is back on a mission to save the Earth, using ancient technology to track down the missing systems of a super-powerful AI that was once the planet's only hope.
With an even bigger world than *Horizon: Zero Dawn*, Aloy has her work cut out just getting around. Luckily, she can rely on her Pullcaster to grapple upward to new heights, or hack some machine creatures to make it possible to ride them.
FAST FACT
There are over forty machine creatures in *Horizon: Forbidden West*, compared to twenty-five in *Horizon: Zero Dawn*. Look out for the scary Slitherfang and the mammoth Tremortusk!

THE HOTTEST HANDHELD!

Meet the biggest thing in handheld gaming since the Switch

Valve's Steam Deck puts the might of PC gaming straight into your hands. On the outside, it looks like a supersize Switch, but on the inside, it has the processing power of a basic games PC and everything you need to run PC games.

How does it work, and can it really play the latest PC blockbusters? Read on to find out!

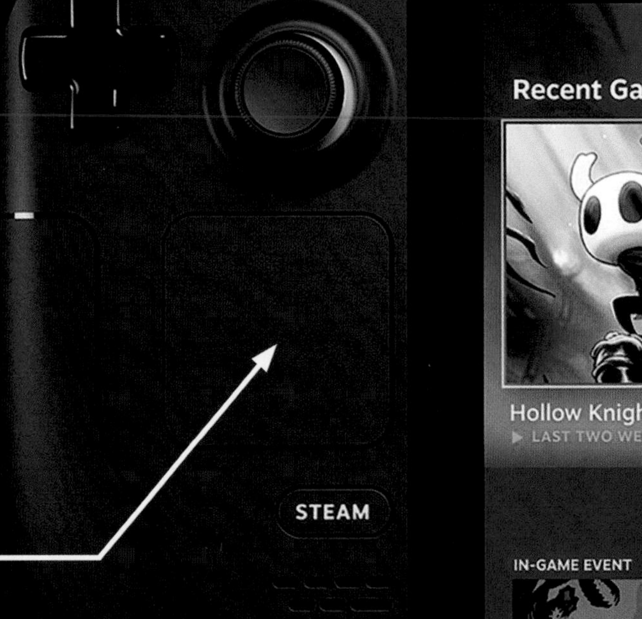

CORE CONTROLS

■ The Steam Deck has two analog sticks, just like most console controllers, but it also has two touch-sensitive pads you can use like a mouse for aiming or moving a pointer.

GAMES AND SOFTWARE

■ Where most games PCs run on Windows, the Steam Deck runs on Valve's own software, based on Linux. Clever coding means it can still run thousands of popular Windows PC games, including *Horizon: Zero Dawn*, *Hades*, *Monster Hunter Rise*, and *Hollow Knight*.

THE SCREEN

■ The 7-inch LCD screen has a 1280 x 800 resolution—which is slightly higher than the Switch. It's also a touchscreen, so you can control some games by tapping.

PULL THE TRIGGER

■ Around the back you'll find two chunky triggers, along with matching bumper buttons. If you like your shooters, the Steam Deck is a dream machine!

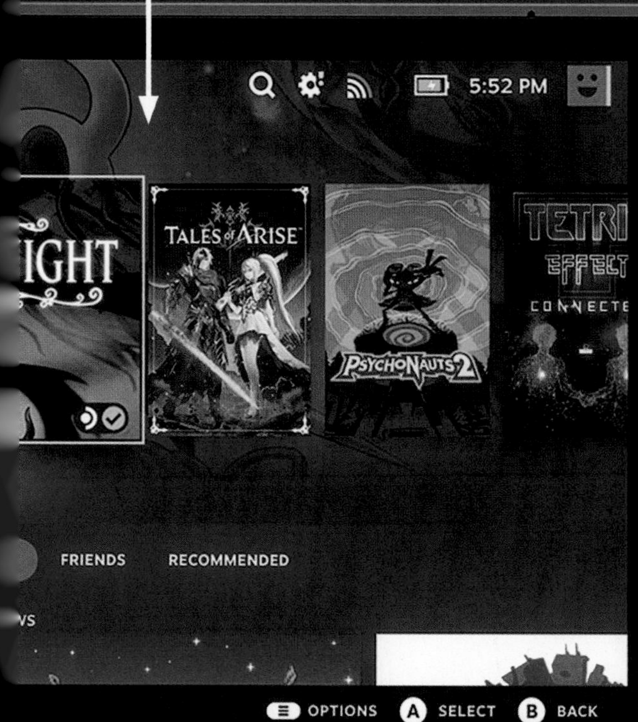

DOCK IT!

■ You can connect the Steam Deck to a TV screen or monitor, plus a mouse and keyboard, using a USB hub or a dedicated dock. This means you can use it like a normal games PC while you're at home!

AWESOME APU

■ The Steam Deck uses a custom AMD processor with a 4-core CPU and an 8-core graphics unit, along with 16 GB of RAM. That processor isn't as fast as the AMD processors in the Xbox Series X or PS5, but it is fast enough to run new games with lower detail levels on the built-in screen.

Prince of Persia: The Sands of Time Remake

Turn back the clock with a classic game

The *Prince of Persia* series has delivered some of gaming's greatest hours, with two stone-cold classics and a bunch of other brilliant games. And now Ubisoft is recreating the groundbreaking *Prince of Persia: The Sands of Time* for a new generation of players. This is the game that transformed the action-adventure with its incredible 3D graphics and smooth acrobatics—and the new version proves that it's still awesome today!

The OG Prince

The original *Prince of Persia* was a jawdropper back in 1989, thanks to its revolutionary animation. Its creator, Jordan Mechner, traced video footage of his brother performing the prince's moves to create the lifelike animation of the prince. Throw in some Arabian Nights sorcery and swashbuckling swordplay, and a gaming star was born.

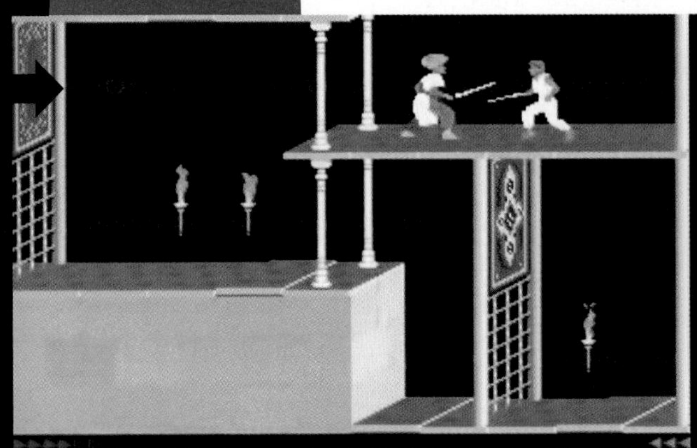

FAST FACT

The first *Assassin's Creed* began as a concept for a sequel to *Prince of Persia: The Sands of Time*. Its designer, Patrice Désilets, came up with the idea of a game featuring an assassin charged with protecting a young prince. The idea was dropped for Prince of Persia but became one of today's biggest gaming series.

The Sands of Time

Fourteen years and two sequels later, Mechner returned to work with Ubisoft on a new vision of the prince. *The Sands of Time* was an instant classic, turning its star into the ultimate acrobatic action hero. It either introduced or transformed all the wall-running, ledge-grabbing, rope-swinging moves that we now see everywhere from *Tomb Raider* to *Star Wars Jedi: Fallen Order* to *Uncharted*, then added the time control magic of the sands.

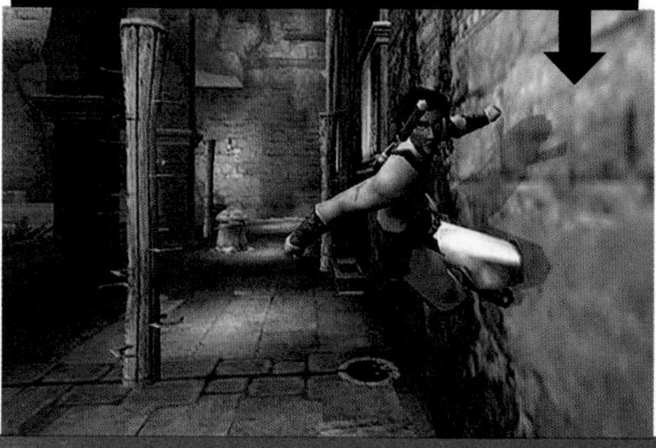

Prince of Darkness

After the success of *The Sands of Time*, the prince had a heavy-metal makeover, with more action and a darker, spikier, more bloodthirsty style. The resulting games—2004's *Warrior Within* and 2005's *The Two Thrones*—had their moments, but they didn't keep you spellbound like *The Sands of Time*.

Prince of Toons

In 2008, Ubisoft took a risk and rebooted the series as a more colorful action-adventure where a lone adventurer and a mysterious girl battle to heal a cursed kingdom and destroy an ancient evil. The new *Prince of Persia* had incredible cartoon graphics, a great story, and fantastic gameplay, but some fans didn't like the change of style.

The Prince Reborn

We've had over fourteen years without a new Prince of Persia, but now the prince is back for a reborn *Sands of Time*. It's a ground-up remake with new graphics, new cinematic cut-scenes, and a great new soundtrack. The controls and gameplay have also been tweaked to bring them up to date.

Underneath all that, though, it's still the same incredible adventure, with one of gaming's greatest heroes in his prime. Let's hope there are more stories of the prince to come!

STAR WARS

Gaming in a galaxy far, far away

Love games? Love Star Wars? You've got it made. Not only have we had the best LEGO Star Wars game this year, but we've got more Star Wars games on their way. Whether you prefer the original trilogy, the prequels, or the sequels, you're in for a treat, and there's a lot more Star Wars to come!

LEGO STAR WARS: THE SKYWALKER SAGA

■ Going further than 2007's *LEGO Star Wars: The Complete Saga*, the latest, greatest LEGO Star Wars brings us all the heroes, villains, and classic scenes from all nine chapters of the Skywalker Saga. You can play through them in any order, unlocking planets packed with side quests and characters to collect.

You'll still be grabbing every stud and gold brick you can find, plus the all-new "Kyber bricks," which you can use to unlock new abilities for each of the game's classes. As well as Jedi knights and bounty hunters, there are protocol droids, scavengers, and scoundrels, each with their own skills and upgrade paths.

CLASSIC SCENES, NEW GAMEPLAY

Though it repeats sequences used in previous LEGO Star Wars games, *The Skywalker Saga* finds new ways to approach them. The escape with the plans from *Star Wars IV: A New Hope* becomes a frantic rush for Princess Leia and the droids, complete with puzzles and Darth Vader on their heels. You might even recognize bits taken from *Rogue One*!

NEVER TELL ME THE ODDS

The Skywalker Saga goes big on all the thrills and spills of the movies, with the most intense lightsaber battles, gunfights, chases, and space combat sequences of the whole LEGO Star Wars series. With more sophisticated aiming and targeting controls, you've never been closer to the action.

FROM REPUBLIC TO RESISTANCE

This is the first LEGO game to cover the whole Star Wars saga, from the conquest of Naboo in *Episode I* to the defeat of Palpatine in *Episode IX*. And don't worry: expansions are covering *The Mandalorian*, *Solo*, *Rogue One*, and more.

FAST FACT

***LEGO Star Wars: The Skywalker Saga* is the sixth LEGO Star Wars game developed by TT Games, and the twenty-second LEGO game in a series that now covers everything from *Marvel Super Heroes* to *Jurassic World* and *Pirates of the Caribbean*.**

STAR WARS HUNTERS

Available on iOS, Android, and Nintendo Switch, *Star Wars Hunters* is a slick arena battle game, where the greatest warriors of the Rebellion and the Empire—along with bounty hunters and the Galaxy's worst scum—meet and duke it out.

Each of the game's brand-new champions has their own unique weapons and abilities, some specializing in blasters and heavy weapons, some preferring the elegance of a lightsaber. Players meet online to fight 4v4 across a bunch of different game modes, from straight-up showdowns to the crazy game of Huttball, in arenas built to look like classic scenes from the Star Wars movies.

STAR WARS: KNIGHTS OF THE OLD REPUBLIC REMAKE

Ask older gamers to name the best Star Wars game ever, and many will tell you that it's *Knights of the Old Republic*. Made by Bioware, who went on to make the Mass Effect and Dragon Age series, it's an epic RPG set thousands of years before the movies, in the days when the Old Republic was under siege from the evil Sith. As a mysterious hero with no memory of their past, you assemble a ragtag team and attempt to find the ancient and all-powerful Star Forge—and find it before the Sith can.

Now's your chance to give the greatest Star Wars game a try, thanks to an all-new remake for PS5. It's been rebuilt from the ground up with the latest graphics tech and smoother gameplay, and it's sure to create a new generation of fans.

STAR WARS: FALLEN ORDER 2

Star Wars: Fallen Order was both a massive hit and the best Star Wars game in years. No surprises, then, that it's getting a sequel, featuring young Jedi Cal Kestis as he battles to escape the Empire and start rebuilding the Jedi order. The sequel's still being made by Respawn Entertainment—the awesome team behind *Apex Legends* and the Titanfall games—and this isn't the only Star Wars game they're working on. They're also making a Star Wars shooter, which could be very special indeed!

STAR WARS: ECLIPSE

The most mysterious Star Wars project of the moment is this stunning-looking adventure, set during the era of the High Republic—the same era as the recent hit Star Wars books and comics. It's not expected to come out for another three or four years, and we've only had an enigmatic trailer to tell us what it's all about.

What we do know is that it's a complex action-adventure where you'll play as a range of different characters, and that you'll see new alien creatures and planets on a tour of the Outer Rim. One thing's for sure: *Eclipse* looks incredible!

CLASSIC STAR WARS GAMES

Before LEGO Star Wars and *Knights of the Old Republic*, we had these three Star Wars classics:

STAR WARS (1983)

The original *Star Wars* arcade game gave early gamers a taste of the movie's big thrills, using revolutionary 3D vector graphics to re-create the final Death Star run.

SUPER STAR WARS: RETURN OF THE JEDI (1994)

The third and best of a trilogy of games, this Super Nintendo classic took us all the way from Jabba's Palace to the battle of Endor, complete with Ewoks, speeder bikes, and a climactic battle against the Emperor.

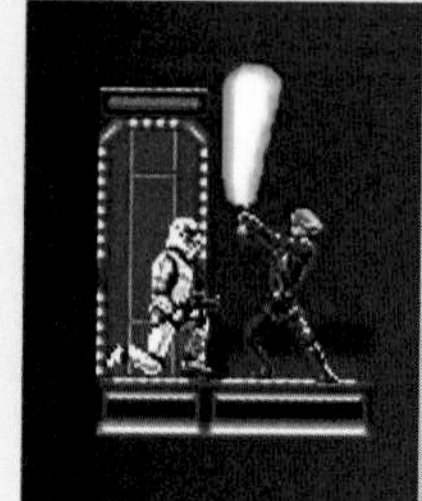

ROGUE SQUADRON (1998)

This superb arcade air combat game follows Luke Skywalker and his Rogue Squadron on sixteen missions against the Empire. *Rogue Squadron* has the authentic Star Wars movie atmosphere, and the sequel, *Rogue Leader*, was even better!

GENSHIN IMPACT

THERE'S A WHOLE WORLD OF ADVENTURE IN THIS FAB FREE RPG

Genshin Impact has been a sensational success, and it's not hard to see why. It's a gorgeous-looking RPG with mighty heroes and a ton of fun things to do. It manages to mix up some of the best bits of *Legend of Zelda: Breath of the Wild* and the classic Tales and Dragon Quest games. It runs on PC and PS4, plus Android phones, iPads, and iPhones. And, best of all, it's free to play!

It's an open-world RPG where you play a character known as "the Traveler." Seperated from your brother or sister—you choose which one you play when the game starts—you find yourself alone in a strange new world full of monsters, magic, and mystery. By making friends and completing quests, you have a shot at finding your lost sibling, and defeating the forces of evil as you go.

QUICK TIPS

FAST FOOD

■ Cooking up a meal can make a big difference. Different recipes will give you a temporary boost to your stamina or improve your attack and defense. Most importantly, meals can recharge your health, even if you chow down in the middle of a battle!

RAISE YOUR RANK

■ Early on, focus on building up your Adventurer's Rank. The higher your rank goes, the more quests and regions you'll unlock, giving you more ways to level up. The best way to boost your rank is to complete story missions, but every battle won or chest looted also counts!

WATCH YOUR STAMINA

■ Sprinting, swimming, climbing, and gliding will all help you explore, but only until your stamina gauge runs out. If that happens, you'll fall to the ground if climbing or gliding, or collapse if you're in the water. Look for safe places to stop and get a recharge.

A WORLD OF HEROES

One of the best things about *Genshin Impact* is that you don't just play the Traveler. You'll recruit more heroes as you play and can also win them by using Wishes.

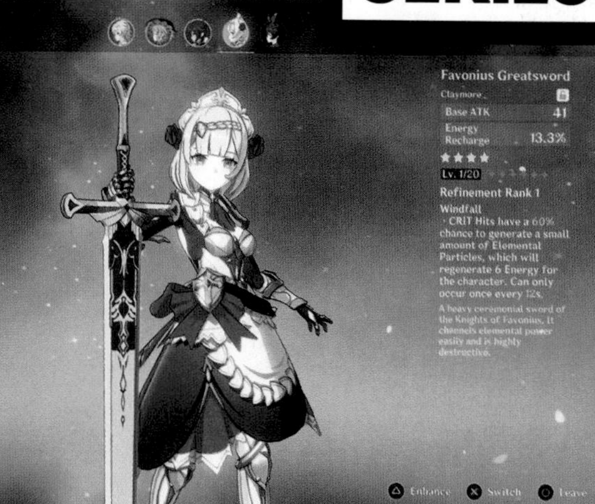

HERO POWER

Each hero has his or her own choice of weapon, as well as some unique abilities and their own fighting style. Most importantly, each is tied into one of *Genshin Impact*'s seven elements, which changes how weak or strong they are against different enemies and attacks.

MIXING THE ELEMENTS

Even better, you can mix up the elements. Use a Cryo attack to cover enemies in ice, then switch to a character with Electro attacks, and they'll electrify the ice. The shock does extra damage and makes your enemies more vulnerable to swords and spears. That's cold!

ELEMENTAL ENERGY

Enemies of one element are weak against attacks from the opposite element, and attacking with elemental forces can change a battle. For instance, fire attacks can burn wooden shields! You can switch from one hero to another to use the best elemental attacks against each enemy.

FAST FACT

The mobile versions of *Genshin Impact* made nearly $245 million in the first month of release, making it the second-biggest mobile game launch in history after *Pokémon Go*!

KEEP 'EM AT A DISTANCE

Some heroes are also designed to use ranged attacks, either by fighting with a bow or by using magic. It's always worth having an archer on the team so that they can take down monster snipers or wear away at tougher bad guys before they get too close.

WISHING ON A STAR

■ *Genshin Impact*'s most controversial feature is its wishes. By spending special points, you can call in a Wish, which might bring you a new weapon to fight with or an artifact that will make you stronger. If you're really lucky, you'll get a new hero to add to your team.

■ Wishes are arranged in packs, a bit like collectible cards, but you never know what you're going to get. The pack gives you some idea of your chances of getting something worth having, but you could end up with the same weapon you already have or an artifact you don't want.

■ Run out of Wish points and you can buy more using special crystals called Primogems, which you can collect just by playing the game. You can also buy Primogems by buying Genesis Crystals for real money in the in-game shop, but you really don't have to! You'll get crystals for completing in-game events or earn Primogems by opening chests and completing challenges and quests. Hold on to your cash!

LEVEL UP

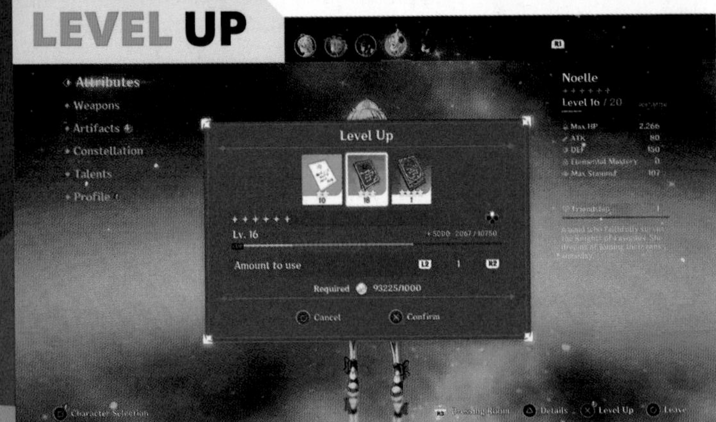

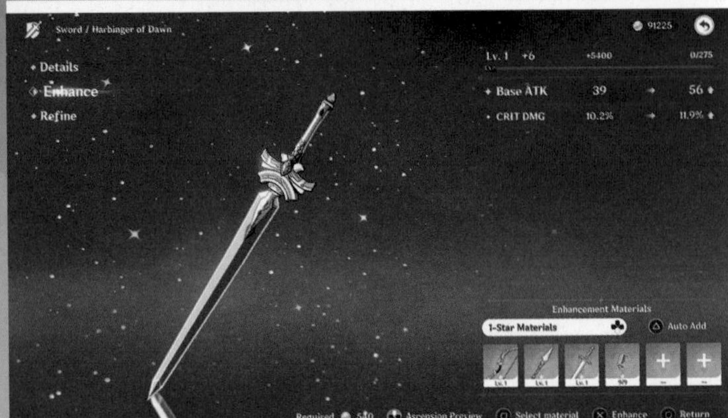

■ Your Adventure Rank isn't the only thing that matters: You also need to level up your heroes, your weapons, and your artifacts or you won't be powerful enough to keep on kicking monster butt!

■ You can update each hero by spending EXP, which you can get from killing monsters and from collecting special EXP materials. You'll get these for completing missions, and you can also find them in treasure chests. Once you have enough EXP and EXP materials, you can spend them on the Character screen and level up your heroes.

■ Eventually they'll reach their maximum level, but you can still make them more powerful. The bigger boss bad guys leave behind ascension materials, which you can spend to help your characters "ascend" and raise their maximum level.

■ It's not just heroes that need leveling, though. Both weapons and artifacts can be leveled up to make them more powerful, though you'll need to collect different materials to do it. Open every chest and grab everything you can to get the right stuff!

GENSHIN'S GREATEST WARRIORS

■ Early on, you'll be stuck with the weaker, basic heroes, but keep making your Wishes and you'll unlock the game's real stars.

RAIDEN SHOGUN

■ Ride the lightning with the top Electro hero in the game. She's ideal for building up high-damage combos and also has useful support capabilities.

TARTAGLIA

■ Tartaglia mixes powerful bow attacks with a deadly set of daggers. His Hydro (water) elemental powers can increase the damage enemies take and even cause them to explode. Yuck!

KAZUHA

■ One of the best heroes to hail from the Inazuma region. Kazuha can double up as a damage dealer or a super-powered support character. Go big on his mighty sword and his strong Anemo elemental attacks.

LIKE THIS? TRY THIS:

DRAGON QUEST XI S – DEFINITIVE EDITION

■ If you're looking for a more conventional RPG with a great story line and cartoon graphics, it's hard to beat *Dragon Quest XI*. It's an epic adventure with its own awesome cast of warriors, thieves, and wizards.

MARVEL'S GUARDIANS OF THE GALAXY

CAN WE PUT THE BICKERING ON HOLD?

No, these aren't the Guardians you know from the movies, but you'll get to love 'em all the same. *Marvel's Guardians of the Galaxy* turns out to be an incredible sci-fi action-adventure, taking Peter "'Star-Lord" Quill, Gamora, Rocket, Groot, and Drax on missions across alien worlds, spooky space stations, and beyond. There's a lot of combat and some clever puzzles, but this is a game that's all about the team. You need to lead the Guardians and transform them from a group of squabbling warriors into a team of heroes that can take on anything!

QUICK TIPS

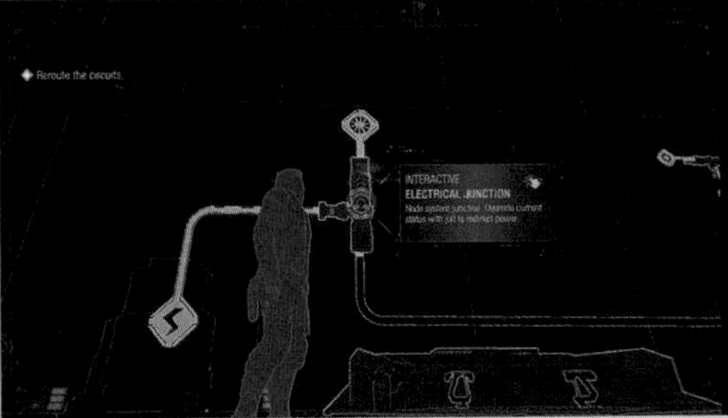

USE THE SCANNER

■ If you can't see an easy way forward or solve a puzzle, use Quill's scanner visor and look for anything that glows yellow. It may be something you can use or a crucial clue.

REMEMBER TO UPGRADE

■ Upgrade Star-Lord and your team as soon as you get enough points. New abilities or more health or firepower can really help you get through difficult encounters.

LOOK AROUND

■ Look for hidden areas or side routes where you might find extra stashes of components, not to mention some sweet collectibles. Components mean upgrades for Quill, so it always pays to search.

LEAD THE GUARDIANS

■ While you play the game as Peter Quill, you have four other heroes (mostly) behind you. If you want to get through this mighty Marvel epic, you need to build and inspire your team!

FIGHT AS A TEAM

■ While the other Guardians will battle on beside you, you can also ask them to unleash their special attacks. Combine their abilities to deal massive damage—and build up your combat rankings!

WORK AS A TEAM

■ Guardian abilities are also crucial to solving puzzles. Groot can grow bridges to cover giant gaps, while Gamora can slice through obstacles or give Quill the boost he needs to reach high areas.

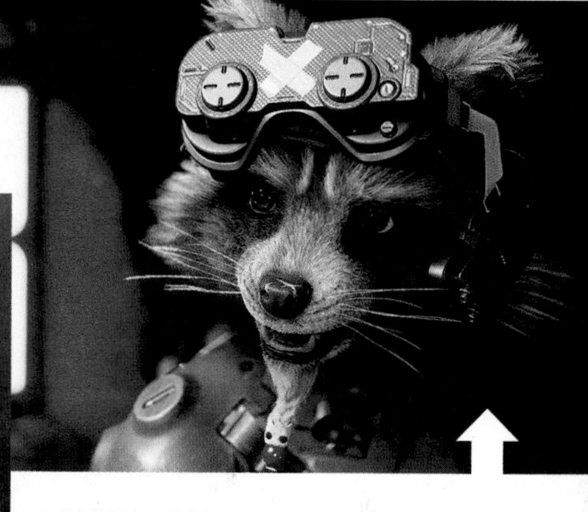

SHARE THE SPOILS

■ You'll earn Ability Points through combat, but don't spend them all on Star-Lord. Level up your teammates and you'll unlock new powers that could help you survive the next fight.

TEAM TALK

■ When you're on your ship, the *Milano*, or even just exploring a new area, your team is going to talk and sometimes argue. Listen for hints that tell you what you need to do, and choose what you're going to say carefully. In this game, your words have an impact!

The game is crammed with sneaky Marvel Easter eggs, from posters on the walls to cool outfits to discover. Each character has at least eight outfits, and Star-Lord has even more!

LIKE THIS? TRY THIS:

LEGO MARVEL SUPER HEROES 2

■ Looking for another Marvel team-up? It's hard to beat this LEGO classic, which packs in the Guardians of the Galaxy and an army of Avengers into one awesome brickbuster of a game.

FIGHT TO WIN IN MARVEL'S GUARDIANS OF THE GALAXY

Use your team effectively and battle through the most challenging encounters

There's a lot of combat in *Marvel's Guardians of the Galaxy*, and it can get pretty tough. Between large gangs of enemies, armored Nova Corps troops, and gigantic, screen-filling monsters, you've got your work cut out for yourself. Even heroes can get overwhelmed! To survive, you need to battle as a team and make the most of some clever game mechanics. Prove you're a Star-Lord and win the fight!

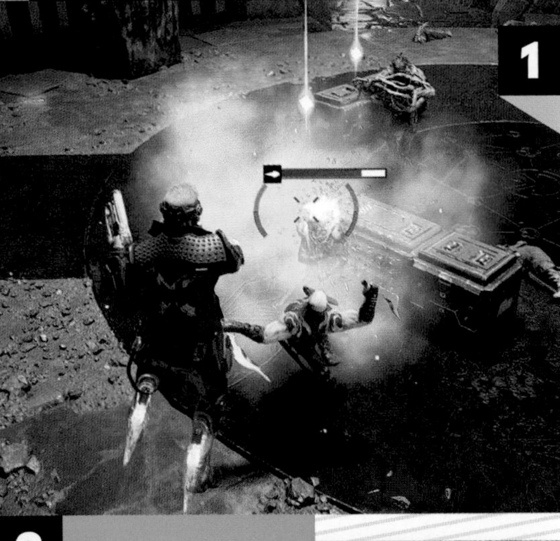

1 Keep moving

■ Star-Lord isn't built for close-up brawling like Drax or Gamora. Keep him moving as much as possible and out of the toe-to-toe stuff. Use his evade skills to dodge incoming fire and, when things get tough, use the Vantage Point and Eye of the Hurricane abiltiies to get some space.

2 Build up combos

■ You need to keep using all of the Guardians' abilities all the time to stagger enemies, make them vulnerable, or finish them off for good. If you're smart, you can build up combos, using Groot to hold an enemy, Drax to make them stagger, and Gamora to deliver a final blow.

3 Get an edge

■ Use whatever you can to destroy the opposition. Sometimes Drax or Gamora can use something in the area to unleash a vicious area attack, or you might find enemies are weak to an ice or lighting attack from your pistols.

4 Losing the battle? Huddle

■ If things look rough, watch the Huddle gauge in the bottom-right. When it's full, press L1 and R1 simultaneously to start a huddle. Listen to your team's thoughts, then pick the answer that matches their mood. You'll not only trigger a cool rock soundtrack but get some battle buffs as well!

nd to battle
ear

5 Gain momentum

■ As you fight and build up combos, you'll also generate momentum. The more momentum you get, the higher your encounter rank—if you survive it! Better still, high momentum can unlock cool finisher moves where all the Guardians join forces to take down one of their tougher foes.

FAST FACT

You might recognize one location, Knowhere, from its appearances in both Guardians movies, *Avengers: Infinity War*, and *Marvel's What If*? It's a mining colony based in the severed head of a giant Celestial.

MARVELOUS!!!!!
A Guardian has fallen. Get close to them and hold △ to assist them.
HEAL

Save your friends

■ Your Guardian teammates will fight hard for you, but they also need some looking after. Check that teammates aren't trapped by certain mines or weapons—shooting the device should free them —and head over and heal them if they fall. You'll need the whole team fighting to beat some bad guys!

METROID DREAD

SAMUS FACES HER BIGGEST CHALLENGE YET

Samus has had her share of scrapes before. She's battled space pirates and crazed AI brains, explored strange worlds, and even beaten a dark version of herself. She's survived alien attacks and infection by a deadly alien parasite, and lost her armor more times than we can count. In *Metroid Dread* she faces her most terrifying challenge yet in a tale of killer robots, ancient scientists, and an all-new Metroid threat.

This is Metroid back at its 2D action-adventure peak, mixing slick gameplay with cinematic visuals that use all the power of the Switch. *Metroid Dread* gets tough and scary at times, but—with your help—Samus will survive her deadly Metroid mission!

QUICK TIPS

BLAST THE SCENERY

Stuck without anywhere to go? Blast, fire your missiles, or bomb any bit of wall, ceiling, or floor that looks slightly suspicious. You'll often uncover a secret area, or even expose a hidden way forward.

LEARN TO COUNTER

Countering is a crucial skill. It can buy you some time when you're being attacked by an E.M.M.I., and you'll often need to block and counter in boss battles. Get the timing right, and you'll pull through.

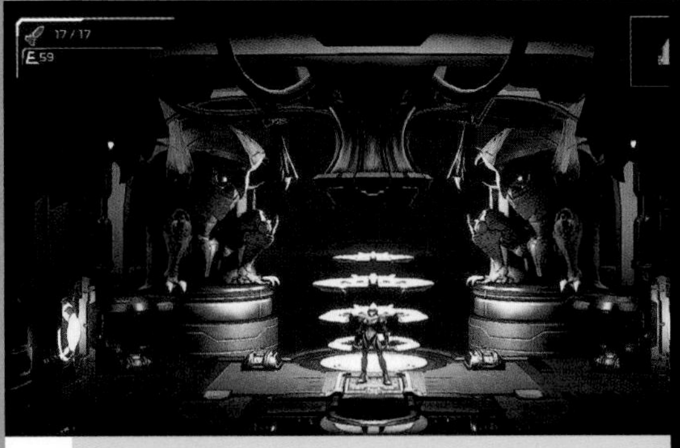

SAVE AND RECHARGE

Metroid Dread can be dread-fully difficult, so save every time you find a save room. The same goes for every health recharge or ammo station. Use them while you have the chance!

GREETINGS FROM PLANET DREAD!

■ Your destination is Planet ZDR, the source of a mysterious video transmission showing a live X-Parasite of the type that attacked Samus back in 2002's *Metroid Fusion*. Seven E.M.M.I. robots have been sent in to investigate, but they've disappeared without a trace. As the only warrior in the galaxy immune to the X-Parasite, Samus needs to find out what's happening on ZDR.

WATCH OUT FOR THE WILDLIFE

■ You won't be surprised that ZDR is crawling with alien critters, or that most of them are looking for a crunchy Samus snack. Blast them with your Arm Cannon or treat them to a missile before they can chow down!

THE E.M.M.I. MENACE

■ The E.M.M.I. robots haven't just gone missing—they've been hacked by the mysterious force at the heart of ZDR. They're too tough to fight with normal weapons, so run away as fast as you can.

BLAST THE BOSS

■ The robots aren't your biggest threat. ZDR also houses some of the most vicious bosses in Metroid history, with more than enough power to wipe Samus out. Build your strength, learn their moves, and target their weak points. Samus needs to show the bosses that she's boss!

POWERING UP

■ Power up your weapons and unlock new gadgets, and Samus is equipped to take on the toughest enemies—even the E.M.M.I. bots. Each region has a Central Unit. Find it, defeat it, and absorb its Omega Cannon, and you can hit the E.M.M.I. where it hurts.

FAST FACT

Samus's iconic Power Suit was made by an alien race, the Chozo, whose ancient buildings, statues, and technology appear across the Metroid games. Samus was adopted and trained by the Chozo after being orphaned by space pirates at an early age.

LIKE THIS? TRY THIS:

AXIOM VERGE 2

■ No, it's not a real Metroid, but this indie favorite is more than a clone. Inspired by some of the best games of the 1990s, it's a retro sci-fi thriller that could have featured Samus in a starring role.

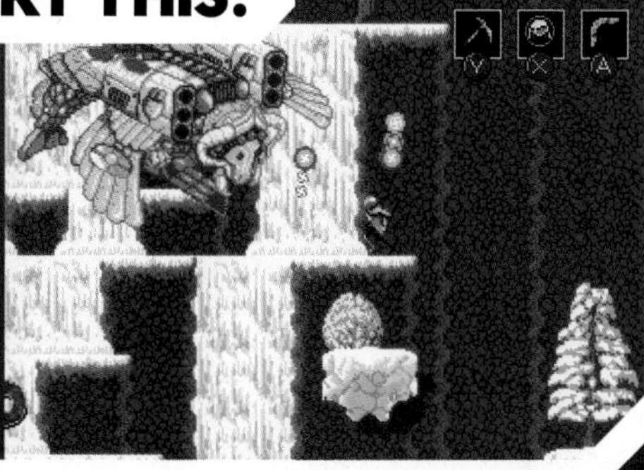

KENA: BRIDGE OF SPIRITS

WHERE DISNEY MEETS LEGEND OF ZELDA

Kena: Bridge of Spirits is one of the most beautiful games ever made. Take a good look at those graphics—if Disney itself tried to make its own *Legend of Zelda*, it might not even look this great! Yet it's all the work of a small studio, Ember Labs, and they've crafted a fantastic game. *Kena* borrows ideas from the greatest adventures, then adds a few fabulous twists of its own.

You play as Kena, a young spirit guide who uses magic to help the dead move from this world to the next. Only, the forest where she lives is corrupted by a powerful spirit, unleashing dangerous monsters on the land. Can Kena and her tiny magic friends, the Rot, purify the forest and help the dead find peace again?

QUICK TIPS

DESTROY THE DEADZONE HEARTS

■ Destroying these nasty-looking plants won't just purify the area of the forest, but also stops monsters from respawning. Do it as soon as you get the chance.

FEED YOUR FRIENDS

■ Karma means upgrades for you and your cute Rot friends. One way to get it is to feed your little buddies. Open crates to find the fruit inside, or see if you can find some fruit and an easy way to ripen it.

RETRACE YOUR STEPS

■ Take time to come back to early areas of the game when you've got more powers later on. New abilities might help you reach areas that you couldn't get to before—and there could be rewards hidden away!

THE WORLD OF KENA

Kena's world is full of magic and wonder, so take the time to explore it and get to know the locals.

THE ROT

The Rot can be awfully cute critters, but they have powers that can help you on your journey. They can gang up and move heavy objects for you, or help you defeat your enemies in battle.

CLEANSING SHRINES

Kena's tale takes her through woodland pathways and mountain villages, and to the hidden places deep beneath the surface. Where did the corruption come from?

FIGHTING EVIL

Combat is tougher and more frequent than you might expect, but Kena has the weapons and the friends to handle it. Prepare for some challenging boss battles!

THE FORGOTTEN FOREST

The Forgotten Forest holds a wealth of secrets, from shrines that need to be purified to an ancient guardian tree. Don't forget to look for more Rot while you're out there.

FAST FACT

Kena was developed by the team at Ember Lab, a talented animation studio. They made their name making ads for MLB, KFC, and Coca-Cola, but won fame with a short film based on *Legend of Zelda: Majora's Mask*. It racked up over 10 million views on YouTube!

LIKE THIS? TRY THIS:

TUNIC

It doesn't have *Kena*'s jaw-dropping graphics, but there's plenty to enchant you in this indie great. It's a love letter to Zelda with a fox hero you can't resist!

Splatoon 3: It's a whole new Inkling world!

New weapons, new specials, and a new furry menace

■ It's a whole new era for the Inklings and their bad-boy Octoling rivals. *Splatoon 3* takes us out of the safety of Inkopolis and off to the Splatlands—a searing desert filled with the ruins of a long-gone civilization. And that's not all that's different in the Splatoon threequel. A new threat has entered the scene, giving the elite Squidbeak Splatoon and its agents their toughest mission yet.

It's a good thing that our heroes are tooled up for the job, with the top guns and gadgets that Sheldon and his Ammo Knights team can invent. What's more, all the freshest Inklings and Octolings are going to need them for the next round of co-op and multiplayer modes.

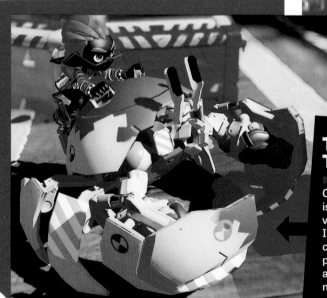

Tank of Terror

■ The fearsome Crab Tank special is the first armored vehicle in splatoon. It's a tough one to crack, soaking up plenty of damage and dishing twice as much out in return.

Amazing Spider-Squid-Kid

■ The Zipcaster special transforms your squid-kid warrior into an inkified ninja who can stretch and stick to walls or rooftops. It's especially helpful for surprising sneaky snipers.

Wail of destruction

■ Why one-shot your foe when you can hit them for six with this update of a classic *Splatoon* weapon? The Killer Wail 5.1 is just the gun you want when you absolutely need to clear a walkway.

FAST FACT

Splatoon 2 **had thirty different splatfests, where Inklings and Octolings settled all the crucial questions. Which is better: ketchup vs. mayonnaise? Chaos vs. order?**

Triple Threat

■ The original inkzooka was a fan favorite in *Splatoon*, leaving many fans devastated when it didn't make the cut for the sequel. In *Splatoon 3* it's back with three times the firepower. Don't stand in its way!

The Inkbow

■ Splatoon's bow is a charger-style weapon firing three jets of ink at once. Silent and deadly, it's perfect for long-range play

Meet the Mammalians!

■ These furry Octarian creatures are Splatoon's most mysterious menace yet. Their fur isn't just evil, it's infectious. One touch will cause your hero to erupt into a ball of fluff. Who knows what these hairy horrors are planning? Could it have something to do with the evil schemes of DJ Octavio?

TEMTEM

THE CREATURE-CATCHING GAME KEEPS EVOLVING

Temtem is a game that's shamelessly inspired by Pokémon, but that doesn't mean it hasn't got its own ideas. As an online game, it has more ways to team up with other trainers, and the team's working hard to add new islands and areas so that players can keep on exploring, along with creatures. You just know you've gotta catch . . . Well, you can guess where we're going with this.

At heart, it's very close to Pokémon, complete with towns, gyms (here called dojos), challenges, dojo leader battles, and routes where you can battle wild Temtem. But *Temtem* makes each of its islands one seamless open world. It also has its own unfolding story, where you battle the fiendish Clan Belsoto and its evil agents. Can you take on their enhanced combat Temtem and win?

QUICK TIPS

KNOW YOUR TYPES

Temtem types matter, so don't waste your best attacks against Temtem with a strong resistance against them. If the targeting circle turns red, either switch attacks, or switch your Temtem.

WATCH YOUR STAMINA

When a Temtem runs out of stamina, they take damage and can't move. Don't keep using your most powerful attacks turn after turn without giving your Temtem time to rest—or swapping them out for a break.

DOUBLE DUELS

Temtem battles always involve two Temtem on each side, so you need a different strategy. It's often more effective to focus your attacks on one Temtem to eliminate them faster.

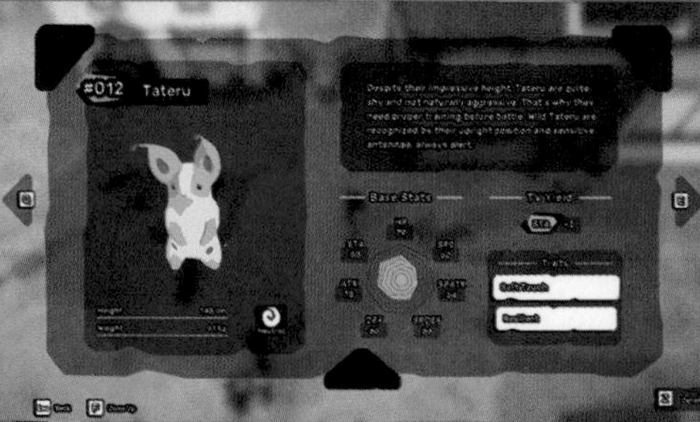

COMPLETE THE TEMPEDIA

Has *Temtem* got its own Pokédex? You betcha! Catch Temtem to fill out your Tempedia and learn their strengths and weaknesses.

TALES OF TEMTEM ADVENTURE

There's more to *Temtem* than catching and training, with a whole archipelago of adventure to explore.

MEET THE BAD GUYS

The Airborne Archipelago is a peaceful place, but those dastardly Belsoto troops are getting everywhere. Can you teach these brutes some manners with the aid of your Temtem friends?

BEAT THE BAD GUYS

Mean and nasty Lady Lottie is up to no good in the ruins of Windward Castle. She's the first Belsoto boss you'll meet, and don't expect any respect!

JOIN FORCES

Because *Temtem* is an online game, you can join up with other players and play co-op. The higher-level player can help the weaker player with their story—which is great if you're getting stuck!

NEW DESTINATIONS

Beyond the first island, Deniz, are five more with their own dojos, champions, and quests to work through, plus new Temtem to collect. Keep training to become a Temtem legend!

FAST FACT

Temtem has its own legendary creatures, though here they're known as Mythical Temtem. There are three in the final game, but it launched in early access without any of the Mythicals in place. All you had were some hints on where they might appear!

LIKE THIS? TRY THIS:

MONSTER HUNTER STORIES

This spin-off of the Monster Hunter series is an RPG adventure with a monster-training twist. Collect the eggs, hatch the monsters, and add them to your team. Don't worry if you can't play the 3DS original. The mobile version looks and plays even better!

The Dark World of Digimon Survive

Only friendship can help these teens escape

■ There's always been a darker side to Digimon, and recent installments have sometimes felt like Pokémon's goth cyberpunk cousin. *Digimon Survive* takes that one stage further, taking its high school heroes to a weird and slightly scary new world.

The game follows a group of teenagers who get lost on a school camping trip and find themselves stranded in strange surroundings, where the familiar places they know seem to have been abandoned long ago and monsters roam the land. Some are friendly and keen to partner up with their new human companions, but others are raring for a fight. Can the kids team up with their new Digimon friends and find their way back home?

High School Heroes

■ *Digimon Survive* stars a case of eight high school students, each with their own strengths and weaknesses. While the game centers on a trio of friends, Takuma, Aoi, and Minoru, you'll have to get to know all the teens and their monster friends if you're going to solve the game's puzzles and survive.

FAST FACT

The original *Digimon* TV series was only planned to run for thirteen episodes as a promotion for the PlayStation game *Digimon World*. Amazingly, it became a huge success in its own right, running over nine seasons, with 476 episodes to date!

Monsters to the Rescue

■ You play as Takuma, who—with his friends Aoi and Minoru—meets up with a cute Dragon Digimon, Koromon, at a mysterious shrine. When monsters attack the students, Koromon evolves into the mighty Agumon to defend them. Agumon becomes Takuma's partner, and soon every teen has their own Digimon friend, whether they like it or not!

Attack and Defense

■ It wouldn't be Digimon if there weren't any combat, and *Digimon Survive* doubles down on the brainy tactical battles series fans of the series know and love. There's a lot of strategy in where you move your monsters and which attacks and abilities you use, and as your Digimon gain experience, they'll level up and even evolve into more powerful new forms.

Solve the mystery

■ When you're not fighting, you spend your time exploring, searching for clues that can tell you what has happened and where you need to go. You'll have to check through some pretty strange locations, and sometimes your smartphone camera might pick up details, clues, and monsters that your eyes would miss.

Work together

■ You'll also need to talk to the other students and their Digimon partners. Some, like the good-natured Saki and Shuuji, will help you out with their own ideas. Their partners, Floramon and Lopmon, will also help. Others, like Kaito and Ryou, might be more hostile, even rejecting their new Digimon chums. Can you bring them around?

HYRULE WARRIORS: AGE OF CALAMITY

QUICK TIPS

KEEP SWITCHING

■ Switch between your heroes to make the most of their powers and deal with objectives in different areas of the map. Sometimes it's quicker to switch to a nearer hero than reach the objective with your current warrior.

BREAK FOR LUNCH

■ If you're finding a battle tough, cook something up before you fight. Different recipes will boost a hero's movement speed, attack strength, health, or XP gained. Don't you know the way to a hero's heart is through their stomach?

HEADING BACK TO THE GLORY DAYS OF HYRULE

Ever wonder what Hyrule was like before Ganon returned and brought disaster to the land? Would you like to see the four legendary Champions in action and take control of the Divine Beasts? Well, you don't want to miss *Hyrule Warriors: Age of Calamity*. It's a prequel to *Legend of Zelda: Breath of the Wild* in the style of Dynasty Warriors—and a must play if you're a Zelda fan.

This is your chance to play your way through the *Breath of the Wild* backstory, playing Link, Zelda, and all the other champions in the biggest, most important battles of the age. You race from one side of the battlefield to the other trying to complete objectives that will swing the fight in your favor and help Hyrule's good guys win the war. It might not be *Legend of Zelda* as you know and love it, but it's truly epic stuff!

HIT THEIR WEAK POINTS

■ Well-timed parries stun your enemies, and so will flurry attacks when you evade their blows. When tougher enemies are stunned, their weak point gauge appears, giving you a chance to dish out lots of damage.

THIS TIME IT'S WAR!

The forces of evil have declared war on Hyrule, and only Zelda, Link, and the four Champions stand in their way. Lead the armies of the land to victory and harness the power of the Divine

SEND 'EM FLYING

Age of Calamity is all about the battles—and the joy of sending a whole bunch of Lizalfos or Bokoblins flying with each swing of Link's mighty sword. Don't just mash the buttons, though. You'll need to use combos and special attacks to take on your toughest foes.

UNITE THE CHAMPIONS

The saga begins at Hyrule Castle, but your heroes have to journey to every corner of the realm. It's a great chance to travel around Hyrule and see what Zora's Domain, Death Mountain, the Akkala Citadel used to look like before Ganon's goons came and messed things up.

UNLEASH THE BEASTS

In *Breath of the Wild*, you freed the Divine Beasts from the evil influence of Calamity Ganon. In *Age of Calamity*, you get to take these bad boys out for a ride. Once you've piloted Vah Ridania, Vah Medoh, and Vah Naboris, you can unlock special side missions for them!

THE MAGIC OF THE SLATE

Remember the Sheikah Slate and its runic powers from *Breath of the Wild*? Well, it's back in *Age of Calamity*, and every hero can use its powers. For Zelda, it's her main weapon, allowing her to smash through crowds of Bokoblins and Moblins with its magical magnetic powers.

FAST FACT

Did you know you can unlock the final big bad guy, Calamity Ganon, as a playable character? You'll have to beat all the story battles and all the main challenges, then complete a final special challenge first!

LIKE THIS? TRY THIS:

FIRE EMBLEM WARRIORS

Age of Calamity isn't the first Nintendo-meets-Warriors mash-up, and it won't be the last! This one mixes the classic battlefield gameplay with scenes and stars from the Fire Emblem series, including fan favorites Lucina, Chrom, Lyn, and Marth.

THE GUNK

There's no time to lose with this evil ooze

Let's call this a situation. Two friends run a deep-space scavenging business, going from planet to planet looking for valuable resources to sell. But then they land on a planet where every form of life is under attack by a gruesome, parasitic ooze. Clear the Gunk and they have a chance to bring the planet back to life, but it's going to be a tough battle . Who knows what this poisonous crud is—or why it's here!

■ The game is full of weird alien landscapes, from glowing jungles to creepy crud-filled caves. There's a ton of exploration to do if you want to clear the world of the deadly gloopy stuff.

■ The Gunk doesn't just attack plants. It can also infect creatures, turning them into aggressive monsters who'll do anything to defend their parasitic goo. Will you fight or flee?

■ Your main weapon in the fight is your high-tech power glove, which can suck the ooze from the plants, rocks, and creatures so that it can't do its parasitic work. Sucking up the ooze will open passages to walk through—or new platforms you can jump to climb on.

Clean the Gunk from the plants and they'll spring back to life. You can save this strange alien world one extraordinary tree at a time!

FAST FACT

***The Gunk* comes from Image and Form, who created the superb Steamworld series. That included puzzle-heavy platform games, strategy games, and even card-battling RPGs, but *The Gunk* is the team's first 3D action-adventure.**

Is the sticky stuff native to this planet, or did it arrive through some sinister plan? Before the game ends, you'll know the secret behind the Gunk!

GAMING'S GREATEST WARRIORS

IF YOU WERE GOING INTO BATTLE, WHICH GAMING HEROES WOULD YOU WANT ON YOUR TEAM?

1

THE MASTER CHIEF

FIRST APPEARANCE:
■ *Halo: Combat Evolved*, 2001

LATEST APPEARANCE:
■ *Halo Infinite*, 2021

SIGNATURE WEAPON:
■ MA5D Assault Rifle

■ How many times does one man have to save humanity before he's recognized as the greatest soldier of all time? Sure, it helps that the Master Chief is over seven feet tall, heavily armored, and makes Chris Hemsworth look puny, but he's also incredibly brave and resourceful and can wipe out a whole alien army before breakfast, even if he has to do it by borrowing their own guns. No wonder they call him a demon!

2

LINK

■ Whenever evil threatens the land of Hyrule, Link steps right up to the plate. Even when he's just a boy with no combat experience whatsoever, he still manages to find the mightiest weapon in the kingdom, wipe out a bunch of bosses, clear area after area of enemy forces, and then go on to fight the most terrifying witch or wizard in town. Most of all, he never gives up, no matter how tough things get or how much people mock his green suit and pointy ears.

FIRST APPEARANCE:
■ *The Legend of Zelda*, 1986

LATEST APPEARANCE:
■ *Hyrule Warriors: Age of Calamity*, 2021

SIGNATURE WEAPON:
■ Master Sword

3

CLOUD STRIFE

Cloud nearly doesn't make this list. He's headstrong, a bit dumb, and prone to rushing into trouble. He constantly questions authority, looks up to dubious characters like Sepiroth, and when he should be practicing his combat skills, he's usually found spiking up his hair. However, there's no questioning Cloud's courage—and who wants to tell the guy with the mighty Buster Sword he isn't going to make the cut?

FIRST APPEARANCE:
Final Fantasy VII, 1997

LATEST APPEARANCE:
Final Fantasy VII Remake, 2020

SIGNATURE WEAPON:
Buster Sword

4

FIRST APPEARANCE:
Street Fighter, 1987

LATEST APPEARANCE:
Street Fighter V: Champion Edition, 2020

SIGNATURE WEAPON:
His fists, what else?

RYU

Ryu is the granddaddy of fighting game champions: the one who got their way before Tekken's Yoshimitsu and Kazuya or Virtua Fighter's Jacky and Akira. He's a big guy with some powerful martial arts skills, and if his Hadoken (fireball fist) and Shoryuken (dragon punch) don't get you, his Hurricane Kick definitely will. And for our money, anyone who can go toe-to-toe with M. Bison and Akuma shouldn't be messed with in a scrap.

SAMUS ARAN

Samus has saved more galaxies from alien parasites and space pirates than Spider-Man has had movie reboots—and that's with over a decade between *Metroid: Other M* and 2021's *Metroid Dread*. One of the pioneering female video game heroes, she's a super soldier and explorer who's never fazed by the weirdest alien worlds or monsters. And the bigger the bosses, the harder she makes them fall.

5

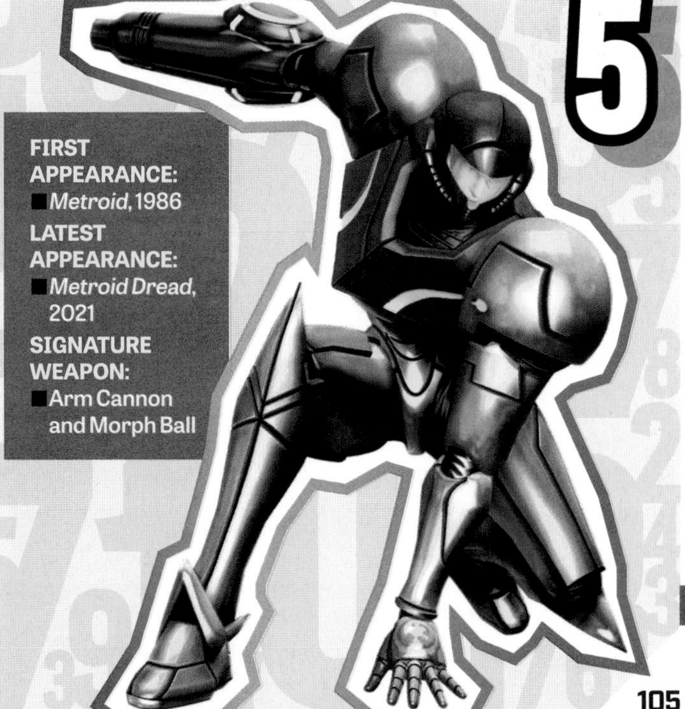

FIRST APPEARANCE:
Metroid, 1986

LATEST APPEARANCE:
Metroid Dread, 2021

SIGNATURE WEAPON:
Arm Cannon and Morph Ball

6

LARA CROFT

Britain's greatest video game star has become something of a national treasure over there—not bad for someone who spends most of her time in mountain caves or in the jungle, blasting endangered species and stealing precious relics. Still, we wouldn't say this to Lara's face, not least because she's as deadly in hand-to-hand combat as she is with her dual pistols, and because we'd rather have her on our team.

FIRST APPEARANCE:
- *Tomb Raider*, 1996

LATEST APPEARANCE:
- *Tomb Raider: Reloaded*, 2022

SIGNATURE WEAPON:
- Dual Pistols

8

SOLID SNAKE

Only James Bond has been in the secret agent game for longer than Solid Snake, and if the two had a fight, we know who we think would win. The star of the Metal Gear series is part one-man army, part ninja assassin: the kind of guy who could spring out of a cardboard box and assassinate an evil genius, then send himself back home by Federal Express. He's also got the coolest voice in gaming. Even as an old dude, he kicks serious amounts of butt.

FIRST APPEARANCE:
- *Metal Gear*, 1987

LATEST APPEARANCE:
- *Super Smash Bros Ultimate*, 2018

SIGNATURE WEAPON:
- MK23 Socom

7

RATCHET

He's the last remaining Lombax in the universe, and we're not surprised, if they all had Ratchet's luck. He's always falling afoul of fiendish robot scientists and evil emperors. He's prone to time-travel misadventures and disappearing through dimensional rifts. Most seriously, he's all too inclined to wield experimental weaponry with strange and unpredictable effects. Still, he's a tough warrior and a survivor, with the coolest robot chum around.

FIRST APPEARANCE:
- *Ratchet and Clank*, 2002

LATEST APPEARANCE:
- *Ratchet and Clank: Rift Apart*, 2021

SIGNATURE WEAPON:
- Omniwrench

9

BOWSER

■ What? You expected to see Mario here? That plumber hasn't got anything on Bowser. The big B always manages to make an army out of a ragtag bunch of turtle troopers, brainless critters, and socially inept masked dudes, and he doesn't know the meaning of defeat. In fact, he's constantly getting handed his spikey shell, yet he always comes back for one more go. Bowser's brimming with bad attitude and has breath bad enough to scorch. In short, he's an absolute winner.

FIRST APPEARANCE:
■ *Super Mario Bros*, 1985
LATEST APPEARANCE:
■ *Bowser's Fury*, 2021
SIGNATURE WEAPON:
■ Fiery Breath

10

BATMAN

■ The Dark Knight doesn't have any superpowers, but he has the smarts, the skills, and the gadgets to mix things up with Superman, Wonder Woman, Green Lantern, and the rest. By rights, he should have been killed long ago, yet there never seems to be a bullet or a bomb with his name on it. He's starred in dozens of games—including some all-time greats—and he's as good with stealth and strategy as he is in a straight fight. Best of all, he always wears black (except when he wears gray, blue, or purple).

FIRST APPEARANCE:
■ *Batman*, 1986
LATEST APPEARANCE:
■ *Batman: The Enemy Within*, 2018
SIGNATURE WEAPON:
■ Batarangs

GODFALL

Fight the fight as a Valorian knight

Godfall is one awe-inspiring action RPG, but while you'll come for the incredible graphics, you'll stay for the fierce combat and fantastic loot. As a Valorian knight, you're somewhere between a soldier and a superhero, wielding magical weapons and wearing legendary suits of armour. These Valorplates do more than just give you useful perks—they change the whole way you have to fight!

TYPHON

■ The Typhon Valorplate increases your chances of inflicting Chill effects on enemies and adds water damage to every blow. The Archon Fury calls in water sentinals to fight by your side.

HARD-HITTING WEAPONS

■ Your knight carries two weapons and switches between them at will. There are five classes: Longswords, Dual Blades, Greatswords, Warhammers, and Polearms. Each has its own moves, effects, and strategies.

GREYHAWK

■ The Greyhawk Valorplate is all about Soul Shatter: a type of damage that builds up when you fight an enemy, and that activates when you deal out a heavy blow to wipe out huge amounts of health. Wearing Greyhawk ramps up the Soul Shatter, while its Archon Fury creates a massive shock wave that hits any enemy in range good and hard.

VALORPLATES

■ Valorplates are sets of armor that you can unlock and equip as you battle through the spectacular ruins of Aperion. Each Valorplate has its own bonuses that help you avoid enemy damage or increase the damage you dish out.

■ On top of that, each Valorplate has a special Archon Fury ability that will ramp up the amount of damage you do against your enemies or unleash a shock wave that can smack them flat on their backs! Build it up and unleash it when you need to take some tough guys out!

BIG PICTURE

SILVERMANE

You start the game with the Silvermane Valorplate, which increases the speed at which your Polarity Attacks, Weapon Techniques, and Shield Attacks charge. Its Archon Fury summons three ghostly warriors to aid you in battle.

SHIELDS

That shield isn't just for show. You can use it to block incoming blows or slam your foes and knock them off-balance. You can mix the shield with any weapon, not just the obviously one-handed swords and hammers.

FAST FACT

The twelve Valorplates are inspired by the twelve signs of the zodiac. For instance, Silvermane is based on Leo, the Lion, while Bulwark is based on Taurus, the Bull.

DIRT 5

PUT YOUR FOOT DOWN AND SPIN THOSE WHEELS

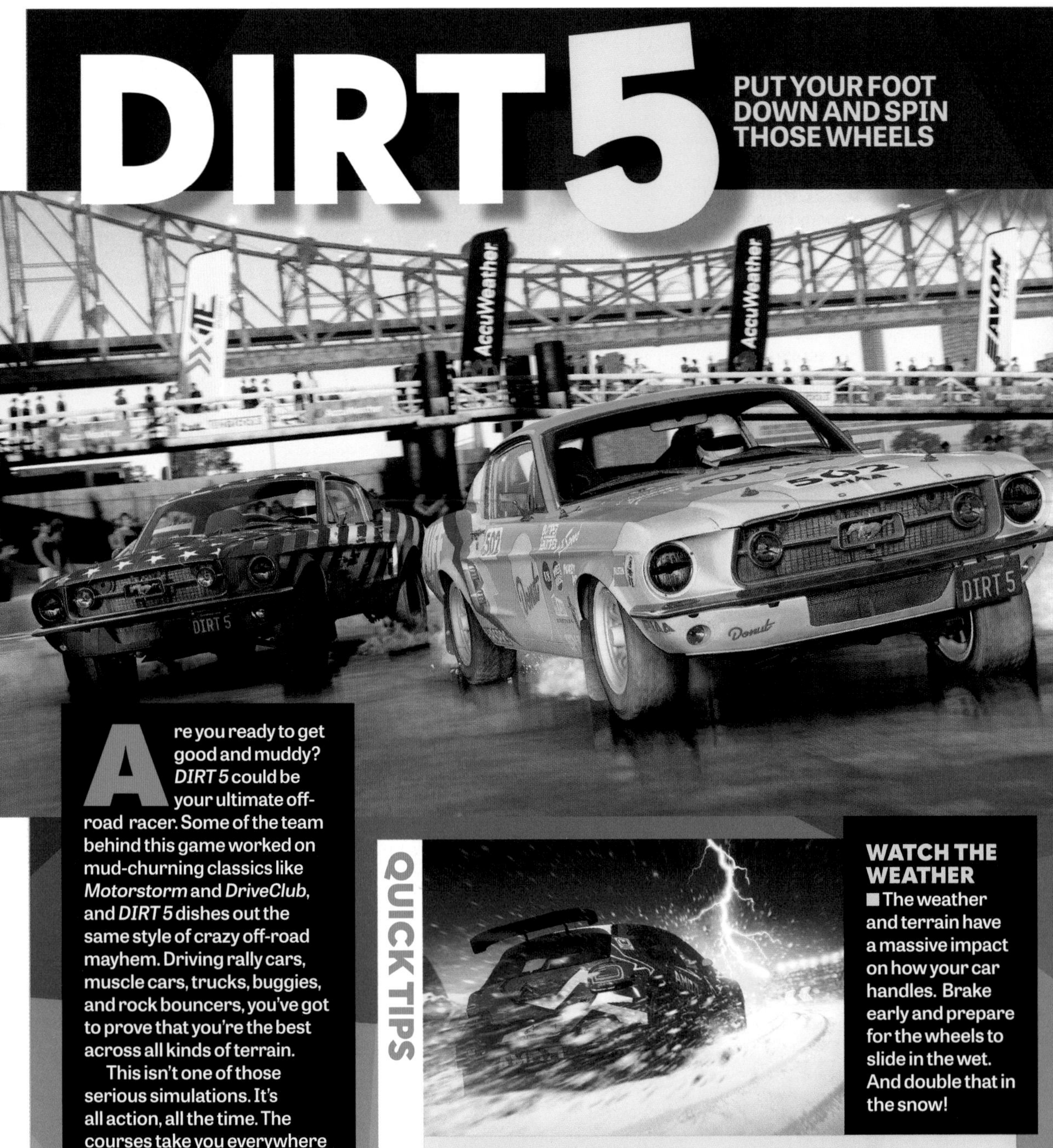

Are you ready to get good and muddy? *DIRT 5* could be your ultimate off-road racer. Some of the team behind this game worked on mud-churning classics like *Motorstorm* and *DriveClub*, and *DIRT 5* dishes out the same style of crazy off-road mayhem. Driving rally cars, muscle cars, trucks, buggies, and rock bouncers, you've got to prove that you're the best across all kinds of terrain.

This isn't one of those serious simulations. It's all action, all the time. The courses take you everywhere from New York City to Europe and China, through desert canyons, frozen lakes, and muddy forests. There's even space for tricks and stunts in the Gymkhana events. Hop in, grab the wheel, and put the pedal to the metal. Only the bold can win!

QUICK TIPS

WATCH THE WEATHER

■ The weather and terrain have a massive impact on how your car handles. Brake early and prepare for the wheels to slide in the wet. And double that in the snow!

CHANGE YOUR WHEELS

■ Buying new cars will give you an advantage in the more challenging races later on, but Speed isn't everything. A higher Handling score is more useful on tricky courses with lots of tight corners.

PLAY TO YOUR STRENGTHS

■ You've nearly always got a choice of events in Career mode, so work out which events suit your driving style. You'll grab more wins and more stamps to help you progress and have more fun.

HIGH-OCTANE ACTION

DIRT 5 features nine different event types that will test you in different vehicles across different types of terrain. Get ready for some really tough driving on the world's most brutal off-road tracks.

ULTRA CROSS

These intense circuit-based races combine tricky terrain, tough corners, and a big field of racers. Try to get out in front as early as you can, and avoid trading paint with the other cars.

RALLY RAID

These point-to-point races take you uphill and downhill through some of the world's most challenging landscapes. Prepare for anything, especially if the weather turns nasty!

PATH FINDER

Head off the beaten track for these challenging time-trial events. You'll be bouncing around across rocky terrain and working out your route along the way. Jumping's fun, but you had better stick the landing!

GYMKHANA

Played out in special stunt arenas, these trick-driving challenges will push you to the limit. You can even create your own stunt courses in the Playgrounds mode.

STAMPEDE

It's maximum rough-and-tumble in these high-speed, high-risk events. You'll be racing through cruel and unforgiving natural landscapes and giving your suspension a seriously hard time.

FAST FACT

Gymkhana might seem nuts, but it's a genuine motorsport, complete with slaloms, drifts, reversals, and 180-degree turns. One of the most famous drivers is Utah rally champ Ken Block, whose Gymkhana viral videos have had over 550 million views!

LIKE THIS? TRY THIS:

WRC11

Looking for a more realistic take on off-road racing? The latest version of the official World Rally Championship game is a blast, with all the rally courses, cars, and crews straight from the real championship.

Gran Turismo to Gran Turismo 7

See how the Real Driving Simulator has evolved

■ Gran Turismo has always pushed itself as the ultimate realistic racer, doing its best to simulate the world's fastest cars—along with those the rest of us get to drive—on the world's greatest courses. The early PlayStation consoles could only do so much, but with PS5, amazing things are possible. Just see how GT has changed!

The PS One Era

■ *Gran Turismo* (1997) and *Gran Turismo 2* (1999) made the most of the original PlayStation. These were jaw-dropping games! They also had more realistic physics than rival racers like *Sega Rally* or *Daytona USA*. The cars handled more like real-world cars, making you work to keep them on the track.

Rebuilt for PS2

■ *Gran Turismo 3: A-Spec* (2001) had even more realistic graphics, thanks to the power of PlayStation 2. Cars looked much more detailed, while amazing lighting effects made the night races come alive. You could now race Formula One cars, along with supercars from Porsche and Lamborghini.

■ *Gran Turismo 4* packed in 700 cars from eighty different manufacturers, along with graphics that made them look even more like the real deal. This was also the first Gran Turismo to simulate the way the car's body rolls when it takes a corner, brakes, or accelerates, and the first to feature Drag Race events. Viva Las Vegas!

Transformed for PS3

With HD graphics and the might of the PS3 to work with, *Gran Turismo 5* (2010) and *Gran Turismo 6* (2013) made it hard to tell the game apart from motor racing on TV. Weather and damage effects were introduced, and we had brilliant new circuits in Rome and Madrid. *GT5* changed the way the game simulated taking corners. Hear those brakes screech! *Gran Turismo 6* added even more cars and tracks, along with features where the PS Vita handheld could work as a rearview mirror.

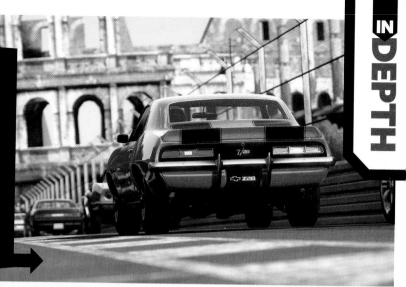

Getting Sporty for PS4

The PS4 never had a full Gran Turismo, so fans had to make do with the cut-back *Gran Turismo Sport* (2017). This went big with online racing and launched with just 168 cars and twenty-nine tracks, though updates took the count up to 324 and eighty-two. Still, the graphics looked better than ever, and the handling was even more lifelike. It was also the first Gran Turismo you could play in virtual reality on PSVR.

FAST FACT

Some of the tracks featured in the original Gran Turismo are so great and loved by fans that they've returned in every Gran Turismo with the exception of GT Sport. We can't stop racing around Trial Mountain or Deep Forest Raceway!

Seventh Heaven

And now we've got *Gran Turismo 7* (2022) on the PlayStation 5. The classic Gran Turismo simulation mode is back, while the graphics look even more astonishingly realistic, thanks to 4D HDR graphics and ray-traced reflections on the cars. If you love cars and want to race with the world's best, it's still the best driving game around!

RIDERS REPUBLIC

THE ULTIMATE EXTREME SPORTS ADVENTURE

Leave the normal tracks, trails, and slopes behind—it's time for some real extreme sports action. *Rider's Republic* mashes seven great national parks together into one mighty open-world wilderness, then turns it into a playground for bikes, snowboards, skis, and wingsuits. If you ever wanted to speed down the slopes of Sequoia Park or glide through the formations of Bryce Canyon, *Riders Republic* is here to make your dreams come true.

It's a crazy game with even crazier events and stunts, culminating in some intense challenges and the Riders Ridge Invitational competition. You can compete and level up solo or with friends, or join in the carnage of the Mass Race competitions, with up to sixty-four players at a time!

QUICK TIPS

YOU CAN'T WIN 'EM ALL

Don't worry if you come second in a race—or even tenth! You can still earn XP and awesome gear.

GO MANUAL

The game has options for auto drift and auto landing, but switch to manual if you can. You'll get extra XP when racing, and it'll help with the trickier events later on.

GO FOR THE BONUSES

Each event has bonus objectives, like popping star balloons or pulling off a certain stunt. Check what they are before starting to grab the extra points.

PEAK PERFORMANCE

The more events you compete in for *Riders Republic*, the more sports and competitions you'll unlock. Ski, snowboard, cycle, and glide like a pro, and you can make it to the top of every sport.

HIT THE SLOPES

Snowboard and ski freestyle events are all about awesome tricks and high scores, while the racing events focus on time trials and fast-paced checkpoint races.

TAKE TO THE AIR

You'll need to earn some stars to unlock the wingsuit and jet wingsuit races, but there's no greater thrill than diving through the rings at breakneck speed.

TWO-WHEELED TROUBLE

Hop on a bike and take part in daredevil downhill races and trick-tastic freestyle events. Get ready for some terrifying hairpin turns and equally scary jumps!

FAST FACT

Riders Republic covers around 100 square miles of territory, including chunks of the Yosemite Valley, Bryce Canyon, Sequoia Park, Zion, Canyonland, Mammoth Mountain, and Grand Teton national parks.

MASS EFFECT!

The game's signature events are its sixty-four-player mass races. These run across three rounds and mix biking, snowboarding, skis, and the wingsuit, so you need to be on your A game across every sport!

THERE'S MORE TO EXPLORE!

Part of the fun of *Riders Republic* is that there's so much stuff to do outside the main competitions. Get on your bike, strap on your wingsuit, or hop on your snowmobile, and see what this massive world has to offer.

LANDMARKS

There are forty-five landmarks to find across the map. You'll get a great view to enjoy, and maybe some other rewards.

LANDMARK
SPINE LINES

Pretty scary stuff. Flutes and spines are formed when snow builds up on rocky ridges or where the terrain naturally funnels into a V. They're most common on monster faces like these in Teton. Pro Rider Tip: As you drop onto the spine, make quick, controlled turns to get a feel for the snow. But remember, when trying to slay a Spine Line you gotta roll with the punches. Whatever happens happens, but the rider who has the most fun wins!

RELICS

Track down any one of the eleven hidden relics and you'll unlock a new vehicle you can use in events. Sometimes you'll get bonus points, but you're always sure of a wild ride.

SHACKDADDY EVENTS

Need a break? Try the weird and downright dumb Shackdaddy Events, weaving through obstacles strapped to a cardboard plane or pulling off tricks on some silly wooden skis.

REACH THE SUMMIT

It can be hard to reach some relics and landmarks if you're traveling on foot, ski, or bike. Instead, press up on the D-pad to access your Sports selection wheel and hop on your snowmobile, or take to the air in your wingsuit and parachute down!

TRICKS AND TIPS

Want to win those races or score big in the tricks challenges? We've got the tricks and tips to help.

DRIFT TO WIN

You can drift and corner faster by pulling the left trigger as you move into the turn. This can help you speed through sharp corners and get through checkpoints you'll otherwise miss.

BOOST OR LOSE

Boosting with the left bumper or L1 button is another crucial skill. Use it to pick up speed when you're pedaling uphill, or to accelerate out of turns in the wingsuit events.

DON'T MISS A TRICK

Take every chance to complete a trick when you're in the freestyle events. Even a quick spin can score you points, or use the shoulder buttons/bumpers for tucks, grabs, handlebar tricks, and whips.

STICK THE LANDING

To rack up the top scores, you really need to perfect smooth landings. Don't try to squeeze in another trick last minute, and learn how to do manual landings if you can.

LIKE THIS? TRY THIS:

SHREDDERS

This trick-focused, powder-packed snowboarding game is a love letter to old console classics like *SSX* and *Amped*. Hit the slopes, work out your run, and shred for glory!

FORZA HORIZON 5

A MEXICAN SPEED FIESTA

The scenery, the cars, the colors! With *Forza Horizon 5*, Microsoft's open-world racing series hits a new peak. This is the game where you can drive the world's coolest supercars on winding mountain tracks, take a Jeep for a spin in the jungle, or race dune buggies along sandy shores. The action never lets up for a second!

What's more, the new Horizon festival is even crazier than ever. What other game makes you drive out of a plane or chase twisters through the desert? And with street racing, stunts, and seasonal events as well, the latest Forza feels like one endless racing vacation.

QUICK TIPS

WATCH THE WEATHER

Time of day and weather make a big difference to the racing conditions and how your car handles. If it's going to be wet and windy, choose a car and setup that can hold the road.

BUILD UP SKILL POINTS

Even when you're just driving from race to race, you can build up skill chains with tricks, near misses, drifts, and more. Skill points can be spent on car mastery upgrades, enhancing your favorite rides.

BUY A HOUSE

Houses might seem pointless, but buying them can unlock bonus perks like fast travel, free prize Wheelspins, or bonus-boosting Skill Songs. Make sure you invest in some prime real estate when you can!

VIVA HORIZON!

The Horizon Festival involves some serious racing, but it never takes its racing too seriously. As well as six series of races to unlock, you have a wild mix of showcase events, quick challenges, and expedition missions. Sometimes there's too much to do!

JOIN THE EXPEDITION

The expedition missions give you some of Forza's craziest moments. If you're not following a plane as it flies through a raging storm, you're speeding in a Baja buggy down the slopes of a volcano.

EXPAND YOUR HORIZONS

Earn Accolade Points by racing and you unlock new adventure chapters, each with a new expedition mission that can open up a whole new class of races. From stunts to street racing, there's something for every kind of driver.

BARN FINDS AND MYSTERIES

You've got more than just open roads to discover. Many of the expedition missions have their own optional challenge objectives, while barns hide classic cars just looking for someone to fix them up.

TREAT YOURSELF

And while you're doing all this, you're earning credits you can spend on new cars, custom paint jobs, upgrades, and more—and you can unlock more hot vehicles by winning or leveling up. Fill your garage!

FAST FACT

The game has eleven different biomes, with their own climates, landscapes, animals, and plants. Look out for different weather and even different critters as you explore.

LIKE THIS? TRY THIS:

GRID LEGENDS

If you want a taste of real motorsports with a brilliant, story-based campaign, *GRID Legends* is an absolute must-have. With everything from truck racing to open wheel to GT racing, it's a driver's dream.

PLACE FIRST IN FORZA HORIZON 5

How to grab pole position and win the race

From judging the right speed to knowing how to corner, winning in *Forza Horizon 5* takes skill. Using driver assists will give you a head start, but if you're going to race online, you'll have to develop your driving abilities and become less dependent on them. And that's when you'll learn that winning isn't just about driving faster, but also driving smarter—as these tips prove!

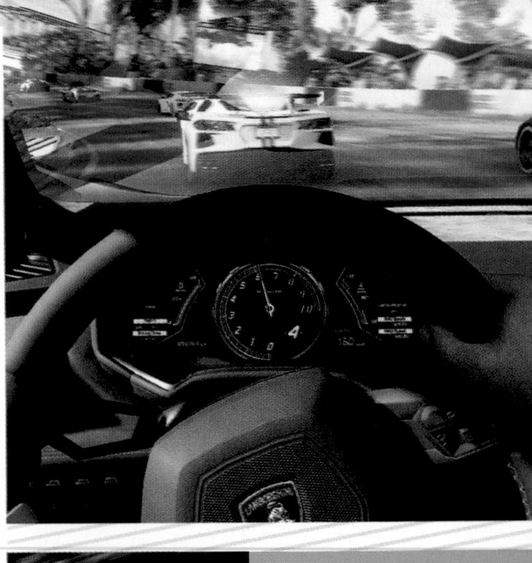

1 Hit the brakes

This isn't some old-school arcade racer where you never have to touch the brake. In *Forza*, you'll need to brake to take corners without hitting the barrier, or without heading off the track or missing checkpoints. You should try to brake later and accelerate sooner than the competition, but that comes with feel and practice.

2 Fastest isn't always best

When you pick a car for a race, don't automatically go for the car with the highest top speed. In a lot of races, handling and how quickly the car can accelerate will be more important, especially when there are tight bends to navigate or a risk of slipping off the road. Sometimes it's better to drive a car you already know and love!

3 Slipstream

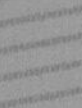

You can get a speed boost by traveling in the slipstream of the car in front. Drive behind them, build up some speed, then shift left or right and slingshot past them! Keep an eye on the road and pick the right moment. You can't stay in front if you hit something hard around the corner.

4 Block the competition

■ Other racers can also try the slipstream trick, or just rely on their car's superior speed to fly past you. This is particularly annoying when it happens on the last straight of the race. Don't let it. Use your rearview mirror or the chase cam view to spot when cars are about to overtake, then steer into their path and block them.

FAST FACT

The fastest car in *Forza Horizon 5* is the Koenigsegg Jesko. It's been seen reaching speeds of up to 308 miles per hour!

5 Practice to win

■ Sometimes, winning takes practice. While you might take first on the first go in some of the easier races, don't be too proud to take a break and then restart if it all goes wrong. You'll slowly learn where the turns are, where it's safe to overtake, and where the biggest risks might be. Use Rewind when you make a stupid mistake, but try to learn from it as well.

Don't race dirty!

■ Racing dirty can be tempting, but smashing into other cars or using the barriers as an emergency brake isn't going to get you on the winner's podium. Learn how to get a good start, move quickly through the pack, and hold on to the lead. The more you can race without trading paint or taking out the scenery, the more wins are going to come your way.

GAMING GOES All-You-Can-Eat

Why buy one game for big money when you can play all you want with a monthly pass?

Buying all your games is now so old-school. For the cost of a few games a year, you could have an all-you-can-eat banquet of hits. Today's games subscription services give you access to a changing lineup of games for a monthly fee. With some you don't even need a console—you can play games through a browser on your laptop, your smartphone, or a TV streaming stick.

Sounds good? Well, there are some drawbacks, but if you're always hungry for new games to play, these services can be a great idea.

How it works

- Instead of buying a game, your parents or an adult signs up to the service and agrees to pay a monthly subscription fee, which could be anywhere from $5 to $15. While they're subscribed, you can play any of the games bundled free with the service and use any other perks that the service has. You can usually leave at any time, but once you do, you can't keep playing the games.

GAMING SUBSCRIPTIONS

The Good

- You get access to loads of games, with new ones added every month. You can try out games you're interested in and see if they're ace or a waste of space.
- You might get access to expensive deluxe versions with all the expansions and upgrade packs included.
- Some subscription services allow you to stream your games to a laptop, TV streaming stick, or smartphone. No console required!
- Subscription fees are a lot less expensive than buying a full game. You could get four months for the price of just one blockbuster game.

The Bad

- You have to keep paying the monthly subscription fee or you won't be able to play your favorite games. That's quite a lot of dollars over the whole year.
- Games can leave your service as well as getting added to it. That's bad news if you haven't finished your game when it happens!
- You won't always get the latest, greatest titles, and there's no guarantee that you'll get all the games you want to play.

XBOX GAMES PASS

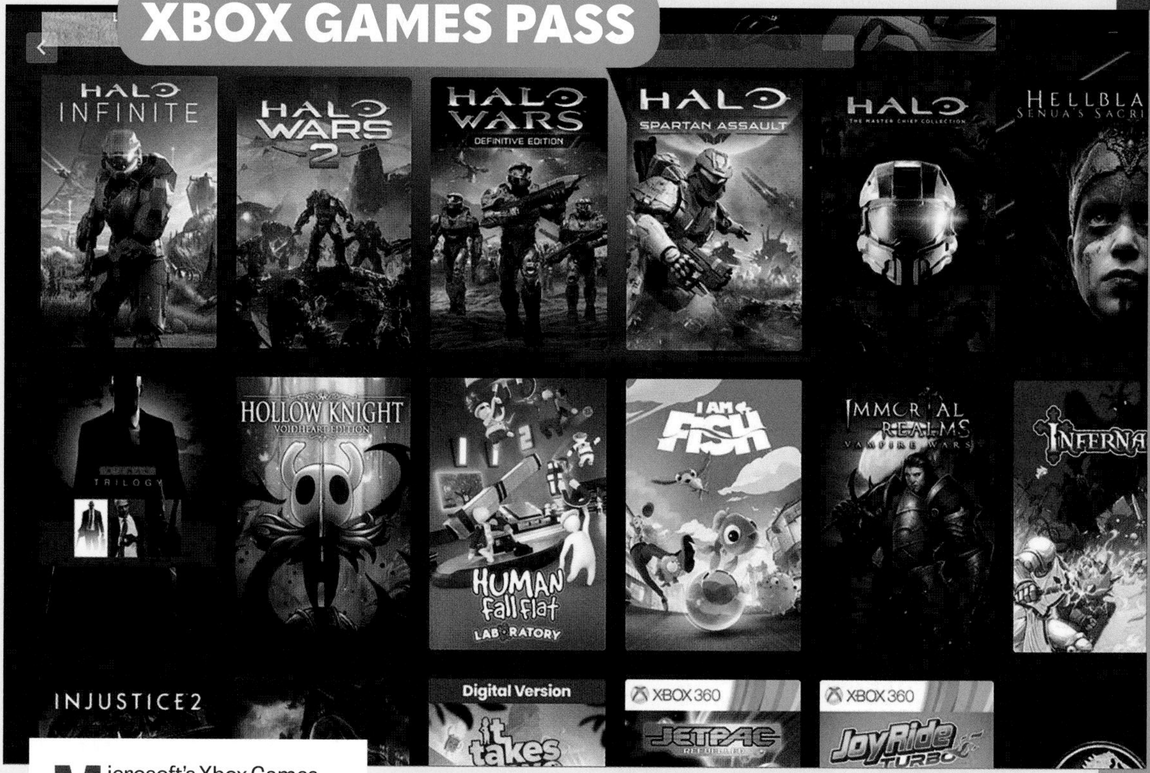

Microsoft's Xbox Games Pass is widely reckoned to be the best subscription service out there. For one thing, it's got a massive library of games from nearly every major publisher. For another, Microsoft puts all their big Xbox exclusives on the service on the day they're released, so you're always going to get to play the next Halo, Forza Horizon, or Sea of Thieves. You'll also get any expansions released for them.

■ The basic versions of Games Pass work for Xbox consoles or PC, but the more expensive Games Pass Ultimate works across both and adds other perks on top. With it you can stream Xbox games to your laptop, PC, or smartphone. Better still, EA and Microsoft throw in an EA Play membership as well!

Don't miss

HALO: THE MASTER CHIEF COLLECTION (Xbox Games Pass)

■ With Games Pass, you can get to grips with the whole Halo saga, going all the way from 2001's *Halo: Combat Evolved* to 2012's *Halo 4*. When you're done with that, you can catch up with *Halo 5: Guardians* before taking on the incredible *Halo Infinite*.

PLAYSTATION PLUS

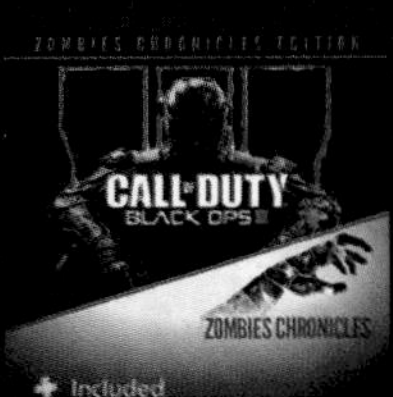

Sort by: Default

Sony has expanded its PlayStation Plus service to bring in the subscription games and console streaming features of PlayStation Now. The most basic PS Plus Essentials plan gives you online gaming and two or three free games a month, but go for PS Plus Extra and you get a selection of up to 400 PS4 and PS5 games to download and play. Step up to PS Plus Premium and you're looking at over 700 games, including PS3, PS2, and PSP games via streaming. Sweet!

■ The only downside? Unlike Microsoft, Sony doesn't put its biggest games on PS Plus on launch day. Sob.

PlayStation Plus

Don't miss

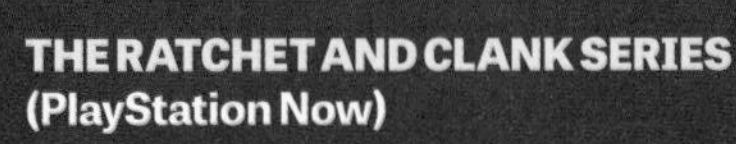

THE RATCHET AND CLANK SERIES (PlayStation Now)

■ PlayStation Plus is a great way to catch up with the classic Ratchet and Clank series, with all of the top PS3 and PS4 titles available to stream. It's also packed with other classic PlayStation hits, along with brilliant PS2, PS3, and PSP games.

EA PLAY

Are you a massive fan of EA's sports games, action games, and Star Wars hits? Then EA Play could be the subscription service for you. The basic version is one of the cheapest options out there, and it's available for Xbox, PS4, PS5, and PC. You get free, all-you-can-play access to loads of classic and recent EA and EA Sports games from what EA calls the Vault, and you also get up to ten hours of play time on selected new releases, so that you can try before you buy.

■ PC gamers can also get EA Play Pro—a more expensive option that adds unlimited play of the latest EA titles as soon as they're released. This isn't available on Xbox or PlayStation.

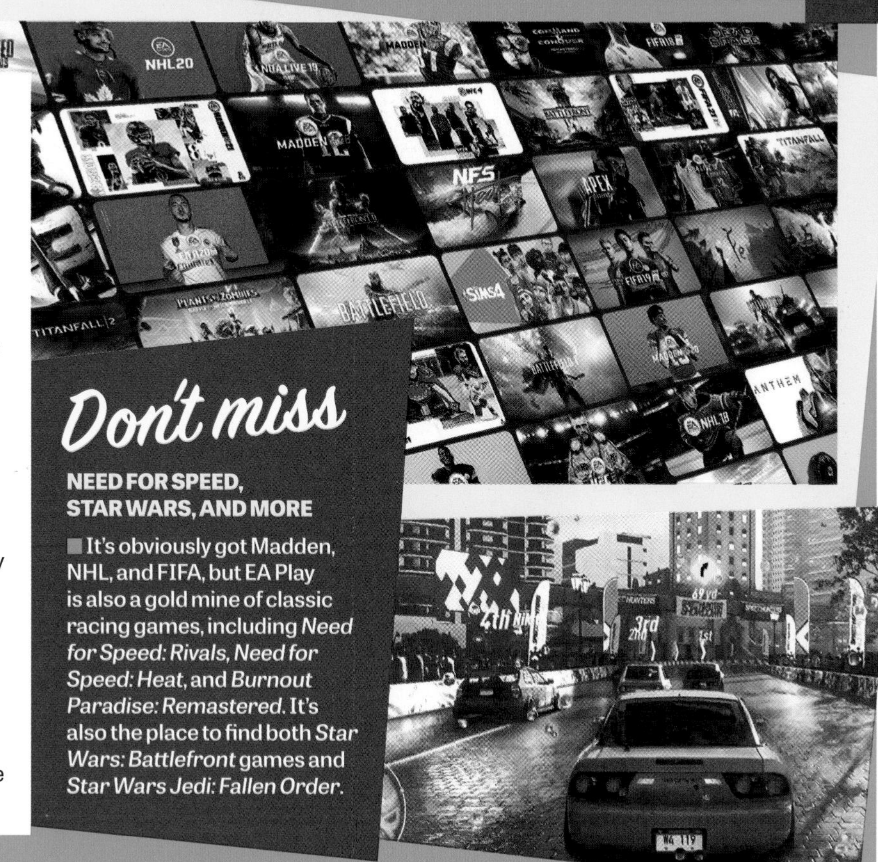

Don't miss

NEED FOR SPEED, STAR WARS, AND MORE

■ It's obviously got Madden, NHL, and FIFA, but EA Play is also a gold mine of classic racing games, including *Need for Speed: Rivals, Need for Speed: Heat,* and *Burnout Paradise: Remastered.* It's also the place to find both *Star Wars: Battlefront* games and *Star Wars Jedi: Fallen Order.*

AMAZON LUNA+

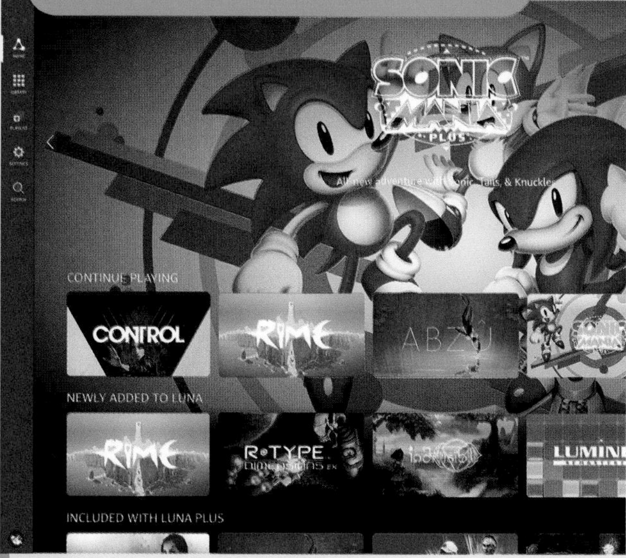

Amazon Luna is Amazon's cloud game streaming service, which works on PCs, Macs, iPhones, and iPads, plus Android devices. It also runs on Amazon's popular Fire TV Sticks and Fire tablets. You'll need a fast internet connection to make it work, but you won't need a console. While Amazon sells its own controller, you can use a mouse and keyboard. Many popular games controllers are also compatible.

■ It's still early days for Luna, but it works well and has a good range of games available to play, with more on their way. It also supports Ubisoft's Ubisoft+ service, though you'll need to pay an additional subscription fee for that.

GOOGLE STADIA PRO

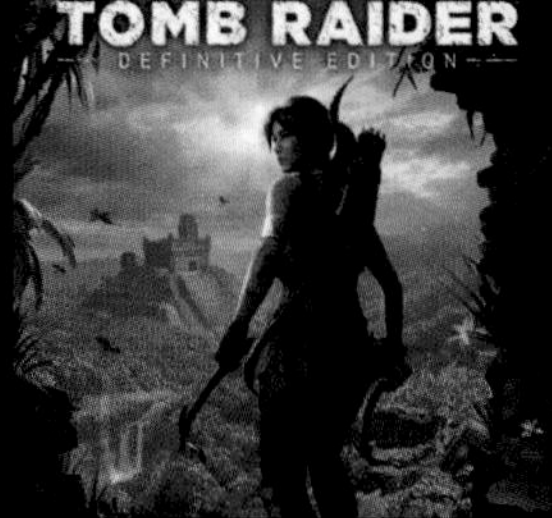

Google Stadia Pro is really more a subscription to Google's cloud gaming service than a subscription option. However, each month Google adds a bunch of free games for Stadia Pro subscribers to enjoy, and as long as you claim them, you can play them for as long as you want. Keep subscribing to Stadia Pro and you'll build up a decent collection of these free games. Plus, Stadia Pro includes other perks like 4K gaming and discounted prices on new games.

■ As long as you've got a fast and reliable internet connection, Stadia Pro works brilliantly across laptops, Android tablets, smartphones, and Google Chromecast Ultra devices. Google also sells an excellent controller, though you can use an Xbox controller or a PlayStation Dual Shock instead. You don't need a console and you can add a Ubisoft+ subscription for an extra fee.

Don't miss

IMMORTALS: FENYX RISING

■ *Immortals: Fenyx Rising* is one of the best action-adventures of the last few years. Find out for yourself with a Ubisoft+ subscription, either on PC, Google Stadia, or Amazon Luna.

APPLE ARCADE

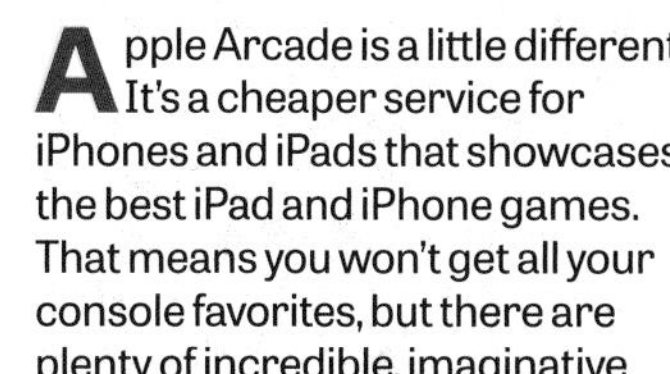

Apple Arcade is a little different. It's a cheaper service for iPhones and iPads that showcases the best iPad and iPhone games. That means you won't get all your console favorites, but there are plenty of incredible, imaginative games to play. Whether you like platform games, puzzle games, racing games, or epic adventures, there will be something for you here, as well as weird and kooky titles like *What the Golf?* and *Things That Go Bump!*

■ It's obviously no good if you haven't got an iPad or an iPhone, but if you spend as much time playing on your phone or iPad as on your console and TV, this could be the service for you.

UBISOFT+

Ubisoft+ is devoted to Ubisoft's own games, giving you the latest releases as soon as they're available, along with a vast selection of classics stretching back almost twenty years. It's available on PC, or Amazon Luna, and Google Stadia through streaming.

■ It's one of the more expensive options out there, so it only really makes sense if you're a massive fan of some of Ubisoft's monster franchises—many of which aren't exactly family friendly. However, it might be the cheapest way to play games like *Immortals: Fenyx Rising*, *Rider's Republic*, and the *Prince of Persia: Sands of Time* remake, along with older Ubisoft hits like *The Crew 2*, *Trials Rising*, *Steep*, and *Rayman Legends*.

MADDEN NFL

BRINGING FOOTBALL BACK DOWN TO GROUND LEVEL

Madden NFL has become a massive monument to football, with so many different modes and options that it's hard to know where to start. First, *Madden 21* crammed in two brilliant new game modes; then *Madden 22* just about perfected them, as well as giving the Franchise mode an awesome overhaul.

Madden still has exhibition matches, where you can replay the week's big real-world games, and a huuuuuge Career mode where you can be a player or a coach. And it wouldn't be Madden without Ultimate Team mode, where you can collect your own dream team of NFL greats. The Face of the Franchise mode tells the story of a new player from the college leagues up, and no other Madden mode gives you fast-paced thrills like The Yard!

QUICK TIPS

STICKS AND TRICKS

The right stick is now the skill stick, giving you a whole bunch of great abilities, such as Juke, Spin, and Dead Leg moves, when you push it in the right direction. Look for prompts and flick that stick!

TAKE THE EASY CONVERSION

Madden 22 will keep on tempting you to run fake plays on conversions rather than just take a straight kick. Just kick and take the easy points—the fakes hardly ever play out.

THE X-FACTOR

Madden 22 goes big on X-Factor superstar abilities you can use to give your team the edge. For instance, when Lamar Jackson enters the zone, his Truzz ability stops any tackles causing a fumble.

FROM COLLEGE TO THE YARD

Madden 22 revamps the Face of the Franchise and The Yard modes from *Madden 21*. Each is an awesome way to get stuck in and learn the basics of the game.

LEARN YOUR LESSONS

Because Face of the Franchise starts in college, it's a great way to brush up on the basics of Madden's complex gameplay. You can get your head around the playbooks and start working on your skills and strategies.

TAKE A CLASS

Face of the Franchise is where you can build your own football superstar, following them from college football all the way to the NFL. You start by picking a position and a class to play. Your class defines your play style and the skills you can use and upgrade.

POWER OF PROGRESS

One of the coolest things about *Madden 22* is that class progress carries over between Face of the Franchise and The Yard. Everything you gain from playing well in one mode will make a difference when you next start playing in the other, so keep unlocking new abilities.

GOING GLOBAL

This year, The Yard has gone global, with a whole series of street football challenges that take you all around the world. Some games hit you with crazy rules, while others have you facing off against some all-time greats.

FAST FACT

Some people think appearing on the Madden cover is a curse. Of the twenty-two players who've had the honor, sixteen have had a bad season straight after. Still, *Madden 21*'s Lamar Jackson and *Madden 20*'s Patrick Mahomes seem immune!

LIKE THIS? TRY THIS:

NHL 22

NHL keeps getting faster, flashier, and even more exciting, with more realistic players, controls, and animations, plus NHL's take on Madden's X-Factor superstar abilities.

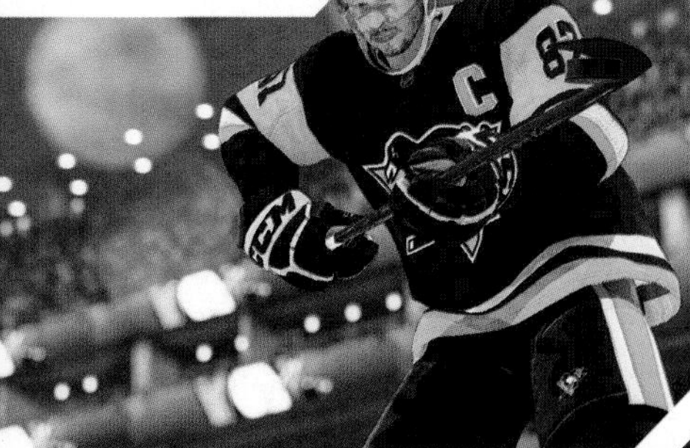

SCORE MORE GOALS IN FIFA 22

Five top tips to get the ball in the back of the net

Want to win at FIFA? A strong defensive strategy will help, but you really need to score more goals. There's more to it than tapping the B or Circle button when your striker comes in range. Position, shot strength, and placement all have a part to play. And if you can master the controls, you can pull off some special shots, which might be all you need to push the scoreline in the right direction.

1 Make space

Ninety-nine percent of the time, charging at the goal will get you nowhere. Learn how to make space for your strikers. Move the ball through the defenders to the wings, sprint up the field, and either go for the shot or pass it to a player in a good position. Move fast and you might take the defenders by surprise.

2 Get a cleaner shot

You'll need some pace to make it to the goal, but take your finger off the sprint trigger before you take your shot. Slowing down and moving into position can help you get a good, powerful, and accurate shot.

3 Go Low

It's harder to score with crosses and headers in *FIFA 22*. Up close, you're often better with a Low Shot: a power shot that travels closer to the ground. Just hold the L and R bumpers (or the L1 and R2 buttons), then hold and release the B or Circle button. Even if it doesn't go in, it might bounce off a defender's legs and give you another shot at a goal.

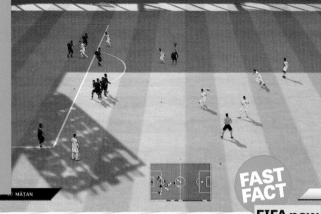

4 Make the most of set pieces

■ Corners are a bit of a wash in *FIFA 22*, but free kicks and even throw-ins can be a great way to get something started and get the ball to your favorite striker. The trick is to move fast and get your timing perfect. Look for angles that could take the goalie unawares.

FAST FACT

FIFA now features over thirty leagues, 700 clubs, and more than 17,000 players from all around the world. Whether your favorite team is in North America, South America, India, Japan, or Europe, FIFA has you covered.

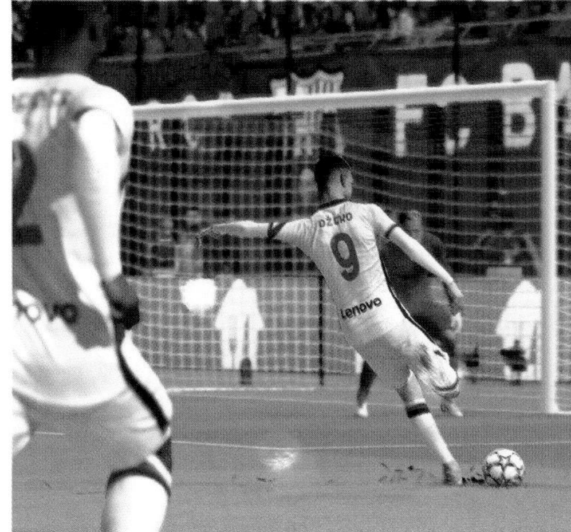

5 Use Finesse

■ Finesse shots are great just outside the box. Just hold the right bumper or the R1 button as you press B or Circle to shoot. If you're really smart, you can go for the Timed Finesse shot. Go for the Finesse shot, then press Circle a second time as your player pulls back their leg. With the right player and good timing, you can pull off some amazing goals!

Don't get caught offside

■ Tempting as it is to blast the ball out to the striker nearest to the goal, you need to be aware of the offside rule. This applies when the player is nearer to the opposing team's goal line than both the ball and the second-last opponent at the same time as the ball is passed to them. *FIFA 22* has a handy blue indicator line to show when you're about to go offside, so take notice and pass to someone else.

NBA 2K

TAKING B-BALL UP TO THE NEXT LEVEL

There's one downside to any hot streak. NBA 2K has been so great for so long that, even when it's awesome, it feels like it's standing still. Luckily, *NBA 2K22* isn't just another brilliant NBA 2K. It builds on all the amazing stuff introduced in *NBA 2K21*, then makes it even better with the power of the next-gen consoles.

What does that mean? How about a revamped MyCareer mode that tries to simulate a star player's lifestyle. Or what about improved WBNA modes that give you MyCareer and MyTeam modes for the women's game? And let's not forget the core gameplay improvements that make *NBA 2K22* even more authentic? Sorry, rival sports games, NBA 2K is still taking you to school!

QUICK TIPS

TOUGH IT OUT
■ The new stamina system means you can't just dribble endlessly while you get in position for your shot. Watch and build your stamina to stay at the top of your game.

EARN BADGES
■ Fill the gauges for Finishing, Shooting, Defense, and Playmaking, and you earn badges to boost your skills. Pick badges that play to your strengths—or make up for your weaknesses on the court.

DOMINATE THE COURT
■ The new animation system means that size matters more in *NBA 2K22*. Taller players can dominate the area around the hoop, and either score or block shots coming in.

NBA 2K: THE NEXT GENERATION

■ Just when you thought NBA 2K couldn't get any more in-depth, *NBA 2K22* proves you wrong. Wherever and however you want to play b-ball, you'll find it here.

HIT THE CITY

■ MyCareer now goes deeper than ever before. You can roam around the city and build your brand, showing off the freshest styles and even developing a music side career.

ON THE COURT

■ The team at 2K Games has transformed the core gameplay to put the focus on skill, smart team play, and strategy. Want to win? You'll need to work out new moves.

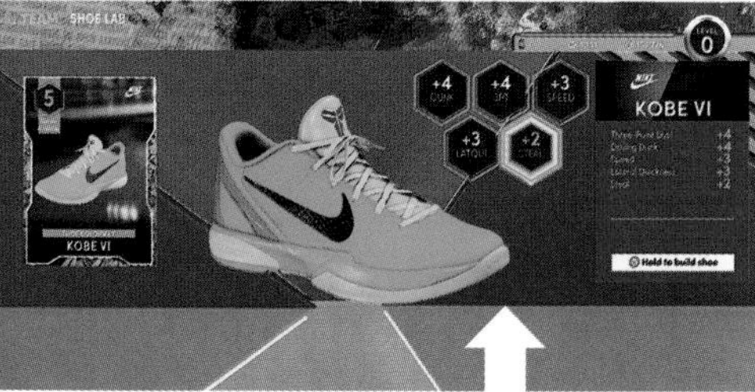

NEW SQUEAKS

■ This must be the first sports game where you can design your own kicks. Hit the Shoe Lab and pick the right upgrades to give your favorite stars a boost.

GET WITH THE W

■ It's time to pay respect to the ladies of the WNBA. Not only do you get a proper WNBA MyCareer mode, but a way to create your own players and a MyTeam mode on top. You can even play your W games online.

The Chicago Sky's Candace Parker is the first WBNA star to front the cover of an NBA 2K game . She appears on the WNBA 25th Anniversary Edition of the game.

WINDJAMMERS 2

■ Looking for another fiercely competitive sports game? Try *Windjammers 2*, a brutally speedy disc-throwing arcade game starring crazy heroes and cool special moves.

KIRBY AND THE FORGOTTEN LAND

THE PINK BLOB IS BADDER THAN EVER BEFORE!

Kirby's not going to take it anymore! First a mysterious vortex appears in the sky and sucks in the pink blob's buddies. Now Kirby is in hot pursuit of a gang of Waddle-Dee-kidnapping bruisers, known as the Beast Pack. These guys are big and tough, but they've reckoned without our hero's shapeshifting powers. By breathing in and swallowing his enemies, he can steal their powers and use them on his quest. Prepare for a blast of Kirby fury!

This is a classic cute cartoon platformer with a difference, as Kirby pulls out all his sword-slashing, bomb-throwing, fire-breathing, hammering tricks to liberate his friends and destroy the Beast Pack. And with optional co-op play and the all-new Mouthful Mode, this might be his best adventure yet.

QUICK TIPS

LOOK FOR SECRETS

■ The Forgotten Land is crammed with secret areas where you might find a handy power-up or a prisoner in need of rescue. Look out for areas just out of reach, and think how you might change shape to get there.

KEEP SWITCHING

■ Different forms have different weapons with different ranges and different effects. Some enemies are weak against fire or ice, or are best tackled from a distance with a bomb blast or boomerang blade.

BASH THE BOSS

■ Stuck against a boss with nothing to throw at them? Look for something to inhale and blast at them. They might even produce something useful when they attack!

SHAPE SHIFTER

What has Kirby got over Mario or Sonic? His copying abilities, that's what! And now he goes beyond the old inhale-exhale routine to cram larger objects in his mighty magic mouth!

OWN THE CONE

I know what you're thinking: What's cool about an oversize traffic cone? Well, Kirby can leap up and spike downward to smash through enemies or cracks in the ground or pipes.

VICIOUS VENDING

Suck in a vending machine and Kirby's a can-blasting cannon, blasting enemies left and right with his fizzy projectiles.

MOTOR MOUTH

In Mouthful Mode, Kirby stretches to take in massive objects. This car's great for boosting through bad guys and obstacles, or pulling off crazy stunt jumps.

GLIDING THROUGH

Suck in the arch and you can soar through the air with the wind at your back. Just make sure you glide through all those hoops!

FAST FACT

Kirby has had over ninety copy abilities since he first appeared in *Kirby's Dream Land* back in 1992. He didn't even learn to copy until *Kirby's Adventure* in 1993.

LIKE THIS? TRY THIS:

YOSHI'S CRAFTED WORLD

Looking for another cuddly platform game where you're not going to get kicked around? *Yoshi's Crafted World* combines ingenious ideas with some gorgeous hand-crafted graphics.

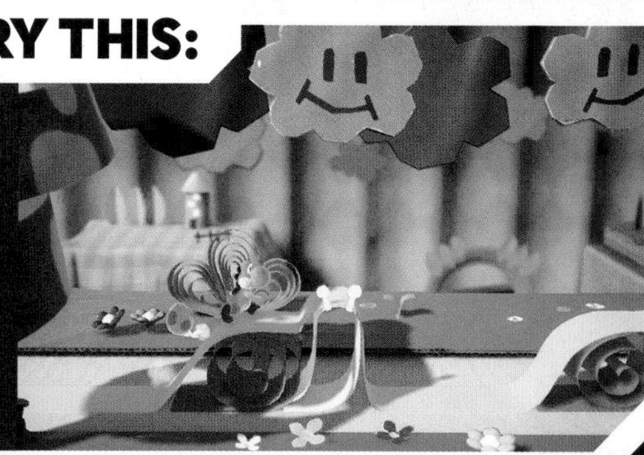

THE GAMES THAT MADE MARIO

The classic games that made—and kept—Mario as gaming's greatest star

The man with the mustache is a true gaming legend! More than just the king of the console mascots, he's the guy who's helped change gaming history time and time again. He's come with us from the earliest days, yet he's still starring in some of the best games of today. So let's give a cheer for Mario and salute his greatest hits.

DONKEY KONG 1981

Mario made his first appearance in Nintendo's arcade classic, playing the barrel-jumping, hammer-wielding hero who had to climb his way to the top of each level to rescue Pauline from the mighty Donkey Kong. The game's designer, Shigeru Miyamoto, dressed him in his bright red overalls to make him easier to see, and added the cap and mustache to avoid animating his hair and face. Donkey Kong has become another Nintendo favorite, while Pauline made a surprise comeback in *Super Mario Odyssey*.

SUPER MARIO BROS. 1985

Nintendo invented the platform game as we know it with Mario's second major hit, while introducing many of the characters, power-ups, and enemies that we still know and love today. It all looks pretty basic now, but the goomba-stomping, coin-collecting gameplay never gets old, helped by the brilliantly precise controls. Nearly everything's here, from the size-changing mushrooms to the fiendish Bowser—it rocked the gaming world!

SUPER MARIO BROS. 3 1990

The third Super Mario for the NES was even better than the first. Shigeru Miyamoto and his team were incredibly inventive, throwing in new moves for Mario, like sliding, throwing blocks, and climbing, along with new power-ups that helped him swim, fly, and hurl hammers. Best of all, *Super Mario Bros. 3* went big on the idea of themed levels, giving us an adventure that crossed icy worlds and sandy deserts, and even lands where everything was giant-size!

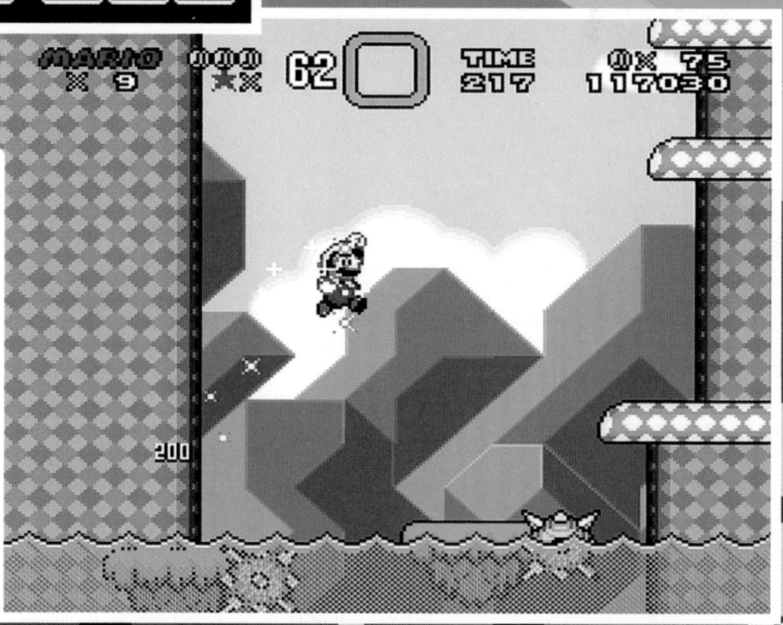

SUPER MARIO WORLD 1991

With a new console—the Super NES—to sell, Nintendo doubled down on everything that made *Super Mario Bros. 3* great. *Super Mario World* had incredible 16-bit graphics and seventy-two levels spread across seven different worlds. It threw in secret exits and secret levels and Mario's new friend Yoshi: a trusty dinosaur with an enemy-catching tongue and a hunger for fruit. Some people think *Super Mario World* is the greatest platform game ever!

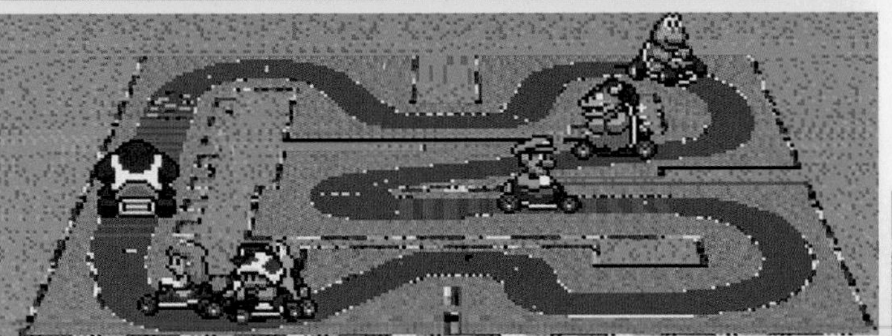

SUPER MARIO KART 1992

We'll say one thing for Mario—he's always been happy to give anything a try, whether tennis, soccer, or golf. His greatest move, though, was to hop into a kart and start the awesome Grand Prix series that we still can't get enough of today. *Super Mario Kart* had it all, with a fantastic set of drivers, brilliant courses, and destructive power-ups, laying the foundations for one of the world's finest multiplayer games.

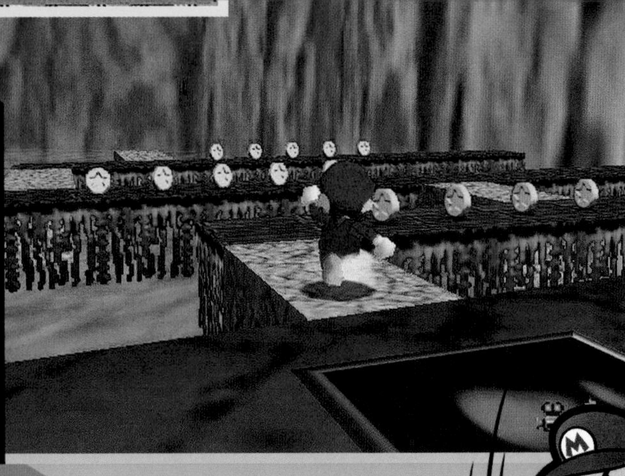

SUPER MARIO 64 1996

Nintendo followed up the Super NES with a console that had revolutionary 3D graphics, but how could you make a side-scrolling platform hero work in a 3D game? By the time he had finished making *Super Mario 64*, Shigeru Miyamoto had the answers. This game brought us the analog stick for movement and an incredibly exciting 3D world to explore, while still having all the classic Mario enemies and power-ups, including Big Boo and Bowser.

PAPER MARIO: THE THOUSAND-YEAR DOOR 2004

Mario has often dipped his toes into other genres, including the RPG. But while *Super Mario RPG* was the first, and came from the makers of Final Fantasy, *Paper Mario: The Thousand-Year Door* is the best. It developed the 2D-meets-3D paper style introduced in the original *Paper Mario*, but gave us bigger and more complex battles in an adventure full of weird puzzles and bizarre paper characters. The series is still going strong, too, with 2020's *The Origami King*.

NEW SUPER MARIO BROS. 2006

Mario had made his mark on 3D games, but some of us wondered if he'd ever get back to his 2D roots. That's exactly what he did in *New Super Mario Bros.* on the Nintendo DS, and it must be said that he did it in style. This game took all the best bits from the classic Mario titles and made them bigger, better, and crazier than ever before, with super-size bad guys and even a giant-size Mario to stomp them. So started a whole new series of superb New Super Mario Bros. games.

SUPER MARIO GALAXY 2007

The arrival of the Nintendo Wii made things tough for Mario. As if making Mario work in 3D wasn't hard enough, Nintendo now had to make a Mario game that used the motion-sensitive Wii remote. Luckily, *Super Mario Galaxy* was a triumph, with our hero blasting into space to explore tiny planets, each with their own enemies, gadgets, and bosses. You could use Sling Stars to travel vast distances or spin your way up and down poles. *Super Mario Galaxy* has all the great ideas.

SUPER MARIO ODYSSEY 2017

Mario never stops working overtime for a brilliant game, and *Odyssey* is one of the plucky plumber's best. It's just as inventive as *Super Mario Galaxy* and just as much fun to explore as *Super Mario 64* or *Super Mario World*. It also gave us a brand-new Mario concept, with the cap you could throw to eliminate enemies or use to possess them for a while. Whether this is the first Mario you play or just the latest, it's another Mario all-time great.

SACKBOY: A BIG ADVENTURE

BECOME THE KNITTED KNIGHT AND FIGHT EVIL

Sackboy has become one of PlayStation's biggest heroes—so it's high time he had his name in the title of a game. The LittleBigPlanet series was always a bit less about the action than it was about its DIY gaming, but *Sackboy: A Big Adventure* is every bit a classic 3D platform game. What's more, it's an absolute blast, proving that your favorite zip-mouthed, sackcloth urchin has what it takes to stand shoulder to shoulder with Sonic, Mario, Crash, and the rest.

This time he's up against Vex, the fiendish lord of fear and chaos, who has kidnapped all Sackboy's fellow sacklings and forced them to build a device that will transform their planet of imagination into a world of nightmares. Only Sackboy can stop him, but has he got the stuffing for the fight?

QUICK TIPS

GRAB ON!

■ Grabbing plays a big part in Sackboy's antics, so if you see a spongey surface, grab it. It might be a wheel or a platform you can hold on to, or something you can pull to reveal something secret.

ROLL WITH IT

■ Sackboy's roll move is handy for getting through small spaces, but it's also great for dodging enemies. He's faster when he's rolling than running on his feet—very useful in the time trial levels.

SEARCH FOR SECRETS

■ Each level is crammed with secret collectibles and hidden areas, so keep your eye out for anything suspicious. Sometimes, flicking a switch or knocking down a cardboard box is all it takes.

SOFT FABRICS, NERVES OF STEEL

Sackboy might not have Mario's acrobatic skills or Sonic's awesome speed, but beneath that cloth exterior beats the heart of a mighty hero. After all, he's got all the qualities a hero needs.

COURAGE

Sackboy will stop at nothing to become the Knitted Knight of legend and stop Vex. Take on the optional Knitted Knight trials to prove you've mastered Sackboy's skills.

RHYTHM

Does Sackboy dance? You betcha! In fact, you'll need a sense of rhythm for some of the game's best levels, where you'll jump, dodge, and roll to the beat of brilliant disco tracks.

STYLE

You can still turn Sackboy into your own creation by collecting outfits and costume parts and dressing the little guy up. There's even a shop where you can buy and try on the latest fashions.

TIMING

Sackboy starts off easy, but it gets pretty tricky as the game goes on. You'll have to watch how the platforms shift and how your enemies move if you want to get through the tougher levels.

AST ACT

Sackboy made his dazzling debut in *LittleBigPlanet* in 2008. His original creators, Media Molecule, went on to make one sequel and the ingenious game creator, *Dreams*.

LIKE THIS? TRY THIS:

YOOKA-LAYLEE AND THE IMPOSSIBLE LAIR

Some of the brains behind classic Rare platformers like *Donkey Kong Country* and *Banjo-Kazooie* created this amazing game. The first Yooka-Laylee is a whole lot of fun as well!

CRASH BANDICOOT 4: IT'S ABOUT TIME

JOIN THE MANIC MARSUPIAL ON A CRAZY JOURNEY THROUGH TIME AND SPACE

Crash Bandicoot is back on the scene—and so are his old enemies, Neo Cortex, Dr. Nefarious, and Uka Uka. They've busted out of their prison in the past and are opening up dimensional rifts, linking up worlds from different universes and different times in a bid to conquer them all. Only Crash and his sister, Coco, can top them, with the aid of the mystic Quantum Masks.

Each Mask gives Crash or Coco different powers, and they'll need them all to get through some of the most fearsome levels of any recent platform game. As well as deadly traps and evil enemies, he'll have to deal with a mad Mardi Gras, dinosaurs, and dragons. Have you got the "N. Sane" skills to get the bandicoot through?

QUICK TIPS

SLIDE BEFORE YOU JUMP

Want to reach the highest fruits or make it to a higher platform? Slide before you double-jump and you'll get some extra height.

GO MODERN

You can play in Classic or Modern styles, and Modern is much easier. With Classic, you only have so many lives, and when they're gone, it's game over! Take the Modern option when you're starting out.

KNOW YOUR CRATES

Watch out for the red TNT crates, which explode on any spin attack (or three seconds after Crash or Coco jumps on them), and the green ones, which are poisonous to bandicoots.

MASKS AND MAYHEM

MASTER THE MASKS

Every level features sections where you'll wear one of the four Quantum Masks. These phase objects in and out of existence, slow down time, flip gravity, or give Crash's spin a boost. Get some practice with each one and learn how to use it—things only get tougher in the later stages.

ENJOY THE RIDE

While there's plenty of tricky 2D and 3D platforming, some of *Crash 4*'s best bits see you racing into the screen on weird contraptions, or getting chased out of it by some monstrous machine! You've got to keep moving, dodge the death traps, and use any boosts you can, or your bandicoot buddy won't survive!

WAYS TO REPLAY

One of the best things about *Crash 4* is that you can keep replaying the levels with different heroes. Tawna has a grapple hook and wall-jumping skills, while Neo Cortex has an air dash move and an enemy-transforming gun. You can even play levels flipped upside down in an N Verted Mode.

FAST FACT

The original *Crash Bandicoot* was an early hit for Sony's first PlayStation. Its makers, Naughty Dog, went on to create the Jak & Daxter and Uncharted games.

LIKE THIS? TRY THIS:

CRASH BANDICOOT N. SANE TRILOGY

Missed out on Crash's classic outings? You can go back and play the bandicoot's first three games in one rollicking remaster. Just be warned: These games are great but really tough!

Psychonauts 2 A journey inside one weird mind

Psychonauts 2 is full of freaky moments, from levels based inside the brains of deranged dentists to psychic abilities that give you the power of mind over matter. It's what you expect in a game about elite psychic agents trained to enter the unconscious minds of other men and women. All the same, nothing can prepare you for a level that sends you into the mind of a brain that's been stuck in a jar for over twenty years!

Get the old band back together

This brain holds information that our hero Raz needs to foil a dastardly plot. But to get it, he'll have to reunite the mind with its five senses, symbolized by a 1960s rock band where the singer has an eyeball for a head.

FAST FACT

Your partner in this level is a tiny spark of light, voiced by Jumanji star and all-round legend Jack Black. It's the third game he's worked on with Double Fine Productions, the team behind *Psychonauts*, *Broken Age*, and *Brütal Legend*.

Take the rainbow road

■ The rainbow bridges link the different parts of this crazy world together and tie in to its musical theme. Each color in the rainbow plays its own musical note as you move along it.

Float like a butterfly, climb like a chimp

■ Tracking down the band and getting them what they need pushes Raz's platforming skills to their limit, not to mention his psychic abilities. Luckily, floating across gaps or clambering up walls is easy for a Psychonaut—even one as inexperienced as Raz.

Let's slow things down . . .

■ Over years of being trapped alive in the jar, the brain has learned to understand time in a new way. It's gotten so incredibly bored—more bored than you've ever been in the most boring lesson from the most boring teacher in your school—that it's learned how to slow it down in a Time Bubble. And it's willing to teach Raz how!

Don't panic!

■ Raz can put his new skill to good use against this level's most fiendish enemy: the Panic Attacks. Treat them to a taste of your Time Bubble, then whack them with your telekinetic attacks. These psychological horrors have just messed with the wrong psychic guy!

SONIC SMASH HITS

We run down the spiky speedster's greatest games

It's now over thirty years since Sonic made his debut, and the lightning-fast blue hedgehog has given us some of the most legendary games ever. Sure, not all of Sonic's efforts have been worthy of their spiky star, but there's a reason why he's outlived every other 3D platform game mascot except Mario. So let's salute Sonic and his ten most awesome games.

10 SONIC ADVENTURE

1998 - DREAMCAST

■ One of the big launch titles for Sega's much-loved Dreamcast console, *Sonic Adventure* was also Sonic's first true 3D game. It might have been an odd mix of slow-paced adventure sections, mini games, and fast-paced 3D action stages, but *Sonic Adventure* had new ideas and a lot of charm. The 3D graphics were a step ahead of what you saw in the mighty *Super Mario 64*. it even had weird virtual pets you could raise.

9 SONIC SPINBALL

1993 - SEGA GENESIS

Sonic and pinball have always gone together, with some of Sonic's finest moments involving bumpers, chutes, and flippers. But *Sonic Spinball* took the idea further, making the hedgehog the star of one amazing arcade pinball game. Use the flippers to launch Sonic around the level and keep him from falling to his doom, while collecting Chaos Emeralds and smashing through the bosses at the top. Forget pinball—Spinball is four times the fun!

8 SONIC GENERATIONS

2011 - XBOX 360/ PLAYSTATION 3W

Many Sonic games have tried to mix the high-speed 2D platforming of classic Sonic with the 3D action of his later adventures, but *Sonic Generations* was the first to make it work. It took two Sonics to make it happen, though, with Classic Sonic racing through levels inspired by the early hits, while the taller, punkier Modern Sonic took on crazy hybrid 3D levels. *Sonic Generations* has aged brilliantly. It even looks and plays great today!

7 SONIC CD

1993 - SEGA CD

By 1993, Sega was preparing to release an ingenious accessory that combined the power of the Genesis console with new graphics processors and the massive storage of CD. And what better way to show it off than a new Sonic game where our hedgehog hero could travel backward and forward through time? *Sonic CD* was big, beautiful, and blessed with an amazing music soundtrack. For years, one of the rarest and most difficult to find Sonics, it's still one of the best.

6 SONIC & ALL-STARS RACING TRANSFORMED

2012 - XBOX 360 -

Sonic has always had a thing for racing, from *Sonic R* on the Sega Saturn to 2019's *Team Sonic Racing*. For the best, though, we have to go back to *Sonic & All-Stars Racing Transformed*. Look, it's basically Sonic does Mario Kart, with a cast of Sega favorites and some magnificent Sega-themed tracks, but it goes one better with a cool transform feature where your car can turn into a boat or plane. This is Sonic racing at its speediest, spikiest best.

5 SONIC AND KNUCKLES

1993 - SEGA GENESIS

Sonic and Knuckles was originally developed to be part of *Sonic 3*, but when the team started running out of time they had an ingenious idea. *Sonic 3* was released without new hero Knuckles the echidna, while *Sonic and Knuckles* was released as a "lock-on" cartridge that could connect to *Sonic 2* and *3*. It added both a new adventure and new levels or characters for each game. The new levels, new hero, and new take on Sonic's classics made Sonic and Knuckles a knockout hit!

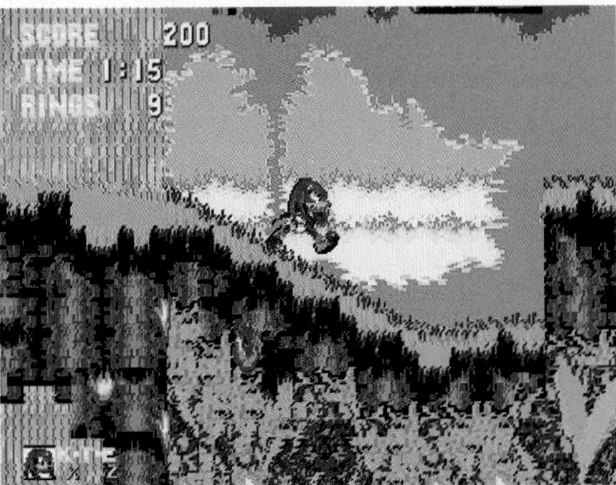

4 SONIC COLORS

2010 - NINTENDO WII - NINTENDO DS

After too many Sonic games starring too many supporting characters and featuring too many silly gimmicks, Sega took Sonic back to his punky roots with the mighty *Sonic Colors*. *Colors* mixed classic, side-scrolling action with shifts into 3D visuals and put the emphasis back on speed, springs, traps, and tricky jumping, with a range of colored wisps that gave Sonic special powers. The result was Sonic's first great game in a good ten years.

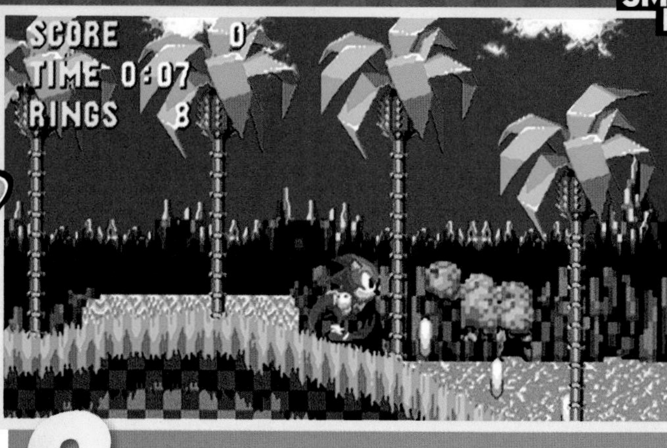

3 SONIC THE HEDGEHOG

1991 - SEGA GENESIS

The original Sonic was developed because Sega needed a mascot to compete with Mario, but Sega's star team of Yuki Naja and Naoto Ohshima produced something even more incredible: a different style of platform game with stunning graphics and an amazing sense of speed. Sonic's lightning-fast moves and spring-loaded levels created a sensation and helped make the Sega Genesis the fastest-selling console in America.

2 SONIC THE HEDGEHOG 2

1992 - SEGA GENESIS

It's not easy to follow a game as groundbreaking as the first Sonic, but *Sonic the Hedgehog 2* doubled down on everything awesome in the hedgehog's dazzling debut. As well as spectacular stages set in a chemical plant, crumbling ruins, and a casino, *Sonic 2* introduced two-player action through a second character, Tails the two-tailed fox. And who can forget gaming's first massive launch event, Sonic Twosday?

1 SONIC MANIA

2017 - NINTENDO SWITCH - PS4 - XBOX ONE

Sonic Colors and *Sonic Generations* should have seen Sonic back on top, yet Sega seemed to drop the ball. But then came Sonic superfan developer, Christian Whitehead, with a game that took Sonic back to his 2D glory days. *Sonic Mania* looks and feels like an old-school Sonic, but it's even better, with fantastic levels crammed with classic Sonic moments and slick retro graphics that bring the classic look to modern consoles. If you can only play one Sonic, make it this one!

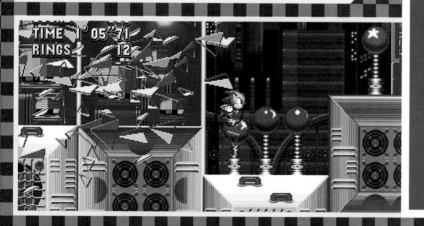

SONIC FRONTIERS

Get ready for a new style of Sonic

Sonic's back, but *Sonic Frontiers* isn't just another Sonic game. This time the hedgehog's heading in an open-world direction, with larger "open zone" levels that just scream out to be explored. The visual style is also changing. Out go the old cartoon graphics, and in comes more realistic scenery that makes you feel like Sonic's charging through an ancient fantasy world. You'd better get up to speed fast—our spiky hero is just getting started!

SONIC SPEEDS

■ Sonic might be a movie star these days, but that doesn't mean he can take it easy. Expect tough sections that will challenge his speed and your timing. Can Sonic survive this new world's threats?

EXPLORE

■ The open zones of *Sonic Frontiers* are crammed with epic waterfalls, dense forests, and mysterious ruins to discover. Just watch out. There are hostile forces out there, and some of them are massive!

NEW HORIZONS

■ We've never seen a 3D platform game with worlds that look like this. From strange shrunken lands to sunlit plains and burning deserts, *Sonic Frontiers* takes the hedgehog's adventures to a whole new level.

FAST FACT

Unlike Mario, Sonic has never been able to swim. He can only walk underwater for short periods. Yet in real life, hedgehogs can handle a quick dunking. Sonic's creators made the mistake of thinking that they couldn't.

SKATEBIRD

FORGET TONY HAWK—HERE'S A LITTLE BIRD WITH SERIOUS SKILLS!

When your big buddy's feeling too sad to skate, what's a little bird to do? How about building a pint-size skatepark and getting all the coolest local birds to check it out? The more you find, the more little parks you'll track down—and the more chance you have of inspiring your oldest friend to turn their life around!

It's a great little background story for a great little skateboarding game, and Skatebird has all the awesome tricks, chains, and high-scoring combos you'd find in a classic *Tony Hawk's Pro Skater*. You'd better bring your A game on the board, as the tricks get tough. But it's also got a lot of heart and charm. These little feathered fellas know how to grind!

QUICK TIPS

FLAP THOSE FEATHERS

■ Your little skatebird has one advantage over human skaters—wings. You can use them to get some extra height or airtime, so flap like crazy when you're building up a score chain.

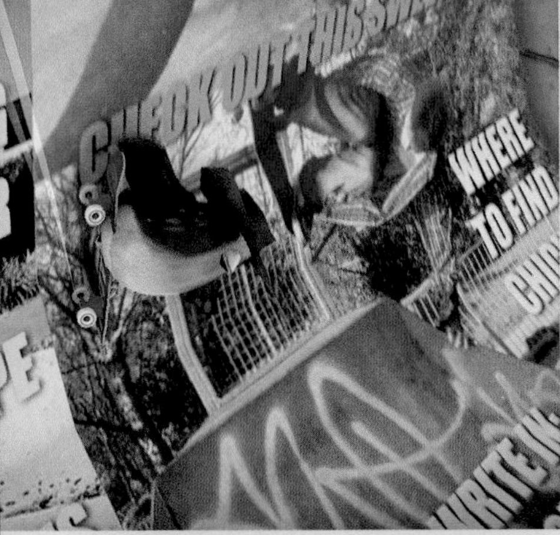

WORK THOSE COMBOS

■ The more tricks you can pull off in a row, the higher your score multiplier rises. Build it up and keep adding more tricks to the chain, but be careful: one false move and you're back to x1.

LOOK FOR LINES

■ Instead of just moving from one trick to another, look for lines you can use to build up a massive score. Hit the quarter pipes to build up speed and grind the bendy straws for all they're worth.

SKATE OR FLY

■ Out tiny feathered skaters need their own mini skate parks, but give them the chance and you'll be amazed by the tricks these little birds can pull off.

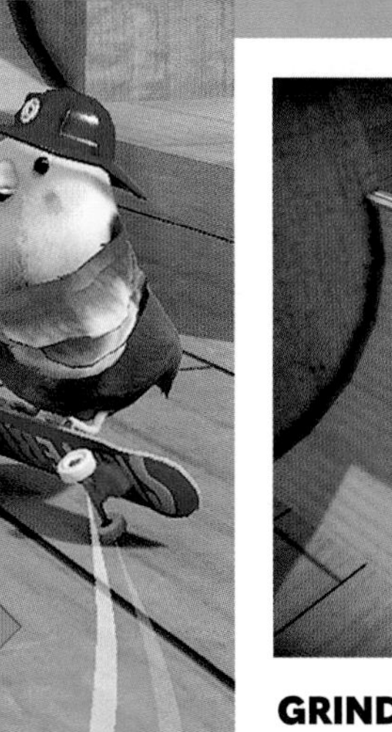

RIDE THE BOARD

■ Birds balance on the board just like a human skater, so you can pull off all the regular kickflips, heelflips, manuals, and shuvits to start racking up those points.

GRIND THE RAILS

■ With a little crafting, everyday objects become the elements of a skatepark. Staplers and bendy straws make rails to grind, while cardboard sheets and magazines become a quarter-pipe or half-pipe.

GET SOME AIR

■ You can use the ramps and half-pipes to pull off all kinds of drops, grabs, and twists. You can also use the edge to slide and grind.

THIS BIRD MEANS BUSINESS

■ Getting tired of your apartment skatepark? Keep playing to unlock awesome new skateparks that take you skating in the office or out onto the rooftops, where the pigeons peck around.

FAST FACT

Skatebird began as a demo for a skateboarding game featuring a skateboard without a rider. Developer Megan Fox had seen a video with a real bird on a tiny skateboard and had the crazy idea to combine the two!

LIKE THIS? TRY THIS:

SESSION

■ Looking for a serious skateboarding sim? Give *Session* a spin. It's designed to be the most authentic skateboarding game out there, with dual stick controls that re-create the thrills and challenges of skating around the world's most legendary spots.

NICKELODEON ALL-STAR BRAWL

ALL YOUR NICK FAVORITES ARE LINING UP TO FIGHT!

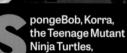

SpongeBob, Korra, the Teenage Mutant Ninja Turtles, Danny Phantom, Lincoln Loud, Aang: which Nickelodeon stars do you think would win in a fight? The answer might be more complicated than you think, at least according to *Nickelodeon All Star-Brawl*. In these two-to-four-player rumbles, just about anything can happen.

This is basically *Super Smash Bros.* with a Nickelodeon cast, but don't let that worry you: The action is as frantic and furious as it comes. With a roster that keeps on growing, new stages, and a range of modes, this one's going to keep you entertained for months!

QUICK TIPS

LEARN THE BASICS

■ The fighting can get crazy very quickly with four fighters on the screen, so make sure you know the basics first. Use the training and practice in the Arcade mode before you even think about battling online.

RECOVER

■ How you recover from a heavy attack can be the difference between winning and losing. Hone your double-jump technique and timing to stay in the fight when you're being booted out.

COUNTER RANGED ATTACKS

■ Don't just stand there and soak up ranged attacks. Use your block or grab moves on the projectiles and you can stop them hitting you—or even return them to their sender.

IT'S TIME TO BRAWL!

Ready to rumble? Pick the battle mode, and you can play on your own or with up to three friends. You can also choose between the standard "stock" and timed matches or the soccer-inspired Sports mode.

PICK YOUR FIGHTER

The game launched with a choice of twenty champions, including stars from *SpongeBob Squarepants*, *Avatar: The Last Airbender*, *Rugrats*, *The Wild Thornberries*, and *Lincoln Loud*. The Shredder and Garfield have been added on since.

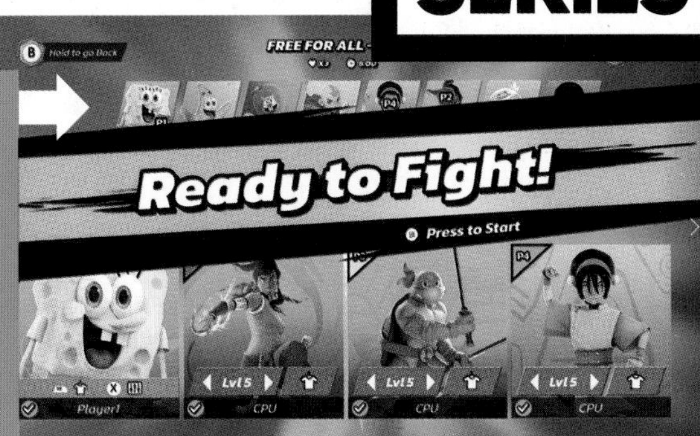

MASTER THE MOVES

Every character has their own special moves that fit into certain strategies and play styles. Korra is super-agile and a combo queen, while Lucy Loud is fast and has some meaty special moves. If you want a good all-rounder, give SpongeBob a spin.

IT'S A KNOCKOUT!

As in *Smash Bros.*, knocking the other players out of the arena is the name of the game. Use your attacks to push up the other fighters' damage percentage, then hit them hard to smash them off the platform and out of recovery range.

SECRETS OF THE STAGES

The different stages also feature unique challenges. Some have complex layouts, moving platforms, elements that can launch or damage you, and other nasty stuff. Learn the stages and use this to your advantage.

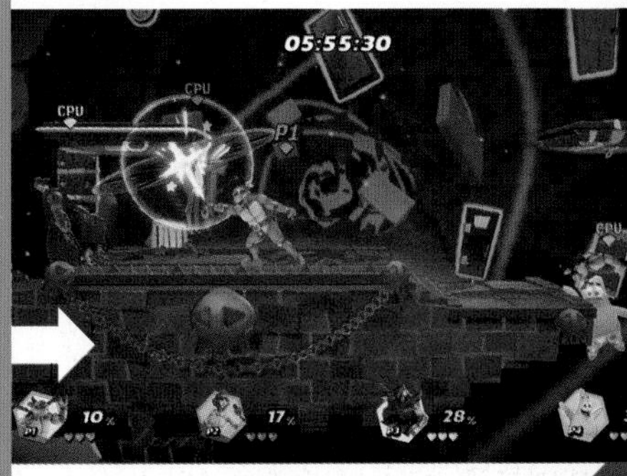

FAST FACT

There are over twenty levels to fight in, each one modeled after a familiar place from one of the characters' cartoons. SpongeBob, for example, has three stages: the Flying Dutchman, the Glove World theme park, and the Jellyfish Fields.

LIKE THIS? TRY THIS:

NICKELODEON KART RACERS 2: GRAND PRIX

Prefer driving to fighting? Play your favorite Nick heroes in this cool, erm, tribute to *Mario Kart*. With some fantastic courses and an awesome lineup of racers, it's one of the cooler clones.

BRAWL BETTER IN NICKELODEON ALL-STAR BRAWL

Don't fumble when it's time to rumble

It might look like a cute cartoon fighting game for kids, but *Nickelodeon All-Star Brawl* is serious stuff. It's already building a reputation in the world of e-sports, and it has surprisingly complex game mechanics and the same online features as some of the biggest beat-em-ups around! Want to win against your friends or make an impact in the competitions? This is how you need to do it!

1 Get some air

Mobility is king in *All-Star Brawl*, so keep jumping between platforms and using aerial attacks and air dash moves. You're going to get countered and hurled into the air, but that's just part of the game. In fact, the most crucial skill in the game is recovering before you fly off the edge of the screen. Jump once, jump twice, and grab on to a platform for dear life!

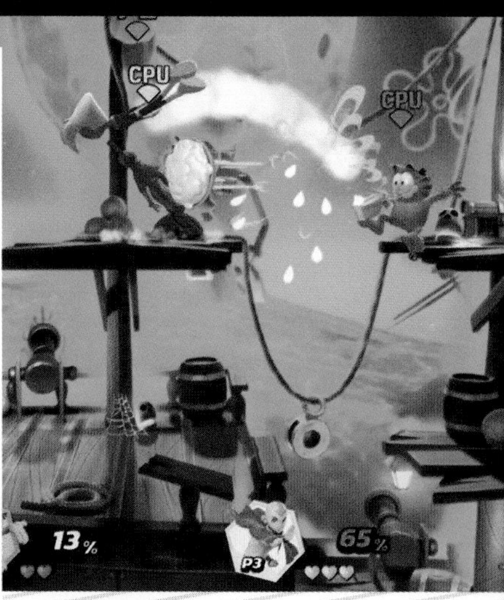

2 Smash and grab

Grabbing moves are often underestimated, and some characters—especially Patrick—are built around grappling. Grab opponents in the air or when they're hanging off a ledge, or grab projectiles and throw them back for extra damage. Patrick even has a Grapple Dive mode he can use to smash opponents into the ground or off the bottom of the stage. It's crazy, but it can help Patrick win!

3 Watch your position

Positioning is everything, and you want to be in the center of a platform, facing toward the side of the stage and smashing your opponents out toward their doom. Try and command the best, central positions. Watch out, too, if using moves like the Turtles' shell spins, that you're not going to lose control and fall off the platform into the void. It's a rookie error!

4 Uppercut and juggle

■ Uppercut moves are great for knocking your opponents off their feet and into the air, where they are weaker. But why stop with just the one upward smash? Jump up after them and hit them with a follow-up move, or try to juggle them with repeated uppercuts and kicks. That way, they soak up a lot of damage, then get booted off the stage.

5 Killer moves

■ Each cartoon champ has one or two killer moves that are guaranteed to smash a weak opponent right out of the park. Use the Arcade mode to find and practice these moves so that you can pull them out of the bag when you need them. It's a shame to lose a match in the last stages because you can't quite find that knockout punch!

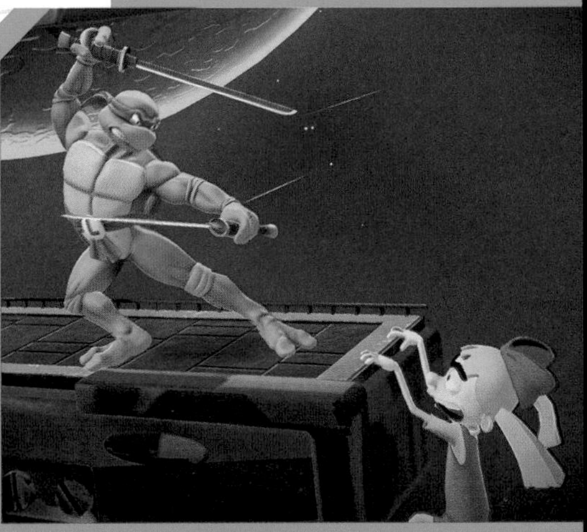

FAST FACT

SpongeBob SquarePants is the longest-running Nickelodeon toon still in production. It's been going strong since 1999!

Top-Tier Heroes

■ As with all serious fighting games, fans have some strong opinions over which fighters are stronger or weaker. In *All-Star Brawl*, Aang, Leonardo, Lucy Loud, Sandy Cheeks, and Oblina are widely reckoned to be the toughest competitors, while Michelangelo is so overpowered that he's actually banned in some tournaments. Avoid Helga, Toph, and Danny Phantom unless you want a challenge, while Patrick only works if you practice his wrestling style.

Multiversus

You won't believe who's fighting in this multiverse of madness!

■ Nintendo's Super Smash Bros. series has created some crazy crossover smackdowns, but it hasn't got anything on this Warner Bros. battler. This is the game where Batman and Superman can take on Shaggy and Tom and Jerry, or where Finn from *Adventure Time* can team up with Arya Stark from *Game of Thrones*, then beat up on Bugs Bunny and Harley Quinn. And with more heroes and villains coming down the line, who knows who's going to join the fight?

A Multiverse of Champions

■ *Multiversus* pulls its stars from some of the world's biggest comics, cartoons, and TV shows, including classic Warner Bros. toons, DC Comics, Adventure Time, *Scooby Doo*, *Steven Universe*, and *Game of Thrones*. You'll find them battling it out in locations like the Batcave, Jake and Finn's Treefort, and Wonder Woman's home island of Themiscyra.

FAST FACT

This isn't the first time Batman, Superman, and Wonder Woman have appeared in a fighting game. Like most DC heroes, they starred in the two Injustice games, facing off against each other and the most notorious DC villains.

Choose your look

All the characters have a choice of different looks. Put Tom and Jerry in their best cowboy or pirate gear, or get Harley Quinn back in her classic *Batman: The Animated Series* look. You can even select their emotes.

Pick your perks

You can customise your character's perks before the battle starts. It's a great way to adjust that champion to fit your own favorite play style or select some useful perks to help you turn a tough match around.

Team up or smash it out

The heart of the game is a team-based 2v2 mode, designed for cooperative online action. But you don't have to team up if you don't want to. You can also play one-on-one games or join feisty four-player free-for-all scraps!

IMMORTALS: FENYX RISING

TAKE ON A TITAN IN THIS AWESOME ODYSSEY

So, the dreaded Typhon—the deadliest of all Titans—has escaped his chains, beaten up the gods, ravaged the mortal world, and turned your brother to stone. Are you going to let it go down like that? As a bold shield-carrier, Fenyx, you're a new demigod in the making, on a mission to release the gods, destroy Typhon's monsters, and put that Titan bad boy back where he belongs!

It might not be the most original game ever, but *Immortals: Fenyx Rising* is a Greek myth open-world adventure, created by the team behind *Assassin's Creed: Odyssey*. While it looks and plays like *Legend of Zelda: Breath of the Wild*, it's inspired by legends that are thousands of years old.

QUICK TIPS

LYRE, LYRE

In each of the four realms, there's a pair of lyres. Learn the tune from the small one, then play it on the big one with your bow and arrows. You're guaranteed some juicy loot for the trouble.

WATCH YOUR STAMINA

You only have so much stamina, and you'll use it up quickly by attacking, dodging, swimming, gliding, or climbing. Running out can be a fatal mistake, so watch the meter and use your potions.

DODGE AND PARRY

You'll meet monsters that hit harder than Fenyx and soak up more damage, so get used to dodging and parrying their blows. A well-timed dodge or parry might leave them open to a counterattack.

SAVE THE GODS, SAVE THE WORLD

Immortals: Fenyx Rising takes place on the Golden Isle—a mythical land with different areas devoted to four of the most powerful Greek gods. Typhon has done his best to wreck the place, and his monsters roam the land. What's worse, he has hunted down the gods and transformed them!

DEITIES IN DISGUISE

It's up to you to release the gods, tracking them down and restoring their legendary essence. They might not be what you're expecting. Aphrodite, goddess of beauty and love, has become a tree. And check out what's happened to Athena, the goddess of wisdom.

BEAT THE VAULTS

Some of the game's greatest treasures—and most fearsome foes—can be found in the Vaults of Tartaros. Each is a tricky level with puzzles to solve, monsters to battle, or complex challenges to complete, but also some incredible rewards!

HERCULEAN TASKS

Restoring each god's essence means taking on a series of epic challenges and tasks. Can you roll a giant pearl down to the ocean to re-create Aphrodite's birth, or destroy the dreaded Hydra? Serve the gods and you'll receive their blessings, giving you new and more awesome perks and powers.

FAST FACT

The team came up with the idea for *Immortals* while developing *Assassin's Creed: Odyssey*. A glitch transformed the crew of a ship into monstrous cyclops, inspiring them to think about a more fantastical take on Greek mythology.

PHOSPHOR

What would any great adventure be without a pet? Early on, Fenyx saves this starving phoenix and names it Phosphor. He can help you solve puzzles and attack your enemies on command, making him just the bird buddy you need when things get rough!

MONSTERS YOU WON'T WANT TO MYTH

Cursed beasts and undead soldiers are only the easiest enemies Fenyx faces. If you want to rid the Golden Isle of Typhon, you'll have to take down some of the greatest monsters from Greek myth and legend.

THE MINOTAUR

The half man, half bull that gave Theseus a tough time is all over the Golden Isle. Watch out for the minotaur's charge, and trick it into charging something hard. Get it stunned, then slash away with your axe and sword.

THE GORGONS

Gorgons might be mean, lazy, and keen to lounge around, but they're no pushover. They can hit you from a distance with a beam of evil energy, while their tail swipe attack can knock you off your toes.

CYCLOPS

The cyclops is really big, strong, and stupid. It loves to throw rocks at Fenyx, so make sure they don't connect. Try throwing some back at the big bruiser. A charged throw can do a lot of damage!

HARPIES

These fast-flying, clawing varmints are best defeated from a distance with your bow, though they're vulnerable to a sword attack if you can get in close. Watch out for their ranged attacks and their dive bombs. If you see them coming in, dodge out of the way!

SUIT UP

Different breastplates, weapons, and helmets bring different perks into play, giving you bonus stamina as you battle, or dealing out more damage. New gear might give you the edge when you're up against a difficult enemy.

BECOME A HERO

The further you go in your quest to defeat Typhon, the tougher the enemies you meet will get. Luckily, you can upgrade Fenyx into every monster's worst nightmare with new weapons, armor, and skills.

KA-CHING!

Beat the game's different challenges to collect Coins of Charon. You can spend these at the Hall of the Gods to upgrade Fenyx's demigod powers and learn new combat skills.

MAKE A BREW

Potions can be used to heal, recharge your stamina, or boost your attack and defense, but you will need to collect the materials you'll need to make them and take them to the Cauldrons of Circe scattered through the land. With some Golden Amber, you can make your potions more effective.

COLLECT THE CRYSTALS

The different resources you collect can be spent on upgrades in the Hall of the Gods. Adamantine shards can be used to upgrade your weapons and armor, while crystals of Ambrosia boost your maximum health. Bolts of lightning, found in the vaults, upgrade your stamina.

LIKE THIS? TRY THIS:

LEGEND OF ZELDA: BREATH OF THE WILD

Saying that *Immortals* owes a lot to the last Zelda is putting it mildly, but both give you a great adventure in an epic world that's yours to explore.

STRAY

Meet the kitty in the robot city

Who would have thought that one of 2021's most exciting PS5 games would be a sci-fi adventure where you would prowl around the streets of a futuristic city as a cat. The developers were inspired by Kowloon Walled City and their love of their own cats to build a game of feline exploration and puzzle-solving, all set in a weird urban world of rain-slicked streets, neon lighting, and androids.

■ This strange city is peopled by robots, with no human beings to be found. Most of the time they'll just ignore you, but you can miaow to get their attention, and if they're nice enough, they'll help you out.

■ There's just one sign that this is no ordinary kitty: that handy little backpack. It gives you somewhere to keep small items or messages, and it's not like you'll need a change of clothes.

BIG PICTURE

You'll meet all sorts of robots, some big, some small, some friendly, and some hostile. You'll befriend one tiny flying drone, called B12, who's happy to help you on your big city kitty quest.

The gameplay mixes exploration with a little stealth and puzzle solving. Cats are naturally small and sneaky, making it easy to get into places where you really shouldn't go. Look for pathways to the rooftops and passages that can get you inside.

Your hero doesn't have superpowers, but it's as fast and sure-pawed as any real cat. It can stay low to the ground and sneak around the streets, or climb onto the rooftops to avoid the crowds.

FAST FACT

Stray's city is based on Kowloon Walled City, a chaotic complex of 300 buildings on the borders between China and Hong Kong. It didn't fall under any government's control, and with over 33,000 people crammed into a space the size of four football fields, it was one of the most crowded places on Earth.

THE YEAR'S HOTTEST MOBILE GAMES

DOWNLOAD THESE BEAUTIES FOR SOME GAMING ON THE GO

AVAILABLE ON:
■ iOS ■ Android

1 LEAGUE OF LEGENDS: WILD RIFT

■ When the world's biggest battle arena game goes mobile, you know you've got to sit up and take notice, and *Wild Rift* has everything that makes the League so great. Riot has streamlined the game, shrunk the map, and tweaked the heroes to make the action even fiercer, and you can still master your favorite heroes thanks to brilliant touchscreen controls. Go wild!

2 PLANTS VS. ZOMBIES 3

■ Dr. Zomboss is back, with his shambling undead horde, and you'll need all your have-a-go garden heroes to stop them smashing up the suburbs. PvZ 3 has all the intense action and tricky tactics you know and love, along with some new plants, zombies, and fiendish brainy bosses, and even some fun online modes. Give those zombies a taste of flower power and don't leaf any of your plants behind...

AVAILABLE ON:
■ iOS ■ Android

3

RUSH RALLY ORIGINS

■ There are some awesome mobile racers out there, but we can't get enough of this wild off-roader. *Rush Rally Origins* crams in all the mud-spattered racing madness you could want, complete with brilliant realistic physics and thirty-six tire-spinning tracks from all around the world. Grit your teeth, slide around the corners, and do your best not to spin out.

AVAILABLE ON:
■ iOS ■ Android

4

AVAILABLE ON:
■ iOS ■ Android

TOMB RAIDER: RELOADED

■ It's time to see one of gaming's greatest heroes from a new point of view in a game inspired by the original, classic Tomb Raider games. Designed from the ground up for phones, *Tomb Raider: Reloaded* gives you a top-down look at Lara Croft in action as she wipes out waves of enemies with her twin pistols and dodges traps and solves puzzles in creepy tombs and caves.

5

GENSHIN IMPACT

■ The smash-hit free RPG is just as good on mobile as it is on console, giving you epic adventures across a huge open world with a team of heroes that grows as you play. The cartoon graphics still look fantastic, and the smart hero-switching combat never gets old. Sure, there are some dodgy loot box mechanics for unlocking new characters and weapons, but don't worry: You don't have to spend a dime.

AVAILABLE ON:
■ iOS ■ Android

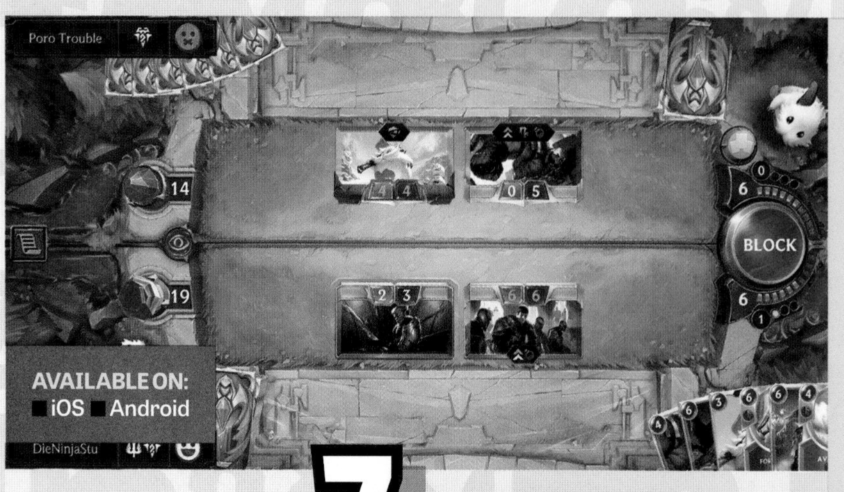

AVAILABLE ON:
■ iOS ■ Android

6 LEGENDS OF RUNETERRA

■ No collectible card battling spin-off has any right to be this good, but somehow *Legends of Runeterra* is the best game of its type since the mighty *Hearthstone* hit in 2014. Like Blizzard's deck-dueling classic, it's easy to pick up and play but incredibly challenging to master, with brilliant artwork on the cards and plenty of exciting special effects. Practice against the AI players, then take your skills online!

7 AMONG US

■ The surprise mobile hit of 2020 just keeps players coming back for more. Rooting out which players are murderous saboteurs keeps everyone guessing, and there are almost as many clever tactics to try as there are amusing *Among Us* memes. Meanwhile, updates and a clever fanbase have bought us new game modes and maps. Unlike its evil impostors, it's very much the real deal.

AVAILABLE ON:
■ iOS ■ Android

8 APEX LEGENDS MOBILE

■ One of the best battle royale games on big-screen consoles is just as amazing on the small screen, with a cut-down selection of the best-loved legends but all the fast-paced action you expect. The team at Respawn has redesigned the mobile game from the ground up, including smooth touchscreen controls. Yet it still has the guns, gadgets, abilities, and tactics of the original console hit. Against all odds, it's the real deal.

AVAILABLE ON:
■ iOS ■ Android

AVAILABLE ON:
■ iOS ■ Android

9

POKÉMON GO

■ Other games have tried to copy *Pokémon Go*'s magic formula, but they fall by the wayside, while the monster-catching classic powers on for another year. Why? Because Niantic keeps on adding new features, events, and activities, and because we can't resist another raid or shiny-spotting weekend. And as the Pokémon and regions keep on coming, why would we want to?

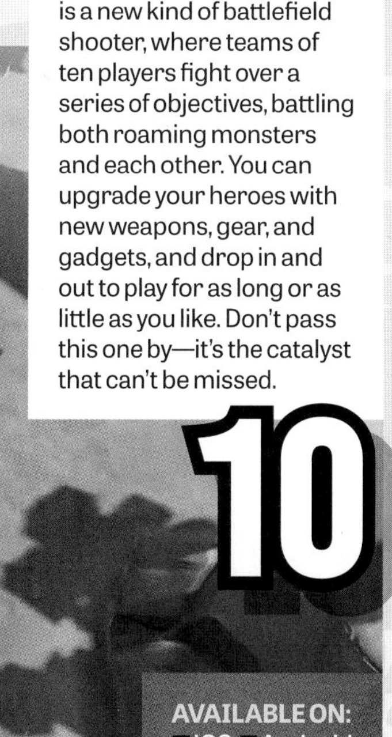

CATALYST BLACK

■ From the team that gave us *Vainglory*, *Catalyst Black* is a new kind of battlefield shooter, where teams of ten players fight over a series of objectives, battling both roaming monsters and each other. You can upgrade your heroes with new weapons, gear, and gadgets, and drop in and out to play for as long or as little as you like. Don't pass this one by—it's the catalyst that can't be missed.

10

AVAILABLE ON:
■ iOS ■ Android

FALL GUYS: ULTIMATE KNOCKOUT

THE FEEL-GOOD GAME WHERE EVERYBODY LOSES AND EVERYBODY WINS!

Fall Guys is the game that put the fun back in online gaming, in a crazy mess of knockabout stages where the only point is to make it through to the next round. Keep going while the other jelly beans fail to make the grade, and you might reach the final stage and seize the crown.

It's the game where *Super Mario* meets *American Ninja Warrior* and *Wipeout*. With more stages and more costumes coming in with each new season, it just keeps getting better. Drop in for a quick go and you'll still be playing an hour later, saying through gritted teeth, "Just one more try..."

QUICK TIPS

TAKE A DIVE

■ So many *Fall Guys* players forget about the dive, but it's a useful move for avoiding obstacles or taking back control when you've built up too much speed.

STICK AROUND AND SPECTATE

■ Don't quit the game as soon as you're eliminated; stick around, watch the action, and have a few laughs. You might even learn something about a tricky stage.

GRAB YOUR CHANCES

■ Don't be afraid to grab, either. Grab the walls and platforms to climb on up and over, or grab other players when they're pushing out in front. It's essential in some games for grabbing eggs or tails.

NO GUTS, NO GLORY!

With each new season, *Fall Guys* brings in brilliant new stages to push your jelly bean heroes harder than ever before.

PIPE DREAM

You never know what's coming next in this Season 6 race event! The tubes transport you at random between different obstacle challenges. Are you getting donut bumpers or bouncy drums?

TUNDRA RUN

The big Season 3 obstacle race is guaranteed to give your jelly bean the shivers. Make it through the snowballs, and you face giant boxing gloves, icy paths, and giant fans. Brrrrr!

STOMPIN' GROUND

You'll have to face off with angry rhinos in this screen-shaking Season 5 round. Can you stay in the arena for seventy seconds, or will the big red galoots toss you out?

FAST FACT

Fall Guys came from nowhere to sell over one and a half million copies in the first day of release and become the most downloaded monthly free PS+ game of all time!

DRESS TO IMPRESS

Do you want to send your contender out in a plain old jumpsuit? One of the joys of *Fall Guys* is its crazy costumes, with players kitting out their beans with the latest fashions, including fantasy favorites, festive winter styles, and even costumes based on the heroes and monsters of *Doom*!

HOW NOT TO FAIL AT FALL GUYS

Becoming a *Fall Guys* champion is tough. Each game starts with sixty players all looking for a win, and it's chaos out there on the field. One minute you can be out in front, the next you're being trampled from behind. It's all too easy to get knocked out of the competition long before you reach the final round.

Luckily, there are some basic tips you can use to survive the early stages and have a chance of picking up the crown. Get your game on and head for the finish line!

WATCH THE CROWDS

The biggest danger in *Fall Guys* isn't the sudden drops or fearsome obstacles but the mass of other jelly beans that threaten to swarm you, trample you, or push you off the edge. Sometimes it makes sense to follow the crowd—other players may have learned the fast way to the finish—but hanging back or taking a different route could mean less traffic and an easier path to the next round.

GO WITH THE FLOW

In stages with moving platforms and obstacles, there's usually a smoother way to make it through. Try to use rotating platforms, moving barriers, and spinning plates to get you where you need to go. Don't fighting against the level; work with what you've got.

LOOK AHEAD

It's hard when everybody's scrambling for the next section, but try to keep an eye on what's coming up next. Platforms might be moving, crowds can be building, and a see-saw section could be tilting one way or the other. Try to get yourself in the right position for the next section, and you won't get held back by an obstacle that lets other jelly beans get ahead.

STAND GUARD

The biggest challenge in the team games is working as a team, so try to see what the other beans are up to. Next, think about what you can do that they're not doing. In stages like Egg Scramble, Hoarders, and Egg Siege, there's an obvious option. Guard the eggs or balls you've captured and stop the other teams from running off with 'em!

TREAD CAREFULLY

Got Thin Ice or Hex-A-Gone as your final stage? Think where you're going and don't just run around like a kindergarten kid on a sugar rush. Jump to keep yourself in the air for some of the time and stop all tiles from disappearing, and plan your routes to keep you moving from tile to tile without getting stuck in a space with nowhere to go.

MIND TRICKS

Perfect Match is a tricky stage, as it's all about using your memory rather than your reflexes. Forget trying to remember all the fruit on every tile. Instead, focus on remembering the order of fruit on a certain column or row. And if you're stuck, just run to the tile that other players have run to. They might have a better memory than yours.

LIKE THIS? TRY THIS:

MOVING OUT

There's no other game quite like *Fall Guys*, but if you like a brilliant four-player couch co-op party game, try the mighty *Moving Out*. You play a team of movers trying to clear everything out of a series of homes. Cue a whole lot of chaos, carnage, breakages, and grumpy ghosts.

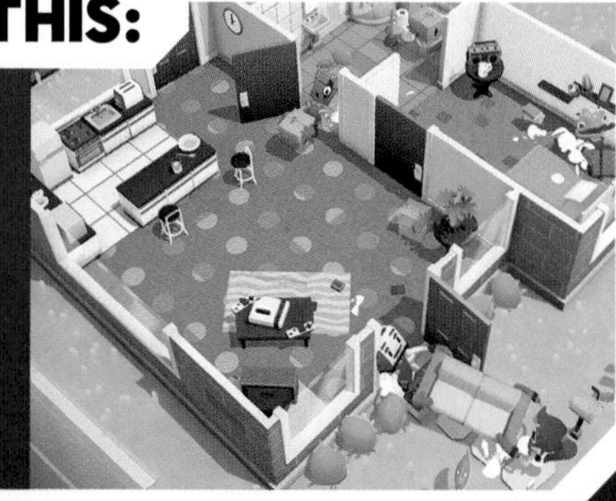

Among Us

Seven signs that scream Impostor!

■ Found a fresh body in Electrical? Think that Pink is looking sus? Nasty smell coming out of the vent in the Greenhouse? Trust your instincts and watch out! We've picked seven sure signs that someone's an Impostor in Among Us, and if you vent the wrong guy, why worry? You're sure to get it right next time . . .

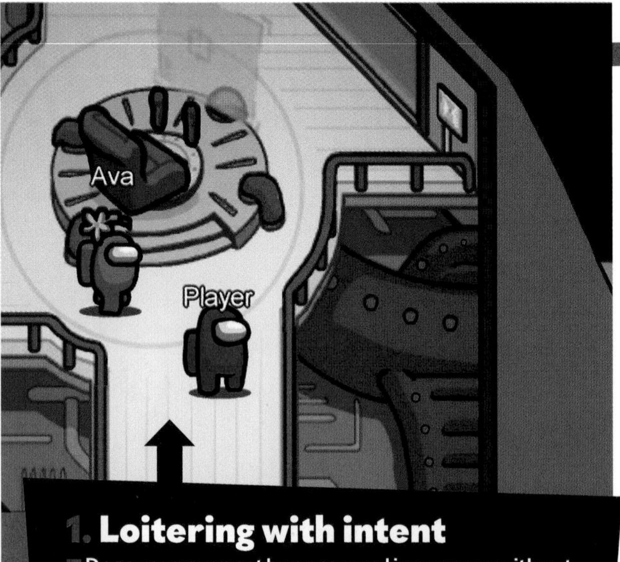

1. Loitering with intent

■ Does your suspect hang around in corners without getting involved in any tasks? Do they seem to be waiting for a quiet moment—perhaps a chance to creep in close and do you harm? If someone is lurking in a room and not moving much, they're either away from the screen or up to something.

2. Keen to vent

■ Has one of your crewmates arrived in the room, though you didn't see them come through the door? Do they seem oddly interested in the vents? Either they've just produced a nasty smell, or they're planning some vent-related action. Watch 'em, and if they pop in or out of the vents, just run!

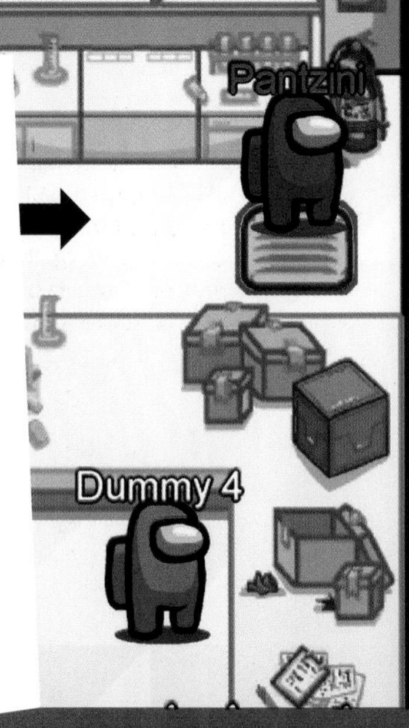

3. Getting too near

■ It never hurts to keep a bit of distance, and if a crewmate keeps getting closer, then they (a) find your new hat strangely attractive or (b) plan to kill you in a minute. Following you or chasing you is a serious no-no, but watch for anyone who gets close, then walks off as soon as there's company.

4. Slow to fix

■ If everyone else is rushing to fix something that's been sabotaged but one crewmate is missing or hanging back, put them on your suspect list. If they're not involved in a task, they might be hoping to score a kill while the crew's distracted.

5. Faking tasks

■ Does a crewmate look awful busy, yet the task completed meter isn't growing any bigger? Maybe they're faking tasks rather than actually getting them done. Call that emergency meeting and let the whole crew decide. And just hope they don't throw you through the airlock!

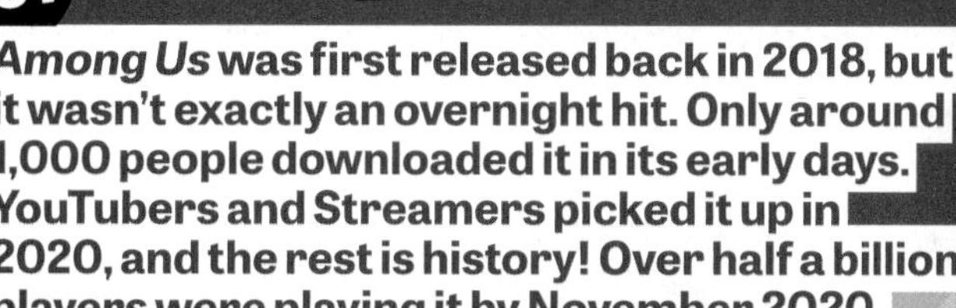

FAST FACT

***Among Us* was first released back in 2018, but it wasn't exactly an overnight hit. Only around 1,000 people downloaded it in its early days. YouTubers and Streamers picked it up in 2020, and the rest is history! Over half a billion players were playing it by November 2020.**

6. Favorite spots

■ Every map has a few favorite kill spots, like Electrical or Security in the Skald. Keep an eye out if someone seems to be spending too much time in these quiet corners with no through passages, and keep your wits about you if you're on the security console. Impostors defend their evil secrets!

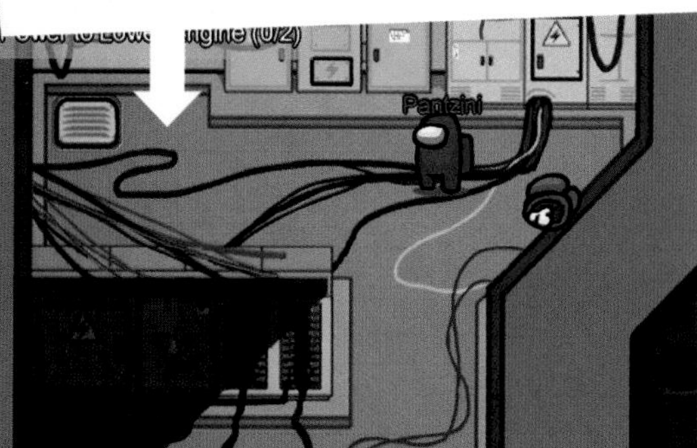

7. Fast to accuse

■ Remember the old maxim "He who smelt it, dealt it"? It's the tactic of many an Impostor, throwing out wild accusations and even calling their own corpse alerts. If someone else is getting picked out, have a good look at who is doing all the finger pointing.

HYTALE

MINECRAFT GOES DUNGEONS AND DRAGONS. NOW, THAT'S WHAT WE CALL A BLOCKBUSTER!

Sure, it looks an awful lot like *Minecraft*, but there's more to *Hytale* than another clone of the Mojang classic. Instead, it's more of a hybrid, mixing beautifully blocky graphics with the bones of an RPG adventure like *The Elder Scrolls*. There's all the monster fighting, treasure grabbing, spell-casting gimmicks you'd expect from that kind of game, but also all the building, harvesting, and crafting you love from *Minecraft*.

In fact, it's even more than that. Once you've played and replayed the built-in adventures, you can make your own and share them using *Hytale*'s awesome tools. Instead of becoming a dungeon delver, why not be the dungeon master?

QUICK TIPS

CRAFT AND UPGRADE

■ Keep upgrading your weapons and armor, but remember you can craft items to fight with or use to heal up. You might even start a nice side job in crafting useful kit for other heroes.

WORK ON YOUR SWING

■ Fighting in *Hytale* takes more skill than it does in *Minecraft*, so get some practice in. Each weapon has its own weight and speed, so swinging a club or axe feels very different to fighting with a sword.

MEET THE MOBS

■ *Hytale*'s mobs are smarter and more varied than Minecraft's simple goons—and you might not have to fight them all. Some can be distracted or befriended with gifts, while others are afraid of fire.

A WORLD OF HY ADVENTURE

Hytale isn't another sandbox survival sim, because it uses elements you know and love from Minecraft as part of an all-action RPG. It's a world where you and your friends can share epic adventures, then go on to build your own!

ENTER THE DUNGEONS

It wouldn't be an RPG if it didn't have dungeons, and Hytale uses clever procedural generation techniques to make new ones up each time you play, so that there's always a new challenge or somewhere different to explore.

GEAR UP FOR BATTLE

Like any RPG, *Hytale* keeps you coming back for more with the lure of better gear. You'll find mighty weapons and enchanted armor on your adventures, or you can use your crafting skills to make your own, progressing through the different tiers to make more and more powerful items.

EXPLORE THE BIOMES

As in Minecraft, there are different biomes, with different scenery, vegetation, resources, and—importantly—mobs. Within them you'll find different quests, but also different mounts to tame and pets to make friends with. You can even head underwater.

D&D MEETS DIY

Want to build your own adventures? *Hytale* has all the tools you need. You can build levels, add monsters, and script what happens as the players battle through. And with loads of new content and a 3D graphics editor to make more, you're not limited to fantasy games, either!

FAST FACT

The makers of *Hytale* had their start running the Hypixel Server, the home of many popular Minecraft modes and minigames. They put the proceeds into making *Hytale*, so you betcha they know what they're doing with this style of game.

LIKE THIS? TRY THIS:

MINECRAFT DUNGEONS

Hytale's great, but it's not the first Minecraft RPG. Mojang's own brilliant crossover combines the magic of Minecraft with the monster-bashing, loot-grabbing action of the classic Diablo games, making for one awesome and addictive dungeon crawl.

STAR WARS: SQUADRONS

DEFEND THE NEW REPUBLIC—OR WIPE OUT THE REBEL SCUM!

Nobody does space combat better than Star Wars, and *Star Wars: Squadrons* is the best starfighter action game in decades. Have you ever dreamed of flying an X-wing like Luke Skywalker or Poe Dameron? In *Squadrons,* you can climb into the cockpit and take part in heroic missions, helping to hijack an Imperial Star Destroyer or save a refugee fleet from destruction.

The action's set just after *Episode Six: Return of the Jedi*, as the New Republic struggles to bring order back to the galaxy after the Emperor's death. Yet in this game, you can also join the dark side, becoming a pilot in the Imperial Navy and flying TIE-fighters, bombers, and Interceptors in the hope of crushing the new rebel government. Which side are you going to choose?

QUICK TIPS

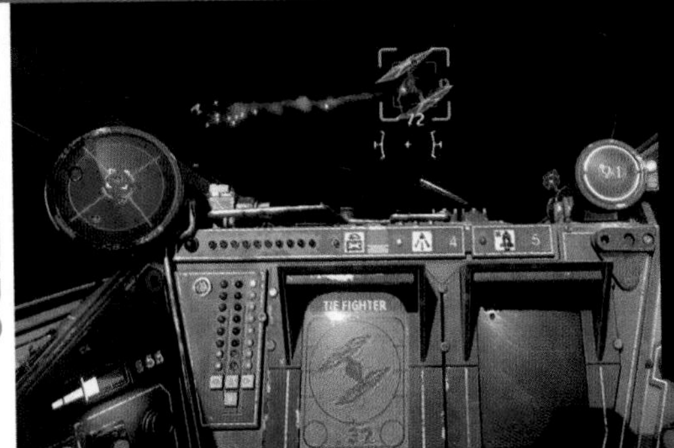

SLOW DOWN AND SHOOT

■ More speed isn't always better. When you're in a dogfight, slowing down will help you turn faster and get a solid aim on your enemy.

SYSTEMS READY

■ You'll need to keep switching power from weapons to engines to shields and back again to fly your ship away from danger or get some extra protection while you attack battleships and cruisers.

CALL IN YOUR DROID

■ When your shields go down, you can take a lot of damage. You'll even see your cockpit cracking up. Ask your droid to make emergency repairs, and don't leave it too late or you'll be going out with a bang!

IMPERIAL MIGHT VS. REBEL COURAGE

There are two sides to every war, and the main campaign keeps shifting between them. Once you join the multiplayer action, you're going to have to pick a side.

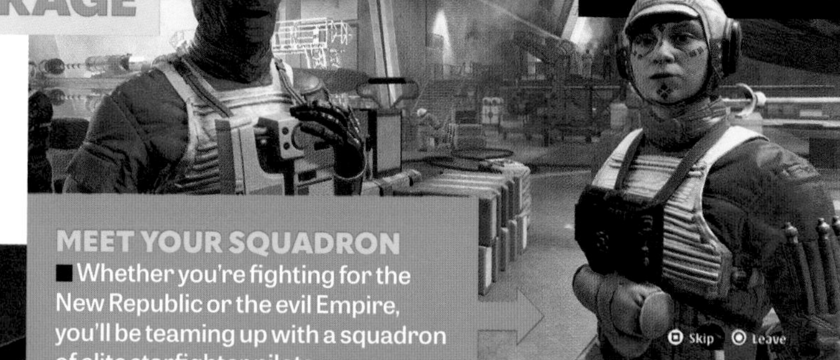

MEET YOUR SQUADRON

Whether you're fighting for the New Republic or the evil Empire, you'll be teaming up with a squadron of elite starfighter pilots.

JUMP INTO THE COCKPIT

The cockpit of every classic Star Wars ship is reproduced in incredible detail, complete with vintage Star Wars displays. If you've got the gear, you can even play *Star Wars: Squadrons* in VR.

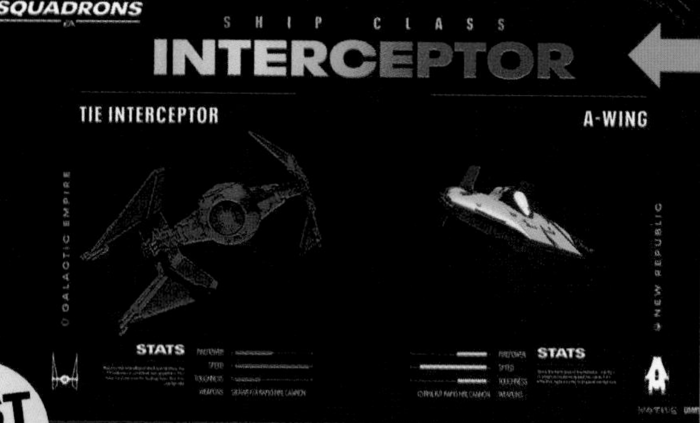

BALANCE OF THE FORCE

Each ship has its own Imperial and New Republic equivalents. TIE Interceptors and A-wings are both built for speed, while the TIE bomber and Y-wing are designed to destroy larger ships.

THE POWER OF THE DARK SIDE

The Imperial Navy has some powerful ships, ranging from the small and maneuverable TIE fighter to the super-destructive TIE bomber. Those rebel scum won't know what hit them!

AST ACT

Star Wars: Squadrons **features Wedge Antilles, the legendary X-wing pilot who's appeared in four of the Star Wars movies, the** ***Star Wars: Rebels*** **series and several previous Star Wars games.**

LIKE THIS? TRY THIS:

STAR WARS BATTLEFRONT II

If you love epic battles in the Star Wars universe, you have to play *Star Wars Battlefront II*. With years of updates on top of an amazing base game, it serves up team-based action from every Star Wars era with all the heroes, villains, and vehicles you could want.

EVERSPACE 2

HEAD OUT INTO THE COSMOS ON YOUR OWN SPACE ODYSSEY

Sure, it hardly looks retro, but *Everspace 2* is a glorious throwback to the days when space exploration wasn't all about harvesting resources or trading, but about being a hotshot space fighter pilot with an itchy trigger finger, too many laser cannons, and zero interest in playing things safe. It was about taking on a squadron of space pirates single-handedly, blasting them to bits, collecting the bounty, and spending it on a brand-new starship with even bigger guns.

Well, with *Everspace 2* the good old days are back again, and there's a whole galaxy of action to discover, with an epic sci-fi story line to pull it all together. Grab a ship, equip it with shields and weapons, then get out there and take out the interstellar trash...

QUICK TIPS

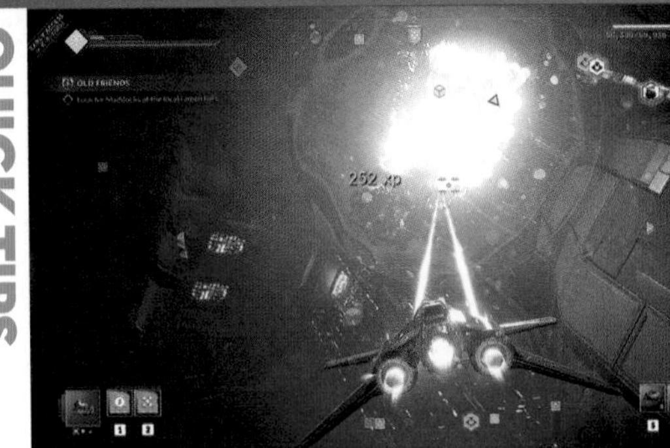

SWITCH WEAPONS

■ Some of your guns do plenty of energy damage, which is good for shields, but for armor you'll need some serious kinetic firepower. Try to fit one of each type of weapon and switch between them to destroy the shields, then the armor.

NO RUSH!

■ You might want to get to your next mission location quickly, but the other destinations that pop up on your screen could hold secret areas or lurking pirates—or even a rich source of useful loot and ship upgrades. Don't rush past, but stop and take a look.

DON'T WASTE THAT SPECIAL

■ Special abilities take time to charge up, so don't throw them away on basic enemies you can defeat with normal weapons. Save them for heavily armored ships or a situation where you're outnumbered and outgunned.

VICIOUS CYCLE

In a lot of ways, *Everspace 2* is closer to a "looter shooter" game like *Destiny 2* than it is a conventional space combat game. You need to upgrade your ship to beat tougher enemies, and you need to beat the tougher enemies to grab more loot to upgrade with!

DEADLY DOGFIGHTS

The heart of the game is its action-packed missions, where you take on groups of enemy ships in deep-space combat. Destroy their ships, then harvest their loot.

UPGRADE YOUR GEAR

With a hold full of cash and cargo to sell, you can stop off at a base or trading outpost and buy weapons, gadgets, and ship upgrades. Kit your ship out to match the way you like to play!

SWAP YOUR RIDE

There's also more than one ship to fly. Ships fit into five different classes, with different strengths and weaknesses and special abilities. Finding a mission tough? Switching ships to something heavier or faster could give you the edge you need.

TAKE ANOTHER MISSION

There's more than one type of mission. You could be battling bandits in an asteroid field one minute, then skimming over alien worlds the next. Some even take place inside deep-space mines. Watch the paintwork!

FAST FACT

In the original *Everspace* you played one of a series of clones, each one sent out to complete the current mission when the old one died. In the sequel, you're on your last clone "life," and you've got one big, epic adventure to get through in one piece!

LIKE THIS? TRY THIS:

NO MAN'S SKY

If you'd rather explore distant worlds than dogfight with enemy starfighters, *No Man's Sky* is the game for you. There are millions of planets to explore, each with their own creatures and secrets to discover, and you have the freedom to trade, build, or battle in a sci-fi universe that's always evolving.

Hyrule's Mightiest Heroes

Meet the stars of *Hyrule Warriors: Age of Calamity*

Link: Defender of Hyrule

Link needs no introduction. While he's had many identities and many forms, he always grows to become the hero of a Zelda game. In *Hyrule Warriors: Age of Calamity*, he's a bold knight of Hyrule armed with sword, shield, and bow. His powerful slashes scatter his enemies left and right, while his super attack is a swipe strong enough to knock down his biggest foes.

FAST FACT

***Hyrule Warriors: Age of Calamity* gives us a chance to get to know Hyrule's heroes before its fall. It also features Hestu, the giant Korok who helps Link out in *Breath of the Wild* in return for Korok seeds.**

Zelda: The Princess with the Power

Princess Zelda wields the power of the Sheikah Slate, using its powers to freeze her foes in time, hit them with bombs or magnetic energy, or block their charges with a pillar of ice. The other heroes can harness the same powers, but Zelda takes them to another level, decimating Ganon's forces in their legions with shattering blows.

Daruk, Mipha, Revali, Urbosa: Legendary Champions

The four great Champions of Hyrule return for *Age of Calamity*, giving fans a chance to see them fighting in their prime. Daruk the Goron, Mipha the Zora, Revali the Rito, and Urbosa of the Gerudo all have their own fearsome weapons and abilities, making them formidable allies on the battlefields of Hyrule.

Impa: Protector of the Royal Family

Impa is a warrior of the mysterious Sheikah tribe, armed with knives, magical abilities, and all the powers of a ninja. She can clone herself in battle, creating a one-woman army of shadow soldiers to tear through the enemy ranks.

HELLO NEIGHBOR 2

THE NEW GUY ON THE BLOCK IS TWICE AS SCARY

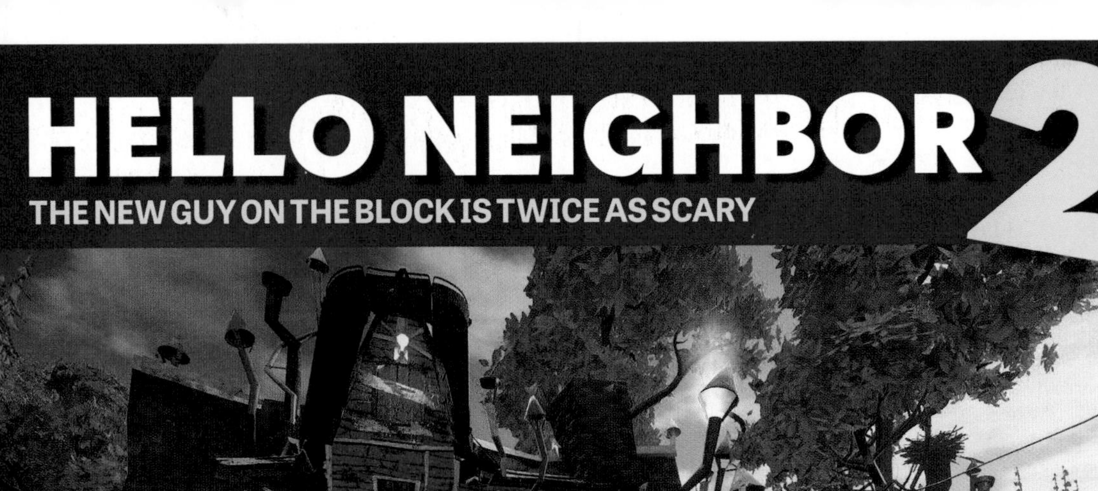

Hide under the covers and call for your mom—the new Hello Neighbor is even scarier than the first one! You're on a mission to track down Mr. Peterson, your twisted neighbor from the original game. But now there's a new menace in the suburbs. A creepy dude in a crow mask is up to something awful, kidnapping kids on Halloween and building something in his house. You need to find out what he's up to, and how your old neighbor is involved.

Get ready for a challenge. This is a much bigger game, with the whole suburb of Raven Brooks to explore, and the area has more than one weird guy with something to hide. You could be in danger everywhere you go! Scared? You should be . . .

QUICK TIPS

SLOW THEM DOWN

If you're chased, slow your pursuer down. Throw something to knock him back or trip him up, or find a gate and bar it closed. Think fast, though. He'll recover and find his own way through.

LISTEN UP

Just like in the first game, you need to use your ears. You can track the town's bad guys through their footsteps and work out when they are getting closer—or keeping busy in a room above.

FIND A PLACE TO HIDE

Bad dude on your tail? The houses and outside areas of Raven Brooks are full of places to hide. Jump in a cupboard, hide behind a curtain, or look for a passage to crawl into. Sit still and wait it out.

WELCOME TO RAVEN BROOKS

Where *Hello Neighbor* took place in and around a small suburban block, the sequel takes you out into the wider world of Raven Brooks. And now you're in danger outside the Neighbor's house, with bad guys who can follow your every move.

INVESTIGATE AND EXPLORE

Raven Brooks is a pretty big place, with different houses and stores to search through, and even the ruins of a fairground and a railroad. Look around. There could be clues to help you solve the mystery.

YOU'RE BEING WATCHED

The crow guy is one smart cookie. He's got his own daily routine to follow and his lair to protect, but he'll keep an eye on where you go and how you get there. Don't be surprised if he learns your tricks and sets up a surprise. Try not to shriek!

CRANKY NEIGHBORS

It's not just the creepy crow guy that you have to watch out for. Some of the other citizens have their own dark secrets and obsessions, and they won't take kindly to you poking your nose around. Worse, rumor has it that a certain Mr. Peterson is coming back to town...

FAST FACT

***Hello Neighbor* came from nowhere in 2016 to become a mini-franchise, with two spin-off games, *Secret Neighbor* and *Hello Neighbor: Hide & Seek*, and even its own animated series.**

LIKE THIS? TRY THIS:

GYLT

Launched as a Google Stadia exclusive, this spooky stealth game hasn't had the audience it deserves. It's gorgeous-looking, smart, and seriously creepy. One of the best scary games to stream.

INSIDE INDIE GAMES

The small teams making incredibly good games

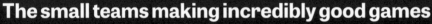

In case you haven't noticed, indie games are big news these days. Games like *Hades*, *Death's Door*, and *No Man's Sky* are beating games from the biggest names in gaming to win awards, while *Fall Guys: Ultimate Knockout* broke records as the most downloaded game ever on PlayStation Plus. Think of some of the big surprise hits of the last few years—*Among Us*, *Hello Neighbor*, *Rocket League*, *Stardew Valley*—they all started out as indie games.

■ What do all these games have in common? They don't come from massive studios with huge teams and budgets, but from smaller teams of developers and artists, and sometimes just a handful of enthusiastic game makers. But because they have more freedom to create their own games and try their own ideas, they are able to produce really smart and innovative games. Sometimes, these games are so clever or exciting that they make you grin from ear to ear.

HOW DID INDIE GAMES GET STARTED?

Back in the early days of home computing, before Sega and Nintendo launched their consoles, most games were indie games. Often one guy, or a small group of coders, would make their own games and sell them directly to their fans. Over time, the more successful coders would start a bigger business or start working with a larger company, who would fund and publish their games. That's a big part of how the whole games industry got started.

Eventually, the costs involved in making games and getting them into stores made it difficult for smaller teams to do it, but in the mid-2000s, this started to change. The internet made it easier to sell games that players could download, while Steam on the PC gave indie game makers a store where they could sell their software. Soon the console makers were getting in on the act, with Xbox Live Arcade, the PlayStation Network Store, and Nintendo's stores on the DS and Wii.

Things really took off with the arrival of games like *Braid* (2008) and *Minecraft* (2009), which won a larger audience and sometimes made their makers very rich. In a way, history was repeating. Almost anyone could make and sell a game, and—before you knew it—some of the best games coming out were indie games.

HOW ARE INDIE GAMES MADE?

Some indie games are built by a tiny team of people, with one person writing all the code that runs the game and others designing levels or creating the art and music. Others are made using existing game engines, such as Unity or Unreal Engine, for the core of the game. Others still use special game-making utilities, like GameMaker: Studio or Construct. Finally, some work just like regular game studios, with teams of artists, coders, designers, and testers—only on a much smaller scale.

It doesn't matter, really. What makes an indie game an indie game is that it's developed by a small team, not one belonging to a major publisher, and that its creators have the freedom to try out their own ideas.

FAST FACT

***Minecraft* is the undisputed most successful indie game of all time. With over 200 million copies sold across every computer, phone, and console you can think of, it's going to be hard to beat!**

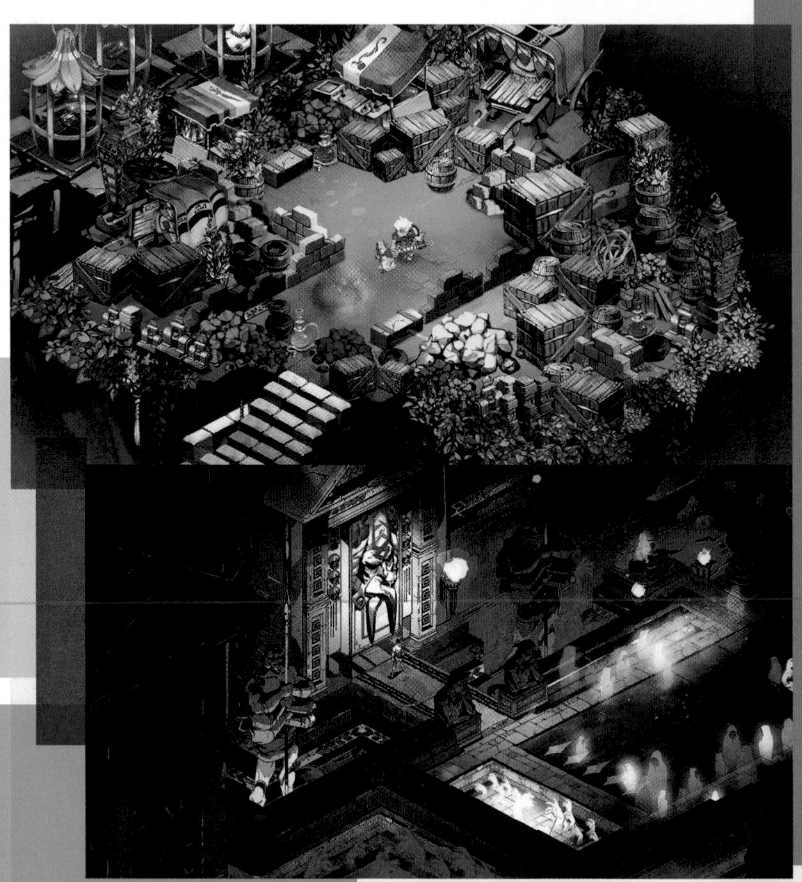

INDIE SUPERSTARS: SUPERGIANT GAMES

■ Supergiant Games was formed by Amir Rao and Gavin Simon in 2009. Both worked for Electronic Arts but decided to quit their jobs and create their own game. Working with musicians, programmers, and developers, they made *Bastion*: an amazing action-RPG with an ingenious voice-over that commented on everything you did in the game. They followed it up with a similar game in a science-fiction world, *Transistor*, and a weird RPG with a sports twist, *Pyre*.

■ In 2020, Supergiant released its best game yet—the ace Greek mythology dungeon crawler *Hades*. It won a bunch of Game of the Year awards and sold millions of copies. Not bad for a small team with fewer than twenty people!

INDIE SUPERSTARS: ACID NERVE

■ Mark Foster and David Fenn make up Acid Nerve, a tiny two-man team based in Manchester, England. To make their debut game, *Titan Souls*, they brought in a single outside artist. A retro-style 2D adventure that focused on battling hulking bosses, it became a hit with fans and game reviewers and made Acid Nerve an indie studio to watch.

■ In 2021, they delivered on their potential with *Death's Door*, a game that fused the team's love of the classic Legend of Zelda series with their love of British humor and Studio Ghibli movies. *Death's Door* was widely talked about as one of the top games

INDIE SUPERSTARS: YACHT CLUB GAMES

Based in Los Angeles, Yacht Club Games is best known as the creator of the Shovel Knight series. The original game, a brilliant side-scrolling platformer, came out in 2014 on the PC, Wii, and Nintendo 3DS, and since then has appeared on nearly every console going. Yacht Club has followed up with more campaigns for the original game, plus spin-offs like *Shovel Knight Pocket Dungeon*, *Shovel Knight Showdown*, and *Shovel Knight Dig*. Its newest game is *Mina the Hollower*, a new retro dungeon crawl adventure with a cool, creepy horror twist.

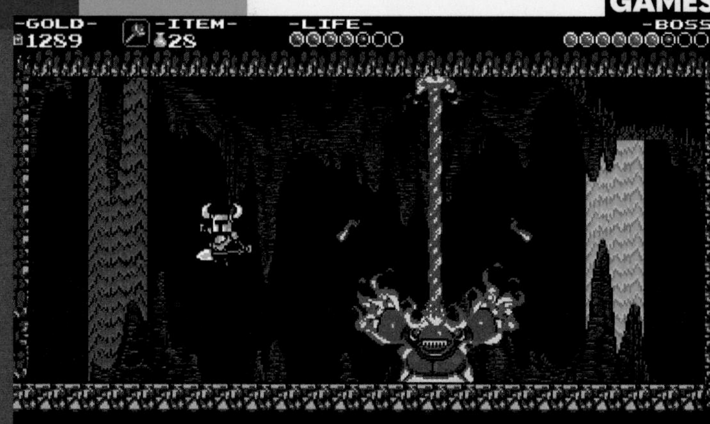

BEHIND THE GAME

Want to know where *Fall Guys* came from? We spoke to Stephen Taylor, technical director for Mediatonic.

"The original idea behind *Fall Guys: Ultimate Knockout* really goes back to loving the sense of clumsy chaos you get from classic game shows. Lead game designerJoe Walsh was really inspired by the likes of *Takeshi's Castle* and *Total Wipeout*; competitions where it wasn't always just about being the 'best' at a challenge, but also enjoying stumbling around and creating hilarious, unpredictable moments. We felt this leant itself really well to a 'battle royale' format, and we wanted to put a more fun, approachable, and super-colorful spin on the genre.

"All sorts of work goes into a game like this! From coming up with early ideas and concept art about what the 'Blunderdome' looks and feel like, to 3D modeling and intricate costume design, to the level designers who come up with all sorts of wild and ridiculous round ideas. A game like Fall Guys takes talent from lots and lots of different disciplines. And of course, being an online multiplayer game, we have a team of engineers who work on our servers, making sure that players from all over the world can join in the fun at the same time, which is no easy feat!"

THE YEAR'S BEST INDIE GAMES

BECAUSE SMALL STUDIOS CAN DELIVER AWESOME GAMES

1

AVAILABLE ON:
■ Nintendo Switch ■ PC

HOLLOW KNIGHT: SILKSONG

■ The sequel to 2017's creepy-crawly classic looks incredible, with a new hero—the princess protector of Hallownest, Hornet, and a whole new world of weird critters to explore. You'll have to master Hornet's acrobatic style of combat as you leap and fight through mossy grottoes and golden towers. And you'll need all your swashbuckling swordplay skills as you meet the spectacular bug bosses.

2

SOLAR ASH

■ *Solar Ash* is the latest game from Heart Machine, the team behind the brilliant *Hyper Light Drifter*, and it's another incredibly stylish action-adventure, with a hero who can jump, glide, and grind their way around the ruins of an ancient world. It's full of weird twisting landscapes that will turn your whole world upside down, and just check out all those freaky glowing colors.

AVAILABLE ON:
■ PS4 ■ PS5 ■ PC

3

TCHIA

Looking for a magical getaway on a group of tropical islands? *Tchia* is the game for you. You're free to jump, climb, and glide wherever you want, clambering up trees or exploring the ocean bed. Or why not chill out and play your ukulele —who knows what might happen? You can also take control of animals and objects to use their unique abilities, or collect a bunch of new tools and clothes.

AVAILABLE ON:
PC PS4 PS5

TCHIA

AVAILABLE ON:
PC PS4 PS5 Xbox
Nintendo Switch

4

DEATH'S DOOR

What happens when an old-school *Legend of Zelda* gets mixed up with *Hades* and a touch of *Dark Souls*? *Death's Door*, that's what. This action-adventure puts you in the role of a crow on the trail of a stolen soul, and with armies of enemies to defeat and huge bosses to battle, you've got your work cut out. It's hero time!

5

TUNIC

This love letter to classic console adventure games—especially *Legend of Zelda*—is the work of a tiny team, yet it looks incredible. It's the tale of a cute Fox hero exploring a mysterious world, and it's packed with puzzles to solve and monsters to battle, not to mention secrets to discover. Don't let the warm and colorful vibe deceive you, either: *Tunic* knows when it pays to play tough!

AVAILABLE ON:
Xbox · PC

6

OLLIOLLI WORLD

The classic skateboarding platform game gets an even better sequel, complete with a glitzy cartoon world and more rad tricks and grinds than Nyjah Huston. You can take on missions to unlock new costumes and rewards, and every level has a range of different paths to explore and pull off more incredible trick runs.

AVAILABLE ON:
Nintendo Switch · PC
Xbox · PC · PS4 · PS5

7

A JUGGLER'S TALE

Can you escape to freedom when you're a puppet, dangling from your strings? That's the big question with *A Juggler's Tale*, where the puppet Abby runs away from the puppet theater into a fairy-tale world. It's a pixel-perfect platformer crammed with odd critters and deadly perils, with a star who tugs at your heartstrings.

AVAILABLE ON:
Nintendo Switch · PC

TOP 10

8 WILDERMYTH

Wildermyth is a different take on the fantasy RPG. Rather than follow one hero on an epic quest, you follow a series of adventures throughout their careers. Each story is generated as you play, reacting to your decisions, so you're crafting it as you go along. With lovable stars, fantastic cartoon graphics, and exciting, tactical combat, this is an RPG you won't want to *myth* (ouch).

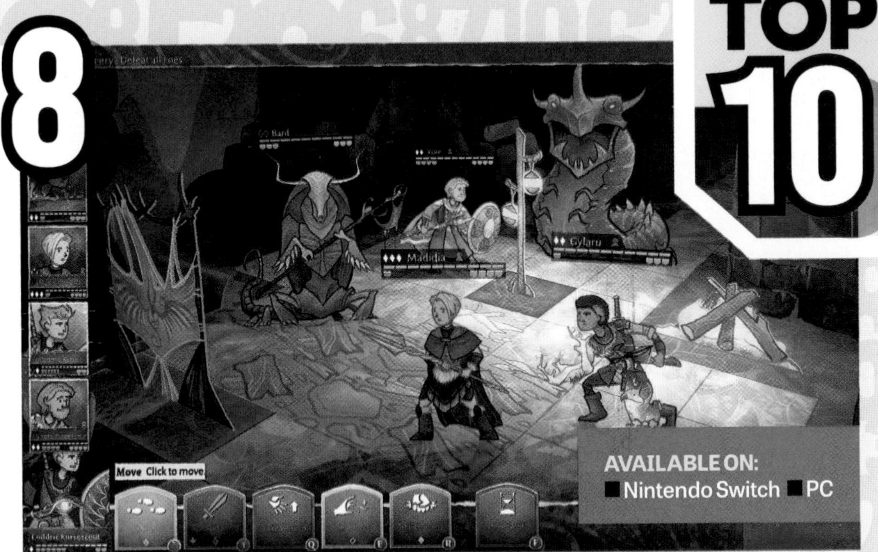

AVAILABLE ON:
■ Nintendo Switch ■ PC

9 PLANET OF LANA

If you love epic sci-fi and Japanese anime, *Planet of Lana* is your jam. It's a big cinematic cartoon adventure, where a girl and a weird but friendly critter head out on a rescue mission across strange alien worlds. Expect scary robots, sneaky puzzles, and some thrilling action sequences, with moments of wonder that will blow your mind.

AVAILABLE ON:
■ Xbox ■ PC

10 ECHO GENERATION

There's something *Stranger Things* about this retro RPG adventure, where a gang of kids investigate a series of supernatural mysteries in their hometown. You'll have to switch between using your detective skills and fighting turn-based battles with mechs and monsters, all in a brilliant pixel-art style that's straight from the nineties setting of the game.

AVAILABLE ON:
■ Xbox One ■ PC

The World of Final Fantasy XVI

The next adventure is just around the corner

Is there anything more exciting than a new *Final Fantasy*? The latest chapter is an all-new saga for the Japanese RPG series, taking us to a new world with new heroes and a new style of adventure. *Final Fantasy XV* mixed fantasy with retro sci-fi, while the *Final Fantasy VII Remake* took us back to a world of sorcery and steampunk. Now, *Final Fantasy XVI* gives us a more traditional high-fantasy saga, full of epic battles, magic, and legendary knights.

Visit Valisthea

The setting is the land of Valisthea, where gigantic crystal mountains of incredible magic energy—the Mothercrystals—tower over six rival realms, flooding each of them with their power. For many years, there has been peace between these nations, but that peace is coming to an end. Dark forces are rising, threatening war across the land.

A Tale of Two Brothers

One of these nations is the Duchy of Rosaria, where two brothers have the potential to change the fate of Valisthea. Your central hero is Clive Rosefield, son of the Archduke and First Shield of Rosaria. His duty is to defend his younger brother, Joshua, Dominant of the Phoenix and, one day, protector of the realm.

Dominants and Eikons

■ Dominants are scattered across the six nations, with each having the power to summon one Eikon—the mightiest and most deadly beings in the land. These titanic figures have the power to defend or destroy, causing carnage on the battlefield when they clash.

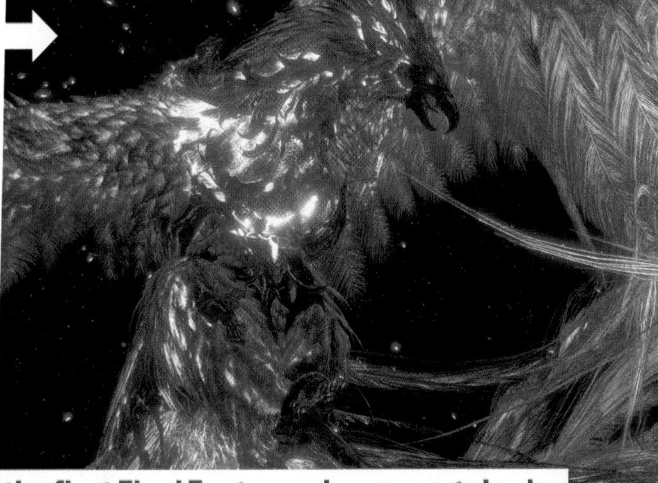

FAST FACT

***Final Fantasy XVI* isn't the first Final Fantasy where crystals play a major part. Giant crystals were at the heart of the plot of *Final Fantasy XIII*, and Mothercrystals have turned up before in both *Final Fantasy XI* and *Final Fantasy XIV*. And the name of *Final Fantasy: Crystal Chronicles* speaks for itself!**

A Thirst for Vengeance

■ You'll play Clive both as the fifteen-year-old First Shield and as an older, battle-hardened warrior on a quest for revenge. As a knight rather than a Dominant, Clive can't summon Eikons like his younger brother, but he can call upon the power of the Phoenix to use its fearsome magic powers in combat.

Haven't we seen you before?

■ Final Fantasy fans will spot that the Eikons are a new variation on the series' Summons—the colossal creatures previous heroes could call in battle to wipe the floor with their toughest foes. In fact, the Eikons themselves include familiar names and faces, such as Shiva, Titan, Phoenix, and Ifrit.

TALES OF ARISE

TALES TO REMEMBER

For centuries, the tyrant Lords of the high-tech world of Rena have enslaved the people of the world of Dahna. Now a Dahnan slave in a mysterious iron mask joins forces with a cursed Renan warrior on a mission to destroy them. And so starts the latest and greatest Tales adventure—a game that should go down in gaming history as one of the best Japanese RPGs!

As Alphen and Shionne, you need to overcome your distrust and take the battle to the five evil Lords, exploring the five realms of Dahna and picking up some new allies and enemies along the way. Combining action-packed combat with magical "Artes," *Tales of Arise* is a fantasy thriller, but also an adventure with real heart.

QUICK TIPS

GET COOKING

■ Use the campsites to have a rest and heal, but also to cook up some recipes. Different recipes have different perks that can improve your chances when you're fighting—and will stop you getting hungry!

DODGE

■ The most important move in battle isn't your attacks or magic Artes, but your dodge move. Use it often to avoid enemy attacks, and—with the right skills and timing—pull off counters.

EXPLORE EVERYWHERE

■ Caves, narrow pathways, ladders, and vines might take you to hidden areas where you can find potions, power-ups, and other goodies. If you don't step off the beaten track, you'll never find 'em.

FIGHTING TOGETHER!

■ You can either play through the whole game as Alphen or switch between the two heroes or their allies at any time. It's worth trying out the different characters to see what moves they can pull off.

ALPHEN

■ Alphen's combat style is all about swords. His basic move is a slash, but trigger his Artes and you'll open up a range of different whirlwind strikes, thrusts, and fiery killer blows.

SHIONNE

■ Shionne is part sorcerer, part sniper. She'll blast away at the enemy, but trigger her Artes and she'll fire off super-powered shots or call down a fireball strike from the sky. She's also great at healing.

BOOST!

■ Other characters that join your party will have their own Artes to use, and each also has a special Boost Attack you can use when they've filled their Boost gauge. Tap a direction on the D-pad to activate the Boost, then watch the fireworks!

DOUBLE-UP!

■ Boost strikes are the most powerful attacks in the game, where two of your heroes team up for one spectacular attack. Build up full Boost gauges for both characters, then watch out for the prompt.

AST ACT

Is this your first Tales? Well, it's the seventeenth in the series, or the thirtieth if you count all the spin-offs. The first Tales, *Tales of Phantasia*, came out in 1995.

LIKE THIS? TRY THIS:

YS IX: MONSTRUM NOX

■ Here's another great entry in an underappreciated series, in which a hero, wrongfully imprisoned, becomes a powerful Monstrum who can destroy evil spirits. It's one action-packed anime-style RPG.

XENOBLADE CHRONICLES 3

Catch up with the story behind the hit Switch RPG

In the world of Aionious, two nations are fighting for survival. Keves has mastered the latest mechanical technology, and their advanced weapons and combat vehicles are destroying the enemy forces. Yet the warriors of Agnus won't go quietly. They have their own powerful magical technology, ether, and they still believe that they can win the war.

It's against this background that *Xenoblade Chronicles 3* follows six soldiers, representing both sides of the war. It's up to you to follow them as they battle and explore and uncover a new threat so terrifying that it might just bring different sides together to fight as one team!

FAST FACT

The Xenoblade Chronicles games tie into an even bigger series, which dates back to *Xenogears*, released on the original PlayStation in 1998. This spun off into the Xenosaga series in 2002, then *Xenoblade Chronicles* in 2010.

NOAH

■ Noah is one of the two main playable characters and a warrior in the army of Keves. He's an ace swordsman, a keen musician, and an "off-seer," who mourns all the soldiers who have lost their lives.

MIO

■ Mio is the second playable hero, and she fights for the Agnus army. Like Noah, she can play haunting tunes on her flute while she mourns for the dead of Agnus as an off-seer on the other side.

SENA

■ Sena fights alongside Mio, using her formidable strength and mighty hammer to defeat the forces of Keves. She's usually found with their friend Taion, a master tactician.

LANZ

■ Lanz is one of Noah's best friends and allies. He's a fearsome fighter who wields a massive sword. Their squad is never complete without Eunie, a powerful healer with a hatred of all things Agnus.

BIG PICTURE

CHRONICLES CATCH-UP

■ *Xenoblade Chronicles 3* is actually the fourth main game in the Xenoblade saga, following on from *Xenoblade Chronicles*, *Chronicles X*, and *Chronicles 2*. None of the games are linked by a story line or characters, so don't worry if you haven't played any of the previous games. All they share is that they're set in the far future, in a world where the last humans live in nations built on the backs of vast, dying titans. They all combine swords, sorcery, and giant robots in one fantastic setting. We promise—it all makes sense when you play!

Ruined King: A League of Legends Story

It takes a dirty half dozen to save Bilgewater from the Black Mist

Six champions are all that stand between Bilgewater and destruction at the hands of Viego, the Ruined King. If you're a fan of the League, you'll know them—you might even have played them before—but here they're on a new kind of adventure, combining action with old-school, turn-based combat.

Bilgewater

This harbor of scum and villainy is home to pirates, smugglers, thieves, and fortune hunters from across the lands of Runeterra. Here there's no government and no hard-and-fast rules. You live on your wits and hope they're sharp enough to make it through the night. It's a dangerous place at the best of times—and the worst are just around the corner.

Illaoi

The prophet of the Great Kraken is a powerhouse in battle. Any enemies she can't break with her mighty fists she'll tackle with her faith and her golden idol, bringing the powers of her tentacled god into the fight.

Miss Fortune

Sarah Fortune avenged the deaths of her family by blowing up the flagship of the reaver king, *Gangplank*, and since then she's brought a fragile peace to Bilgewater as a captain among captains and their pirate crews. That's hard work enough for this pistol-packin' buccaneer, but now the city faces a new threat from the Shadow Isles.

Braum

The big-hearted, massive-muscled hero of the Freljord is a great protector, defending and supporting his comrades with the aid of his mighty shield—an ancient and enchanted vault door. He might have left his beloved Northern lands behind, but he won't leave Bilgewater to fall.

FAST FACT

***Ruined King* is the first single-player game to come out of *League of Legends*, starring six of its 140 champions. Over 100 million players play *League of Legends* every month, with as many as 50 million playing on a single day!**

Pyke

Once a renowned Harpooner, Pyke now hunts the worst thugs and criminals of Bilgewater—those who prey on the weak and vulnerable. And when dark forces threaten the city he calls home, Pyke brings all his supernatural abilities to the battle.

Ahri

As a legendary fox spirit, Ahri survives on the emotions and memories of her human victims, taking something from each rotten soul she consumes. Being a mage, she can control the energies of sorcery, releasing them in magical orbs of explosive power.

Yasuo

The Ionian swordsman is a master of his blade, wandering the world to atone for the death of his own brother, killed in an act of self-defense. With Yasuo's sword and his mysterious powers over wind, our champions have a fighting chance of beating back the Ruined King.

The Shadow Isles

Once the home of a noble civilization, these sinister islands are now shrouded in a permanent black mist, which steals the life force of the living and attracts the restless spirits of the dead. This same black mist now threatens the people of Bilgewater. What does it have to do with a cursed king and ancient legend? What can our motley crew of champions do to stop it?

RUNE FACTORY 5

FARMING, FISHING, AND FIGHTING MONSTERS—IT'S ALL JUST ANOTHER DAY'S WORK!

There's never a dull moment in the life of a Seed Ranger. One minute you're looking after the sheep or harvesting your crops, the next you're heading out of town to battle monsters with your besties. That's just how life goes in this lovable series, which mixes the farming fun of Harvest Moon and Stardew Valley with the magic and mayhem of a classic RPG.

In *Rune Factory 5*, you're a young man or woman with no memories, starting a new life as a peacekeeping Ranger in a small town. You've still got to make a living from the land, but you're also there to defend the people against the local monsters and investigate any news of new monster threats. Still, you'll make friends to fight beside you and earn new magical gear, so who's complaining? It's livin' the dream, fantasy style!

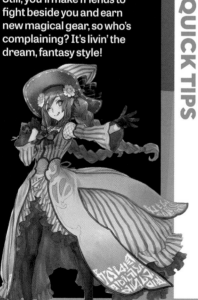

GOOD EATING

■ The food you grow isn't just for show—or even just for selling. Learn to cook, and you'll get recipes to buff your Hit Points, Rune Points, and resistance to effects. It might even help you win some hearts!

MAKE SOME MONSTER FRIENDS

■ Don't assume all monsters are bad guys. Some can be won over with food or presents, and they'll follow you back home. They'll help out with the farming and even join you on adventures!

GO FISHING

■ Fishing will net you something to sell early on and open up some useful recipes even later in the game. It won't earn you the big bucks like farming, but it's still worth casting out a line.

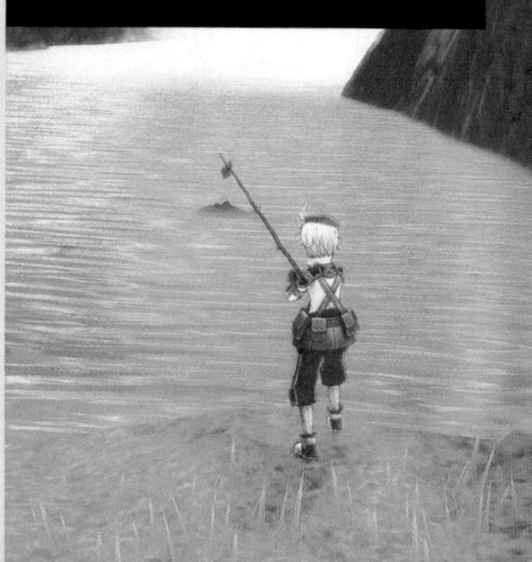

LIFE AS A RIGBERTH RANGER

So, you've got a new life as a Seed Ranger in the small town of Rigberth. There's no time for sitting around. You've got a town to defend and dungeons to explore, and that takes a lot of preparation.

TOP CROPS

Hey, even a Ranger's gotta eat, and your Ranger salary won't pay all the bills. You'll need to plant, look after, and harvest your crops, then sell them to bring some money in.

GEAR UP

Invest in a crafting table and a forge, and you can start making your own tools and weapons, which will make your farming more effective and help you when you're fighting monsters.

KILLER COMBOS

Make friends with the locals, and they'll join you in battle, opening up a whole new bunch of combo moves. This is a first for the Rune Factory series and makes it crucial that you buddy up.

AFTER WORK

When you're not whacking evil creatures, fishing, or tilling the soil, you'd better work on your relationships. With the right gifts and favors, a friendship can become a romance, and you might hear wedding bells!

MEET YOUR DATE

You've got a choice of potential sweethearts, ranging from your average town girls or handsome knights to demon-girls and well-groomed werebeasts!

FAST FACT

Rune Factory started off as a spin-off of the much-loved Harvest Moon series. Yoshifumi Hashimoto, one of the producers on the series, once called it "Harvest Moon where you wield a sword."

LIKE THIS? TRY THIS:

MOONLIGHTER

Looking for another cute RPG where you live a double life? In the lovable *Moonlighter*, you're a shopkeeper by day, dungeon delver by night, slaying monsters and grabbing gear to sell!

STACK THE

Play the greatest collectible card games

Video games based on collectible card games, or CCGs, have become incredibly popular, and you don't have to be a card-dueling genius to see why. They're fast to learn but challenging to master, and they're great for playing solo or head-to-head with friends. There are tie-ins with your favorite comics, TV shows, and movies—and spin-offs of some of your favorite games—and they're as much fun on a phone or tablet as they are on a laptop or console. Deal us in!

HOW DO THEY WORK?

These games seem simple, but there's a lot of smart stuff going on beneath the surface. In most, players usually take turns to draw cards from their deck and play them to attack the other player or block the cards the other player is using to attack them. There are also cards with spells or special abilities, which might, say, give another card a boost or let you draw more cards. You battle it out until one player is defeated—and the other player wins!

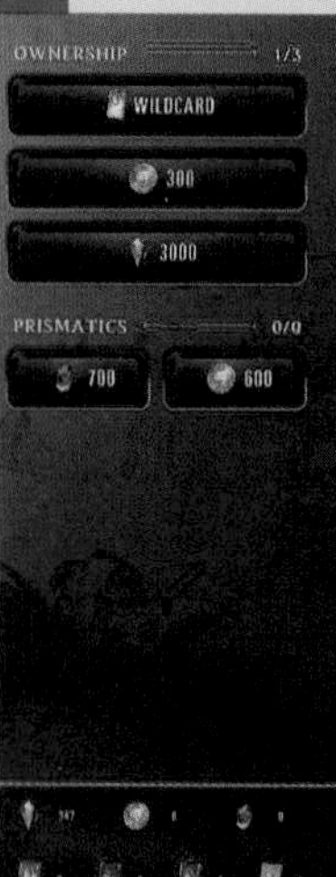

However, there's another crucial part to the game: building your deck. The more you play, the more you can win cards to add to your collection, which you can use to create your own decks. There's a whole extra layer of strategy here, as some combinations of cards can be incredibly powerful and open up new strategies to try. Build a great deck and learn how to use it, and you might become a CCG master!

DECK!

HOW DID THEY START?

■ The whole CCG phenomenon started with the original tabletop version of *Magic the Gathering* in 1993. Players loved collecting the cards, with their awesome fantasy art, as much as they loved dueling other players, and *MTG* became a massive global craze. This inspired other CCGs, including games based on *Star Wars* and *Pokémon*, as well as the Japanese classic *Yu-Gi-Oh!*

■ Strangely, for all its popularity, *MTG* didn't take off as a video game. Instead, the first video game CCG to hit big was Blizzard Entertainment's *Hearthstone*. Based on the classic Warcraft games, it went on to inspire a new generation of CCG video games, not just on console and PC, but on tablets and smartphones, too!

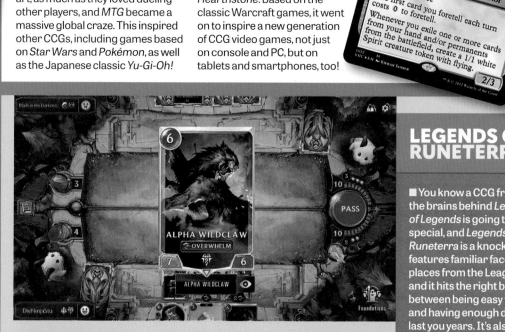

LEGENDS OF RUNETERRA

■ You know a CCG from the brains behind *League of Legends* is going to be special, and *Legends of Runeterra* is a knockout. It features familiar faces and places from the League, and it hits the right balance between being easy to learn and having enough depth to last you years. It's also one of the best games for building up your decks. You get a lot of great cards as rewards just for playing, and you don't have to buy packs of cards without being able to see what's inside them. It's the king of CCGs.

HEARTHSTONE

Blizzard's groundbreaking CCG is still one of the best, because it takes a lot of the hard work out of playing without removing any of the strategy. You can go a long way into the game without ever buying any add-on packs, and when you do pay for expansions, these pack in new cards along with new challenges and story-based quests. The World of Warcraft card game still has the WOW Factor!

MAGIC THE GATHERING

There's no better way to learn how to play *Magic the Gathering* than to play the latest video game version, *Magic the Gathering: Arena*. It's slicker and easier to get into than previous efforts, with some brilliant tutorials and challenges to help you get to grips with the different cards and rules. Plus, you can play for ages—and enjoy the cool art—without spending a cent.

It is one of the more complex CCGs out there, though, which is why there's a mobile game, *Magic the Gathering: Spellslingers*, that's faster-paced, with fewer complex rules. With wisecracking heroes and villains and exciting special effects, it's a great CCG for gaming on the go!

PAY TO WIN?

The most controversial thing about video game CCGs is that, as with tabletop CCGs, you're often encouraged to spend real money on cards to build up your decks. Often, this means buying "blind" packs of cards, where you're not even sure you'll get the cards you're looking for. The better games give you other ways to earn new cards without splashing out extra, or provide them through themed expansions with a lot more stuff to do. Whatever you do, don't buy anything without permission from a parent or guardian—or whoever pays the bills!

SLAY THE SPIRE

■ This hit PC and console CCG mashes up *Magic the Gathering* with a "roguelike" RPG in one awesome hybrid game. You've got to work your way up through a tower of monsters and demons, using the cards in your deck to fight them off. The further you go, the more cards you'll collect and the more powerful you become, but the enemies you face grow more deadly! Die and you're back to square one. *Slay the Spire* is super easy to pick up and play but a real test of your brains and nerves—and once you've paid for the game, that's it!

MONSTER TRAIN

■ *Monster Train* is a lot like *Slay the Spire*, only this time you're in charge of a train full of demons and monsters under attack from the forces of good. Can you keep them from making their way up from floor to floor and hacking away at the magic pyre that powers your hog? With each battle, you'll win new cards to add to your deck, but you also need to think about your defenses if you want to keep your monsters on the right tracks.

YU-GI-OH!

■ *Yu-Gi-Oh!* might not be as big as Pokémon, but it never goes out of style. The *Yu-Gi-Oh! Duel Links* game for iOS and Android has all the characters and creatures you know and love, plus cool quizzes and in-game challenges. *Legacy of the Duelist* for PC, PS4, and Nintendo Switch lets you replay some of the greatest-ever *Yu-Gi-Oh!* moments, And now they're joined by *Master Duel*, which takes the *Yu-Gi-Oh!* experience to a whole new level. Turn the page to find out how!

YU-GI-OH! MASTER DUEL

PLAY YOUR CARDS LIKE A MASTER

BRAVEDRIVE
[Cyberse/Effect]
Once per turn, when your Cyberse monster declares an attack: You can discard 1 monster; that attacking monster gains 600 ATK, until the end of this turn.
ATK/ 1500 DEF/ 1000

When you think of what Yu-Gi-Oh! did to define the digital trading card game, it's a shame that it has had its thunder stolen by the likes of *Hearthstone* and *Legends of Runeterra*. Not anymore. With *Master Duel*, Yu-Gi-Oh! is back with a vengeance! This is where you can build your decks, develop your skills, and take on the world's top players. It's also a great way to learn how to play Yu-Gi-Oh! and get some practice with its vast range of cards and complex features. Don't be afraid—you can master *Master Duel*, and you don't have to pay big bucks to do it!

QUICK TIPS

SPEND WISELY

Don't blow all your gems on unlocking standard packs of cards. Instead, save them for the bonus and secret packs, which are better for opening up new strategies and giving you a wider range of cards to play.

LEARN WHEN YOU LOSE

When you're starting out, you're going to lose, especially in player vs. player matches. Don't make it a big deal, and try to learn from the winner. What strategies did they use to stop you? Which combos hit you where it hurts, and how could you have defended yourself?

USE PHASE 2

Lots of players pass over Main Phase 2, but it can be a great time to summon a monster or use any trap or spell cards you still have in your hand. There could be something you missed in Main Phase 1 that could help you respond to any cards your opponent has laid down!

IT'S TIME TO DUEL!

Yu-Gi-Oh! is a complex collectible card game with a lot to learn. You could take years mastering its strategies. Luckily, *Master Duel* gives you an easier way to learn the fundamentals, then experiment with your own decks and cool card combinations.

PLAY SOLO

The tutorials won't tell you much beyond the basics, but the Solo play mode is perfect for learning about tactics, different styles of play, and offensive and defensive moves. Keep playing against the computer-controlled characters before you take on a human opponent.

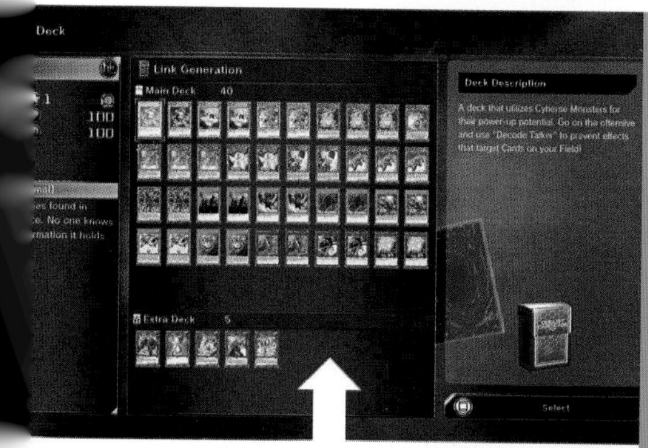

ADVANCED TECHNIQUES

With practice, you can get to grips with the more advanced techniques, using traps to surprise your opponent and turn the game around, or finding combinations of spells and monsters that can help you build an unstoppable winning momentum!

CRAFT YOUR DECK

Building and structuring your deck is absolutely crucial. The three starter decks—Power of the Dragon, Synchro of Unity, and Link Generation—give you a choice of simple and more advanced play styles, but you can tweak all three to add new strategies and combos.

SECRETS AND RARITIES

Look out for secret packs and rare cards that can open up new card combinations or have the potential to turn the tide of battle when you look like you're about to lose. But remember—it's not always about being number one. It's about dueling with bravery, honor, and respect!

FAST FACT

The original *Yu-Gi-Oh!* anime first ran on Japanese TV in April 1998. In the anime, the game Yugi plays is called Magic & Wizards. *Yu-Gi-Oh* itself means "Game King" in Japanese.

LIKE THIS? TRY THIS:

FAERIA

How about a collectible card game with a twist? Faeria cleverly combines the usual deck-building and dueling with a tile-based board game and an RPG. It's one ingenious hybrid!

TRIANGLE STRATEGY

THINGS TURN SALTY IN THIS CLASH OF KINGS

Would you go to war over iron and salt? Well, metals and minerals have been the cause of many a conflict, and it's the same in this superb strategy RPG. Here, three mighty kingdoms rule a continent between them, with the Grand Duchy of Aesfrost rich in iron, the Holy State of Hyzante overflowing with salt, and the Kingdom of Glenbrook managing the trade between them. After decades of feuding, there's a fragile peace. But as a young noble of Glenbrook, Serenoa, prepares to marry a princess of Aesfrost, treachery puts the three kingdoms at war with each other once again.

Between battles, diplomacy, exploration, and adventure, there's a lot going on in *Triangle Strategy*. Not only do you have to win the key fights, but also the hearts and minds of friends and potential allies. Listen to your companions, hone your powers of persuasion, and make choices that could change the history of your world.

QUICK TIPS

DON'T PANIC OVER DYING

Don't worry if you lose a favorite unit in battle. This isn't Fire Emblem; death isn't permanent, and you can still go on to win the fight.

SURROUND 'EM

Triangle Strategy goes big on follow-up attacks, where one successful attack on an enemy causes extra attacks from units who surround them. Surround tougher enemies and smash them!

WATCH THE ORDER

Keep track of which units are moving next using the display at the bottom of the screen. If a tough enemy is closing in on a weak unit, move them or bring someone in to defend them.

BIG DECISIONS

As Serenoa, the young head of House Wolffort, you need to lead both on and off the battlefield. That means making some tough choices that could steer the story in a new direction.

PICK YOUR TEAM

As the game goes on, you'll have more units than you can put on the battlefield at once. It's up to you to select the best fighters for the battle and level up their skills.

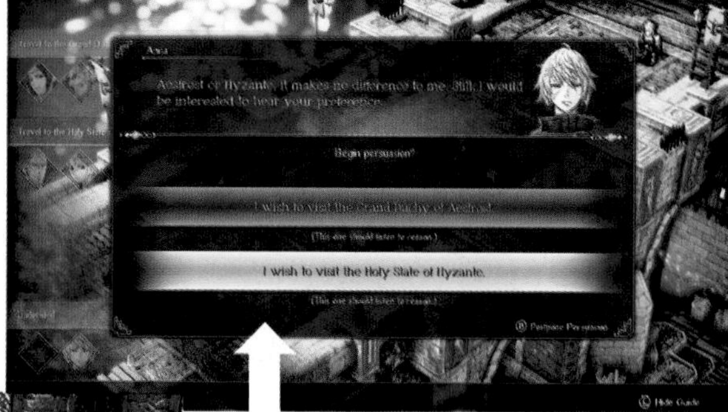

TALKING TACTICS

When it's time to fight, you need to move your warriors and use their unique abilities to full effect. Hughette, for instance, is a deadly shot if you can get her somewhere high.

POWERS OF PERSUASION

When making the big decisions, you rely on the opinions of your closest friends and allies. Everyone gets a vote, but you can help them make their minds up.

PEACE TALKS

Being head of a noble family, you'll have to meet with princes, kings, and holy leaders. You can choose your questions and answers, and what you say can save lives—or destroy them!

AST ACT

***Triangle Strategy* comes from the same team that bought you *Octopath Traveler* and *Bravely Default*, and uses the same mix of retro 2D characters and slick 3D scenery.**

LIKE THIS? TRY THIS:

FIRE EMBLEM: THREE HOUSES

If you haven't played Nintendo's own strategy RPG, you're missing out on a stone-cold classic. As a new teacher at a magical military academy, can you prepare your students for the outbreak of war?

HOW GRAPHICS EVOLVED

Gaming graphics have come a long, long way

To get from *Space Invaders* to games like *Spider-Man: Miles Morales* has taken video games over forty years. That journey has seen us move from blocky shapes and pixels to amazing 3D graphics that look like they've come from a movie, all thanks to some genius game programmers and the latest gaming hardware.

1974

SPRITES

■ The early arcade games created characters from sprites: grids of blocky pixels designed to look like a basketball, a space invader, Pac-Man, or Mario. Over time, the game programmers worked out how to animate these grids of pixels to make the characters look like they were running, jumping, dropping a bomb, or swinging a mighty sword, and when you put these sprites on top of a blocky pixel background, you could start making cool-looking games.

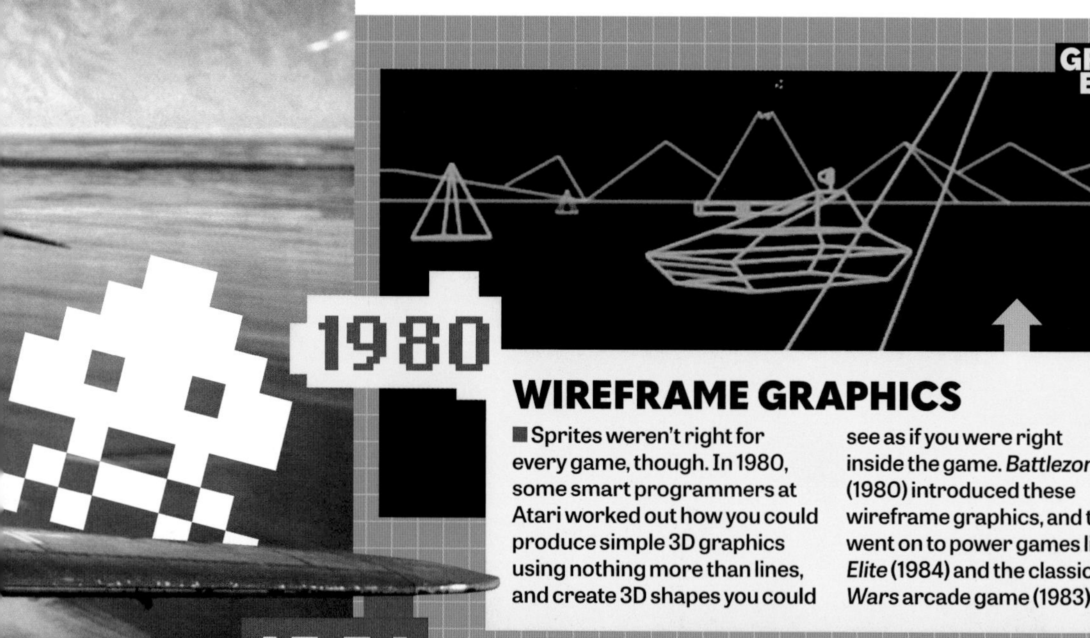

1980

WIREFRAME GRAPHICS

Sprites weren't right for every game, though. In 1980, some smart programmers at Atari worked out how you could produce simple 3D graphics using nothing more than lines, and create 3D shapes you could see as if you were right inside the game. *Battlezone* (1980) introduced these wireframe graphics, and they went on to power games like *Elite* (1984) and the classic *Star Wars* arcade game (1983).

1981

SCROLLING

The earliest games took place in one location with a simple background, and if they wanted to go to a different location, the screen would go blank quickly and switch to a different scene. Scrolling changed all that, so that the game could follow a spaceship in *Defender* (1981) or Pac-Man in *Pac-Land* (1984) and the background would just move behind them. *Super Mario Bros.* took the idea to town, and the rest is gaming history!

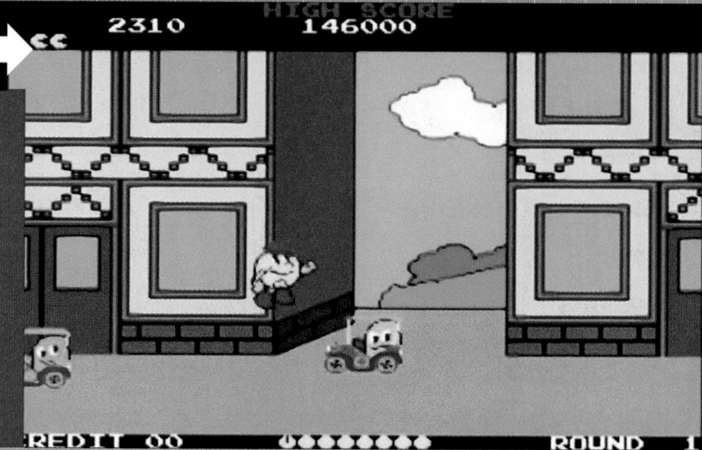

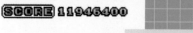

1984

FAKE 3D

Arcade games of the mid-1980s wanted to give us awesome 3D graphics and make you feel like you were on a dangerous adventure. Only, nobody had worked out how to do it. Then game designers like Yu Suzuki at Sega, who worked out that you could scale sprites, making them bigger as they came toward you. Suzuki created games like *Hang On* (1984), *Space Harrier* (1985), and *Outrun* (1986) that put you right in the action.

1988

ATTACK OF THE POLYGONS

■ By 1988, the world was ready for some real 3D graphics, as new coding whiz kids worked out how to take the old wireframe graphics, shade them, and fill them with color to create more realistic 3D shapes made up of polygons. Sure, the spaceships and cars that filled these polygon worlds looked a bit basic, but as time moved on, we went from *Winning Run* (1988) and *Hard Drivin'* (1999) to fantastic early 3D hits like Sega's *Virtua Racing* (1992).

1991

BRING ON THE TEXTURES

■ Shaded, colored polygons looked good, but then programmers found a way to attach different patterns and more sophisticated graphics called textures to each surface of the 3D shape. With the textures in place, game designers could build much more real-looking game worlds. Games like *Ultima Underworld* (1991) and *Wolfenstein 3D* (1992) still had pretty basic textures, but then the original *Doom* came along and—in 1995—was the closest any game had come to realistic 3D graphics.

1996

3D GETS REAL

■ Games like *Doom* still used big, scaled sprites for their characters and monsters, but soon smart developers worked out how to make these out of polygons as well. *Super Mario 3D*, *Quake*, and *Tomb Raider* all came out in 1996 and featured fully 3D characters in fully 3D worlds, just like most of the games we love today.

1998

LIGHT AND SHADE

These true 3D games looked pretty brilliant for the time, but they still looked weirdly flat. That's because game programmers hadn't mastered realistic lighting or how to simulate how game worlds and characters looked with different lights—or if they cast realistic shadows. At the end of the nineties, games like *Thief: The Dark Project* (1998) and *Quake III Arena* (1999) figured some of this tricky stuff out, leading to games with more convincing lighting effects, like *Doom 3* (2004) and *Half-Life 2* (2004).

JUST LIKE A MOVIE

Within a few years, programmers had learned to use all these tricks, and more, to create games that looked more like real life—or at least more like a slick Hollywood movie. Games like *Crysis* (2007), *Gears of War* (2006), and *Halo 3* (2007) really upped the pace with believable game worlds and more human-looking (or monstrous-looking) stars. Since then, programmers have done even more to simulate how light bounces off different surfaces and how we see the effects, making games look even more incredible!

2019

RAY TRACING

And now games can use a technology—ray tracing—that used to be found only in the big movie studios. Ray tracing calculates how different rays of light bounce off all the different surfaces in a scene before hitting your lucky eyeballs, and can produce much more realistic lighting effects, shadows, and reflections. PC games like *Battlefield V* (2019) and *Control* (2019) were first to use it, but check out *Spider-Man: Miles Morales* to see ray tracing at work in one amazing game.

ANIMAL CROSSING: HAPPY HOME PARADISE

DON'T YOUR VILLAGERS DESERVE A DREAM HOME?

Animal Crossing: New Horizons keeps getting bigger and better. Brewster has finally opened his café, the Kapp'n is back with his island tours, and Harv's Island is the closest thing your village will get to a mall. You can even get your fortune told!

Yet Nintendo reserved some of the best stuff for the *Happy Home Paradise* expansion. Here you join Lottie and the Paradise Planning team, building and designing vacation homes for a growing list of clients. And when you're not busy creating their perfect chill-out pads, you've got your work cut out making hospitals, restaurants, and schools. DIY and decorating have never been so much fun!

QUICK TIPS

EAT OUT OR GRAB A CUP OF JOE

■ Keep coming back to your café and restaurant. You may be given a new recipe or find a new client with a special mission for you.

PAIR THEM UP

■ Got two potential clients with the same request? Why not make them roommates? You can make two people happy with half the work.

NEED POKI? JUST REMODEL

■ You need a special currency, Poki, to buy new furniture and decorations, but you can always get more by remodelling homes you've already made. Just talk to the village about remodeling, and you'll get one even happier client and a pile of cash. Ka-ching!

BUILD THE PERFECT HOME

■ So, you've got a new client wanting their own special vacation home? Pay attention and take the design step by step, and you'll get a happy homeowner every time.

PICK YOUR SPOT

■ Listen carefully to your client. Where and how do they want to spend their vacations? See if you can find the right island spot for them and give them the style of home they're looking for.

FIX THE YARD

■ Don't forget to fix up their outdoor spaces. Look for the plants and exterior items that are going to make them feel good as soon as they arrive.

DECORATE

■ Selecting the right furniture and decorations comes down to your sense of style and whether you've listened to what your client wants. Give them what they ask for if you want a happy customer!

ENJOY THE GRATITUDE

■ Once you've finished, tell your client that their home is ready and watch as they take a tour. Not only is it great to see your stuff being enjoyed by a friendly face, but they'll tell you how great your work is. Nice!

FAST FACT

***Happy Home Paradise* is a sort of sequel to *Animal Crossing: Happy Home Designer*, which came out in 2015 on the 3DS. This time it's not a separate game, so you can take the furniture and items you unlock back to your island home!**

LIKE THIS? TRY THIS:

MY TIME AT SANDROCK

■ There's no other game like *Animal Crossing*, but with *My Time at Sandrock*, you can put your building skills to use while helping out a struggling western town. There's hunting, mining, and romance as well!

ANIMAL CROSSING: NEW HORIZONS

A Year on Your Island Home Away from Home

When life gets rough and you need somewhere to escape to, *Animal Crossing: New Horizon* is the place to be. Whatever the time of year, there's always something fun going on – and a bunch of friends to share it with!

STARTING OUT

■ You start out with nothing more than a tent and sleeping bag, but get to work and you'll soon have your own sweet island camp. Before you know it, you've got stalls springing up and some places to hang out with your new island buddies.

SPRING

BUNNY DAY

■ Bunny Day's the big spring celebration, and there's a whole load of stuff to collect and make. Get it all and you'll get some pretty colorful DIY recipes—if Zipper T. Bunny doesn't drive you crazy first!

CHILLING OUT

■ You can't be all work, no play all the time, so enjoy the spring sunshine by chilling out with a friend or two.

BUILDING A TOWN

■ There's a lot to do as the island takes on more folks —a bigger population needs a proper store. Luckily, Tom Nook and the kids, Timmy and Tommy, are primed to fill the hole. And it's not long before the island has its first museum, complete with spots where Blathers can show off your best fish, fossils, butterflies, and creepy-crawly bugs.

SUMMER

WEDDING SEASON

■ A new season brings new challenges, like the Wedding Season photo shoot. You need a bunch of different themed items for each part and some serious design skills, but at least there's a party to enjoy!

FIREWORKS

■ By now the island's going strong, so it's time to celebrate! Get dressed up with some kooky gear and join your best friends for the fireworks. There's a party starting every Sunday night.

LIVE THE DREAM

■ Want a vacation from your island? You can catch a flight with Dodo Airlines and visit a new island or use Luna's hypnotic powers to see what other players are up to in your dreams.

ENJOY THE SUNSHINE

■ And there's plenty of time to relax near home. Relax by the beach, head out for a swim, or just wander around the island and catch up with your friends and neighbors.

FALL

HALLOWEEN

After a while, the weather turns a little cooler and the leaves start falling from the trees. And there's an extra chill in the air when Jack arrives, craving candy on Halloween. Get dressed up in your best scary costume, grab those lollipops, and give your friends a fright! If you don't give them some candy treats, they might want to play a trick or two on you. Big screams all around!

TAKE TIME OUT

Fall is a great time to relax and take things easy, even when you've got a lot of things to fix up around the town. Take a few hours off to shoot the breeze, or even go healthy with a bit of yoga. Who knows? Your sporty friends might want to join in!

FAST FACT

Animal Crossing's laid-back musician, KK Slider, is based on a real guy. Nintendo modeled the character to look like Kazumi Totaka, who wrote the game's music and also directs the sound on many of Nintendo's biggest hits. Of course, Totaka doesn't have the floppy ears!

GIVE THANKS ON TURKEY DAY

There's a lot to be thankful for on your island, and who better to help you celebrate than Franklin the Turkey? Don't worry—you won't be cooking this big bird. He needs your help to get some recipe ingredients and make a Thanksgiving dinner you won't want to miss. Clam chowder? Fish? Pumpkin pie? It's all on the menu.

WINTER

SNOWMAN

As fall turns to winter, snow is falling and a white blanket covers the ground. Get the ball rolling and you'll soon have one half of a snowman. Roll another, smaller ball and put them together, and he will come to life with a grin. You'll get rewarded with some brand-new DIY recipes, so keep making snowmen once a day.

HURRAY! IT'S TOY DAY!

The highlight of the festive period is Toy Day, when you get a chance to make like Santa and spread some joy around for your island friends. Help Jingle out with some awesome wrapping paper, and make sure to keep some gifts back for your buddies.

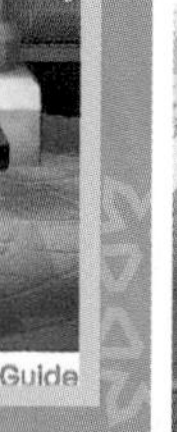

NEW YEAR

One year ends and a new one begins, and what better place to celebrate it than your island? You'll find a countdown clock sitting in the island plaza, and there's a big fireworks display when midnight comes.

VIVA FESTIVALE

The fun's only just getting started. Festivale is an all-day carnival of costumes, craziness, and color. Find the colored feathers, trade them to Pavé the peacock, and join in the jubilations! After all, a new spring is in the air.

GLOSSARY

4K
■ A screen or image with an ultra-high definition resolution, giving the picture even more detail than high definition (HD).

Achievement
■ An award added to your online profile for completing goals or objectives in a game.

AI
■ Artificial intelligence. Intelligent behavior simulated by a computer to, for instance, control how enemies behave toward a player or control other players on your team in a sports game.

Battle royale
■ A type of action game where sixty or more players are dropped onto a single, large map and fight until just one survives.

Beat 'em up
■ A fighting game where two or more fighters battle in hand-to-hand combat.

Boss
■ A bigger, tougher enemy that players have to fight at the end of a level or mission in a game.

Yu-Gi-Oh! Master Duel

Splatoon 3

Campaign
■ A series of levels or objectives connected by some kind of story, usually making up the single-player mode of a game.

CCG
■ Collectible card game. A style of game based on real-world card games where players collect an army of cards and use them to battle other players.

Checkpoint
■ A point in a game where your progress is saved. If you die, you'll return to the checkpoint.

Combo
■ In a fighting game or action game, a series of button presses that triggers a hard-hitting attack or counterattack.

Co-op
■ A game or game mode where players can work together to complete objectives or win the game.

CPU
■ Central processing unit. The main processor of a computer or games console that does most of the work of running games.

Gran Turismo 7

Crafting
■ Using materials collected within a game to make useful items, armor, or weapons.

Cut-scene
■ An animated sequence or video sequence in a game, used to build atmosphere or tell the story.

DLC
■ Downloadable content. Additional items, characters, or levels for a game that you can buy and download as extras.

Easter egg
■ A secret feature or item that's been hidden in a game, either for fun or as a reward for observant fans.

Endgame
■ A part of a game that you can carry on playing after you've completed the main campaign or story.

FPS
■ First-person shooter. A style of game where players move around a map, shooting enemies from a first-person perspective, with a view straight from the hero's eyes.

GPU
■ Graphics processing unit. The chip inside a computer or console that turns instructions from the game software into 2D or 3D graphics you can see on the screen.

Indie game

■ Short for independent game. A game created by a small team of developers—or even a single developer working alone.

JRPG

■ Japanese role-playing game. A Japanese-made role-playing game with the kind of gameplay and graphics you'd expect from a Final Fantasy, Persona, Xenogears, or Dragon Quest game.

Level

■ A portion or chapter of the game set in one area with a beginning, an end, and a series of goals and challenges in between.

Map

■ An in-game map to help you find objectives, or a level where players can fight in a multiplayer game.

MOBA

■ Multiplayer online battle arena. A multiplayer game where two teams of players select champions and go into battle for a series of objectives until one team wins.

Noob

■ A new and inexperienced player without the skills and knowledge of an experienced gamer.

NPC

■ Non-player character. A character in a game controlled by the computer. NPCs often provide help or guidance, sell useful stuff, or help tell the story of the game.

Metroid Dread

Open-world

■ A style of game where players are free to explore one or more large areas and try out different activities, rather than complete one level after another.

Patch

■ An update to a game that fixes bugs or adds new features.

Platformer

■ Platform game. A type of game where you run across a series of platforms or a challenging landscape, leaping over gaps and obstacles and avoiding or defeating enemies in your path.

Port

■ A version of a game made for one console or computer that's been converted to run on another.

PvE

■ Player vs. environment. An online game or game mode where players work together to beat computer-controlled enemies.

PvP

■ Player vs. player. An online game or game mode where players work against other players, either on their own or in teams.

Retro

■ A game or visual style that looks back to older games from the 1980s or 1990s.

Roguelike

■ A style of game where players fight through a series of randomly generated levels, killing monsters and collecting weapons and equipment.

RPG

■ Role-playing game. A type of game where the player goes on an epic quest or adventure, fighting monsters, leveling up their character, and upgrading their equipment on the way.

Marvel's Guardians of the Galaxy

Season pass

■ An add-on for a game that allows you to download and play through any expansions or DLC released after it launches.

Shoot 'em up

■ A style of game based on classic arcade games, where players work their way through waves of levels full of enemies, blasting away at them and avoiding their attacks.

Speedrun

■ A gaming challenge where players compete to finish a game or level in the shortest possible time.

Streaming

■ Watching a video or playing a game through a live connection to the internet, rather than downloading it and then playing it from a console or computer.

VR

■ Virtual reality. Playing games through a head-mounted screen with motion controls so that it looks and feels more like you're actually in the game world.

XP

■ Experience points. Points scored in a game for completing objectives, beating challenges, or killing monsters, and often used to upgrade the hero, their skills, or their equipment.